BY WHAT LAW?

SOCIETY
OF BIBLICAL
LITERATURE

DISSERTATION SERIES

David L. Petersen, Old Testament Editor
Pheme Perkins, New Testament Editor

Number 128

BY WHAT LAW?

by
Michael Winger

Michael Winger

BY WHAT LAW?
The Meaning of Νόμος
in the Letters of Paul

Scholars Press
Atlanta, Georgia

BY WHAT LAW?

Michael Winger

Ph.D., 1990
Columbia University

Advisor:
Robin Scroggs

Library of Congress Cataloging in Publication Data

Winger, Joseph Michael.
    By what law? : the meaning of nomos in the letters of Paul /
    Joseph Michael Winger.
    p. cm. — (Dissertation series / Society of Biblical
    Literature ; no. 128)
    Originally presented as the author's thesis (Ph.D.).
    Includes bibliographical references.
    ISBN 1-55540-592-4 (alk. paper). — ISBN 1-55540-593-2 (pbk. :
    alk. paper)
    1. Law (Theology)—Biblical teaching. 2. Bible. N.T. Epistles
of Paul—Criticism, interpretation, etc. 3. Bible. N.T. Galatians
II. 15-21—Criticism, interpretation, etc. 4. Bible. N.T. Romans
VII, 14-25—Criticism, interpretation, etc. I. Title. II. Series:
Dissertation series (Society of Biblical Literature) ; no. 128.
BS2655.L35W56 1991
227'.048—dc20   91-10194
                                                   CIP

Printed in the United States of America
on acid-free paper

Ποῦ οὖν ἡ καύχησις; ἐξεκλείσθη. διὰ ποίου νόμου;
τῶν ἔργων; οὐχί, ἀλλὰ διὰ νόμου πίστεως.

Then what becomes of our boasting? It is excluded.
By what law? The law of works? No, but by the law
of faith.

– Romans 3:27

Contents

Tables and Figures

Preface

This dissertation stands at the intersection of my two chief professional interests: law, which I have practiced, off and on, since 1973, and scripture, which has been my abiding concern since I entered the Union Theological Seminary in 1980. That scripture was as interesting as law I perceived immediately; that the two are connected became apparent as time passed. Both bear tradition, one as the framework—but only the framework—of secular order, the other as the framework (only the framework) of religious order.

The place of law in Paul's thought is an old problem that has received considerable attention in the last decade, as the works of Dunn, Hübner, Räisänen, Sanders and Westerholm, among other, testify. Generally it is taken for a religious problem, not a secular one. In investigating the lexical meaning of the Greek term νόμος I have found some evidence that the two realms are at this point—as at so many others—not entirely distinct; rather, the secular meaning of νόμος carries over to Paul's religious discourse with the term, and helps to explain much that he says with it.

Or so I argue. My basic aim was more modest: simply to explore the lexical semantics of a key term, a foundational issue which was, as it seemed to me, somewhat neglected in the many works which have addressed the term's theological implications. The major questions about the relations of law, tradition and scripture—and about how these are to be understood in the light of the gospel—still lie ahead of me. I believe I have, in this dissertation, cleared some ground for excavation of those topics, much of which excavation will have to take place in Paul's letters.

My debts are many. First, to the New Testament faculty of Union Theological Seminary: Robin Scroggs was my principal advisor, and always a challenging one; Agneta Enermalm-Ogawa was the second reader, and especially helpful in guiding me through the linguistic thickets I found myself drawn into; Raymond E. Brown was my teacher long before I began the dissertation, a model of scholarship and clear expression. Alan F. Segal of Barnard College and Robert E. Somerville and Dean Roger Bagnall of Columbia University, the other members of my committee, were careful readers and insightful critics. Eugene A. Nida of the American Bible Society made helpful comments on early drafts of the appendix to Chapter 1.

I am particularly grateful to Joel Marcus of the Princeton Theological Seminary for his reading and criticism of Chapters 5 and 6.

For my introduction to Greek and to the New Testament I thank Thomas L. Robinson. Finally, everything that I do in these subjects bears the imprint of J. Louis Martyn: whenever I think I am closing in on Paul's meaning, the voice in which I hear myself trying to speak is Lou's. May I sometimes succeed!

To my wife, Dr. Jane A. Curtis, and to our children, Emma Curtis Winger and David Curtis Winger, I hope I have expressed my gratitude in ways much clearer than the words of this preface.

Chapter One

UNDERSTANDING Νόμος: AN INTRODUCTION TO THE PROBLEM

St. Paul, according to the earliest extant comment on his letters, wrote "some things that are hard to understand."[1] Succeeding centuries have not disturbed this conclusion; even (or especially) those who consider that they understand Paul grant that very many of his readers have not understood him.

A number of these "things that are hard to understand" appear in Paul's remarks about νόμος, or, as it is almost always translated, "law." For example:

. . . the power of sin is the law. (1 Cor 15:56)

For I through the law died to the law, that I might live to God. (Gal 2:19)

. . . if a law had been given which could make alive, then righteousness would indeed be by the law. (Gal 3:21)

Then what has become of our boasting? It is excluded. By what law? The law of works? No, but by the law of faith. (Rom 3:27)[2]

So then, I of myself serve the law of God with my mind, but with my flesh I serve the law of sin. (Rom 7:25)

In addition to these sayings which are enigmatic in themselves, Paul also appears to take contrasting views at different times about the relation between "law" and such other vital concepts as "faith," "righteousness" and "spirit."

---

[1] 2 Pet 3:16.

[2] Here νόμος is often translated "principle" (*RSV, NEB*; contrast *JB, NAB*).

Thus, in Gal 3:23 Paul says that "we were confined under the law . . . until faith should be revealed"; but in Rom 3:27 he speaks of a "law of faith," and in Rom 3:31 he says that "by this faith . . . we uphold the law." Again, in Rom 3:21 he says that "the righteousness of God has been manifested apart from law," but immediately adds that "the law and the prophets bear witness to it." And of spirit, Paul says both: ". . . we are discharged from the law, dead to that which held us captive, so that we serve . . . in the new life of the spirit" (Rom 7:6), and also, eight verses later: "We know that the law is spiritual . . ." (Rom 7:14). These passages take us beyond the merely puzzling into major theological issues: the nature of faith, of righteousness, and of spirit, issues which thus become intertwined with the nature of law.

Underlying all of these difficulties is a question which Paul himself does not address, and which provides the topic of this dissertation: what does Paul mean by "law," νόμος?[3] This question has usually had two basic answers. The first answer is that Paul means (at least most of the time) "the Mosaic law,"[4] or the Old Testament,[5] or perhaps "the whole of Israel's sacred tradition."[6] The second answer is that Paul is speaking of law generally; this is the basis for Luther's sweeping conclusion that "a Christian, properly defined, is free of *all* laws and subject to *nothing*, internally or externally."[7] These two answers are not inconsistent; Paul could be using Mosaic law as an instance of law in general; or, even if Paul himself is thinking only of Mosaic law, his arguments might nevertheless be applicable to law in general.

For several reasons, however, neither of these answers is adequate. First of all, the disagreement over whether Paul refers to Mosaic law, to scripture as a whole or to all sacred tradition is troubling. Second, while these possibilities (separately or together) are satisfactory for most of Paul's uses of νόμος, there remain a few, such as νόμος ἁμαρτίας in Rom 7:25, where they are more dubious; yet it is equally dubious that νόμος ἁμαρτίας means law in general.

Third, both answers neglect a distinction useful in lexical semantics, between a term's *meaning* and its *reference*. I take up this distinction in detail

---

[3] Paul almost always says simply νόμος (or ὁ νόμος), without qualification and without explanation. The context usually provides hints as to Paul's meaning, but not always; see, e.g., 1 Cor 15:56.

[4] Hübner, *Law*, 17; BAGD, s.v. 3; Luther, *Works*, 26.122 (on Gal 2:16).

[5] Davies, "Paul and the Law," 92; E. P. Sanders, *Paul, the Law*, 3; J. A. Sanders, "Torah."

[6] Räisänen, *Paul*, 16.

[7] *Works*, 26.134 (on Gal 2:16) (emphasis added). Somewhat similar is Burton's view (*Galatians*, 455-59) that νόμος means generally "divine law"—often, however, misunderstood "as a purely legalistic system" (ibid., 457). According to Burton, it is this misunderstanding which Paul criticizes, not "divine law" as such.

in an appendix to this chapter, but a related illustration in English will make the basic point. We may take "law" to *mean* something like "a rule established by authority";[8] in the sentence, "The law gives every accused person a day in court," the term "law" *refers* to some particular law within the general meaning of the term.[9] With this in mind, we may ask: if Paul does use νόμος for "Mosaic code," is this *meaning*, or *reference*? Is this use of νόμος distinct from all others? Or does it depend on some general sense of νόμος which Paul applies to the particular object, "Mosaic code"?

These possibilities are not sharply opposed; we shall see that the relations between meaning and reference are complex. What is at stake can be put thus: in what ways (if any) does Paul's use of νόμος to refer to "Mosaic code," or to "scripture" or "sacred traditions," involve elements of general meaning which are common to other uses of νόμος? An answer to this question will give a basis for exploring the relation between the two theses that (a) Paul is talking about Jewish law, scripture or tradition, and (b) that he is talking about law in general. When we translate νόμος as "law" (or "Gesetz," or "loi"), it becomes natural to assume that Paul's discussion has a general meaning, even if at the same time Paul refers specifically to Jewish "law." This natural assumption is suggestive; it is true that a specific reference, for instance to Jewish scripture, does not rule out a more general significance. But the assumption requires testing at two points: first, what is the general meaning assumed in a reference to a particular νόμος? Second, does that general meaning play any role in Paul's argument? If, for instance, Paul rejects νόμος because it came through angels, by the hand of a mediator (Gal 3:19), that is probably an argument specific to Mosaic law.[10] But if Paul rejects νόμος because it is "purely legalistic,"[11] and if this "pure legalism" is intrinsic to the meaning of νόμος, then that is an argument of general application. Therefore an inquiry into the meaning and reference of νόμος as that term is used by Paul may shed light not only on what Paul means to say to his particular audiences, but also on the ways in which we may fairly apply his utterances.

---

[8] *American Heritage Dictionary of the English Language* (Boston: American Heritage, 1971). Although the meaning of "law" is much disputed by jurists and philosophers, this definition will be sufficient here.

[9] Depending on the speaker's degree of knowledge about law, "law" might refer generally to "the law of the United States," or specifically to some statute or court rule that allows a defendant to appear in court.

[10] Such an argument would have implications for most other νόμοι, whose connection with God Paul would doubtless see as still more indirect. But the argument does not apply to νόμος *as such*; it might not apply to a νόμος of Christ (Gal 6:2)—depending on what *that* expression refers to.

[11] Burton, *Galatians*, 457.

The distinction between meaning and reference allows us to recognize Paul's focus on Jewish νόμος and still explore the relations between Paul's use of νόμος and the general usage of νόμος in Paul's world. In that world νόμος had a range of senses, as the lexicons indicate,[12] and as a survey of Greek literature more-or-less contemporary with Paul can easily amplify: from the νόμος of a city or people[13] to νόμος as reason[14] to νόμος as custom[15] to νόμος as force.[16] Are any of the ideas associated with these senses present in Paul's use of νόμος? I shall try to find out in this dissertation.

An investigation of the meaning of νόμος in Paul may also help to determine its referents. As I have noted, there is wide agreement that Paul refers to something Jewish, but no agreement over whether that is "law," "scripture," or "tradition." If we can establish a meaning for νόμος, that may help to clarify

---

[12] E.g., LSJ, s.v.: "*usage, custom . . . statute . . .*"; BAGD, s.v.: "gener., of any law . . *a rule* governing one's actions, *principle, norm* . . . esp. of the law, which Moses received from God . . . Holy Scripture gener. . . . fig. of Christianity as a 'new law' . . ." (I discuss these definitions below, in Chapter 2).

[13] E.g., Diodorus Siculus, *Library of History*, 1.69.6, 70.1; 12.17.1-2, 20.3; 13.35.3; Dionysius of Halicarnassus, *Roman Antiquities*, 2.27.3, 74.2; 4.41.2; 10.1.2, 57.5, 60.6; Epictetus, *Discourses*, 2.20.26. Although Philo typically uses νόμος for Jewish νόμος, he also allows a comparison to the νόμοι of other peoples: *De Vita Mosis*, 2.7 §44.

[14] E.g., Dio Chrysostom, *Orations* 1.75:

ὁ δ' ἐγγὺς οὗτος ἑστηκὼς τῆς βασιλείας παρ' αὐτὸ τὸ σκῆπτρον ἔμπροσθεν ἰσχυρὸς ἀνήρ, πολιὸς καὶ μεγαλόφρων, οὗτος δὴ καλεῖται Νόμος, ὁ δὲ αὐτὸς καὶ Λόγος Ὀρθὸς κέκληται Σύμβουλος καὶ Πάρεδρος, οὗ χωρὶς οὐδὲν ἐκείναις πρᾶξαι θέμις οὐδὲ διανοηθῆναι.

And this one standing by Royal Rule, just before her very sceptre, a man strong, gray and noble: he is called Law; but he has also been called Right Reason, Counselor and Coadjutor. Without him none of the others may act or think.

Cf. Marcus Aurelius, *Meditations* 7.9:

κόσμος τε γὰρ εἷς ἐξ ἁπάντων, καὶ θεὸς εἷς διὰ πάντων, καὶ οὐσία μία, καὶ νόμος εἷς, λόγος κοινὸς πάντων τῶν νοερῶν ζῴων, καὶ ἀλήθεια μία·

For there is one universe out of all things, and one God through all things, and one substance and one law, the common reason of all intelligent beings, and one truth.

[15] E.g., Philo, *De Iosepho* 34 §202; Josephus, *Life* 39 §198, equating ἔθη τὰ πάτρια with παλαιοὶ νόμοι; *Ag.Ap.* 1.35 §317, *J.W.* 5.9.4 §402, 7.3.4 §50, equating ἔθη and νόμος.

[16] E.g., Epictetus, *Discourses* 3.24.106, νόμος as ἡ τῶν ἀπροιρέτων, τῶν οὐκ ἐμῶν, "the realm of things not chosen, which are not mine." Cf. Josephus, *Ant.* 4.8.48 §322, death as νόμος φύσεως, and *J.W.* 5.9.3 §367: νόμον γε μὴν ὡρίσθαι καὶ παρὰ θηρσὶν ἰσχυρότατον καὶ παρ' ἀνθρώποις, εἴκειν τοῖς δυνατερωτέροις . . . , "there is an established law, as strong among beasts as among humans: yield to the stronger . . ."

the nature of Jewish νόμος. For instance, if νόμος for Paul should mean "an inflexible rule,"[17] translating it by "law" or "code" might convey that idea better than "scripture" or "tradition." On the other hand, if νόμος for Paul should include the idea of custom,[18] then "tradition" might be preferable.[19]

As I proceed, the technical literature of both linguistics and philosophy will inform both my terminology and my method. For many readers this technical background may be of little interest, and therefore I have tried to write the principal chapters of this dissertation (2 through 6) so that they can be understood on their own. My analysis of terminology and method appears in the appendix to this chapter; there I consider the concepts of *meaning* and *reference* in greater detail, distinguishing these two from each other, and both from what a speaker *asserts* about what a term either *means* or *refers to*. This discussion is followed by a consideration of methodologies for identifying meaning.

In Chapter 2 I take up the meaning of νόμος in Paul's letters, first surveying the analyses of lexicons and scholars, and then presenting my own investigation.

In Chapter 3 I turn to reference, surveying all of Paul's uses of νόμος and identifying the various ways in which the term refers to non-linguistic entities.

Next I will look more carefully at the principal referent for νόμος in Paul's letters; I shall call this referent simply "Jewish νόμος," in order to avoid too hasty a choice among the alternatives law, scripture and tradition. Two questions about Jewish νόμος occupy Chapter 4: first, when νόμος *refers* to Jewish νόμος, does it also have a distinct *meaning*? and second, what is Jewish νόμος?

The analyses in Chapters 2, 3 and 4 are based on a survey of all of Paul's uses of νόμος. The conclusions reached in these chapters are tested in Chapters 5 and 6, through the detailed examination of two passages in which νόμος is prominent: Gal 2:15-21 and Rom 7:14-25.

A summary, in Chapter 7, concludes the dissertation.

---

[17] Compare the use of νόμος for "force" (above, n. 16).

[18] See the passages cited in n. 15 above.

[19] Conversely, if we can identify the referents of νόμος we should have a better idea of its meaning; this is the way lexicographers usually work. But the identification of Paul's referent (or referents) for νόμος is sufficiently difficult that it will prove helpful to begin, instead, with meaning. See further "Procedures for the Analysis of Meaning" in the appendix to this chapter.

Appendix to Chapter 1

Terminology

Two terms describe what I am investigating, and a third describes what I am not investigating: *meaning, reference,* and *assertion.*[1] I wish to know what νόμος means and what it *refers* to in Paul's writings; in the course of investigating these questions it will be necessary to discuss what Paul *asserts* about νόμος, but this discussion will be incidental to my investigation of *meaning* and *reference.* The role which νόμος plays in the created world, a topic of eternal interest to theologians and exegetes, is not my topic; I turn instead to the preliminary task of specifying what that νόμος is whose role is of such importance to Paul and his interpreters.

My three terms are analytically distinct, although we shall see that in practice the distinctions may be difficult to locate. They can be illustrated by the sentence:

---

[1] Terminology is apt to be a source of confusion here. With *meaning* and *reference* I am generally following the usage employed by Nida (*Semantic Structures*, 15). Louw (*Semantics*, 54-55) employs "meaning" more-or-less as I do, and "referential meaning" in the way I employ *reference*, but he uses "reference" itself differently; Lyons (*Semantics*, 1.177) employs "reference" more-or-less as I do but reserves "meaning" for non-technical use and employs the distinct terms "sense" and "denotation" for different aspects of what I cover by "meaning" (ibid., 197-215; I discuss these aspects below, at nn. 10-11). As for *assertion,* that does not appear to have a technical usage among semanticists (although Lyons occasionally employs it, as at *Semantics*, 1.177); Dr. Nida has suggested in a letter to me (August 17, 1988) "that linguists and logicians tend to use the term 'proposition' for which [I am] using 'assertion.'"

In this dissertation, each of these terms is intended to have the meaning which I give it here.

(1) The bicycle has a flat tire.

Here the *meaning* of "bicycle" is something like "a vehicle with two wheels in tandem, usually propelled by pedals . .";[2] the *reference* is evidently to some particular bicycle, which a broader context would presumably specify ("I have a bicycle; the bicycle has a flat tire"); and of this particular bicycle it is *asserted* that it has a flat tire.

Meaning and Reference

The distinction between *meaning* and *reference* is, generally, that the meaning of a term is (for the community which uses it) implicit in the term, while the reference is supplied by the context in which the term is used.[3] Usually a general *meaning* allows a variety of particular *references,* as "bicycle" can refer to any individual bicycle. According to Nida,

> The meaning of a word consists of the set of distinctive features [in my example, two wheels and pedals] which make possible certain types of reference, while reference itself is the process of designating some entity, event, etc. by a particular symbol.[4]

It would not be quite correct, however, to say that a word's meaning is independent of any particular context; if a word has multiple meanings, the meaning in any particular context is that which is indicated by the context.[5] Consider:

(1') The car has a flat tire.

Although "car" by itself might mean a railway car, this meaning is excluded here by "has a flat tire." It is still the case, however, that the term "car" on its own contributes a range of meanings, independent of the context; in this case the context both specifies one meaning out of that range,[6] and

---

2 *Random House Dictionary*, s.v. bicycle.

3 In Louw's words (*Semantics*, 51), "the meaning for which a word serves is only that which the word itself, on its own, contributes to the context." Here I use "context" in the restricted sense used by Ducrot and Todorov (*Dictionary*, 333), "the strictly linguistic surroundings of an element [a word or phonic unit] within an utterance" (brackets in the original). Ducrot and Todorov also speak (ibid.) of "speech situation," meaning "the physical and social setting in which the act [of communication] takes place . . ."; others (e.g., Silva, *Biblical Words*, 138-49) use "context" to include "speech situation" as well as "strictly linguistic surroundings."

4 Nida, *Semantic Structures*, 15.

5 Ullmann, *Semantics*, 168.

6 In other cases the context may be ambiguous—sometimes inadvertently, sometimes, as in John 3:3, deliberately.

(presumably) also specifies which particular car is referred to. I shall have more to say about multiple meanings below.

Meaning: Things or Concepts?

How can a term's *meaning* be stated? According to Nida, "meaning" is not a matter of the relation between *word* and *thing*, but rather of the relation between *word* and *concept:*

> Although many persons recognize that meaning is essentially a relation, they tend to view it as a relation to some entity in the practical world. The meaning of the word *chair* is thus considered to be the relation of the symbol to the thing called 'chair,' and the meaning of *house* is the relation of the word to some particular dwelling which can be referred to by this symbol. In reality, however, the referent of a verbal symbol is not an object in the practical world; rather, it is a concept or set of concepts which people may have about objects, events, abstracts, and relations. If this were not so, it would be impossible to have words for things which have never existed except in the mind, e.g., *mermaids, unicorns,* and *the gods of Olympus.*[7]

Applied to our example, this suggests that the ideas of two wheels, pedals, and so forth—ideas that we could entertain without having ever seen any object combining them—are basic to the meaning of "bicycle." Nevertheless, I do not want to dismiss completely the possibility that knowledge of physical objects may also be important to meaning. Suppose a vehicle with two wheels and pedals but so designed that only one wheel touches the ground at a time, the other wheel being raised in the air until it comes down to take its turn on the ground. Such a vehicle might fit the dictionary definition of "bicycle," but I think most people would agree that it must be something else. To be sure, we could add to our definition some qualification such as "with both wheels ordinarily touching the ground at all times while the vehicle is in use"; but this new concept is evidently one we have drawn from our prior knowledge of the objects called "bicycles."[8]

"Bicycle" is a relatively simple term, used for a relatively well-defined class of objects; the entities for which νόμος is used are far more diffuse. Perhaps, then, we should think of concepts as prior in the meaning of νόμος. But this might not be so. It might be, for instance, that for Paul and his audience νόμος means first and foremost the Pentateuch: that singular object. Or νόμος might mean, alternatively, any rules of conduct enforced in courts: a

---

[7] Nida, *Semantic Structures,* 14 (emphasis in the original).

[8] Other fantastic objects might also be imagined, which would require that further conditions be added to exclude them from the definition of "bicycle."

wide range of things, but still one that might be known by experience prior to the development of a conceptual description. Or νόμος might have all of these meanings, and also a figurative sense developed by taking a concept which came originally from the meaning "rules of conduct enforced in courts" but is now divorced from that meaning and is simply "any force difficult to resist"[9]—such as physical desire.

I have tried here to select examples plausible for Paul; I shall pursue these matters in the course of this dissertation, particularly in Chapter 4, where I try to define "Jewish νόμος." For now I will only add that I do not think it necessary to choose between regarding meaning as a relation to things or to concepts. Lyons is helpful at this point. He holds that a term has *both* "sense," which is the term's relation to other terms in the same language,[10] *and* "denotation," which is the term's relation to "persons, things, places, properties, processes and activities external to the language system."[11]

Reference Incorporated in Meaning

Now let us return to the relationship of *meaning* to *reference* as analogous to that of *general* to *particular* (see above, at n. 3). This analogy is complicated by cases in which a term's *meaning*—the context-independent sense of the term—itself includes a specific *reference*. This might be unusual for bicycles, to return to my illustration; still we can certainly imagine that for some group

---

[9] See Chapter 1, n. 16.

[10] Lyons, *Semantics*, 1.206. This, differently defined, corresponds closely to "concepts," for concepts can only be conceived in language.

[11] Ibid., 207; on "sense" and "denotation" generally, see ibid., 1.197-214. Note also Kripke, who argues in *Naming* that "natural kinds," including not only "gold" (116-19, 123-25), "tigers" (119-22) and "heat" (131), but also non-existent kinds such as "unicorns" (156-57), are analogous to names: they have denotation but not connotation (134-35; in Lyons's terms, "connotation" is "sense").

Besides the distinctions between sense and denotation, linguists distinguish between *semantic* and *pragmatic* aspects of meaning. The distinction is not easy to describe; Levinson devotes thirty pages of his textbook (*Pragmatics*, 5-35) to an assessment of competing definitions, concluding (ibid., 32) that the "most promising" description is that pragmatics is "a theory of language understanding that takes context [i.e., speech situation] into account, in order to complement the contribution that semantics [which is context-independent] makes to meaning." Cf. Carnap, *Semantics*, 8-11; Lyons, *Semantics*, 1.114-19. Most of pragmatics is concerned with the meaning of utterances rather than single words, but Levinson (*Pragmatics*, 8-9) illustrates lexical pragmatics with the distinction between "rabbit" and "bunny": *semantically* equivalent, they differ *pragmatically* in that "bunny" is "appropriately used either by or to children."

We could similarly say that the use of νόμος as an equivalent for "Mosaic code" *in a Jewish speech situation* is pragmatic. For my purposes, however, the distinction between semantics and pragmatics has not seemed helpful, and I will not employ it here.

of people there is a particular bicycle which, because of some special qualities (perhaps it seats ten people) is known simply as "the bicycle." Then for that group "bicycle" has a special meaning, or technical sense; used with no specification, it *means* that particular bicycle. The *meaning* incorporates a *reference*.

This could be the case even though the members of this circle are perfectly familiar with the general sense of "bicycle," and in fact, in some contexts, use the term in that general sense. Then we would say that bicycle has two meanings, one of which incorporates a reference, one of which does not. Moreover: in the example just given the bicycle specially referred to is one within the ordinary meaning of "bicycle"; we could therefore consider this use of "bicycle" to be, rather than a separate meaning, the ordinary meaning with a specific reference supplied by the context. It might however be that "bicycle" comes to be applied to some unique object which is not, strictly speaking, a bicycle (perhaps it has three wheels). In that case, when "bicycle" is used of the unique object it has not only a unique referent but a unique meaning—related to the ordinary meaning, but not the same.

This may seem an unlikely possibility for bicycles, but it is quite real for νόμος among first-century Christians and Jews. If they used νόμος for Pentateuch, did that necessarily mean that they regarded the Pentateuch as a νόμος?

Meaning and Assertion

There is more to be said about the distinction of *meaning* from *assertion*. Two additional sentences will be helpful:

>   (2) Bicycles have two wheels.

and:

>   (3) The bicycle is a popular means of travel.

In (2), the *reference* is now to bicycles in general, and the *assertion* now specifies part of the *meaning*.[12] In (3), on the other hand, the *reference* is also to bicycles in general, but the *assertion* does not specify the *meaning* of "bicycle."[13] Sentences (1) ["The bicycle has a flat tire"], (2), and (3) are all of

---

[12] The general reference in this sentence is signalled by the use of "bicycles," plural, but the same sense could have been expressed by:

>   (2') The bicycle has two wheels

in which "bicycle" is now generic. (1) and (2') are thus identical in form.

[13] Here, as generally, I am using *meaning* for lexical meaning: that is, the meaning of a particular term. *Assertions* will also both depend on and contribute to *meaning* in other senses, as when we speak of phrases, sentences and larger units as having meaning; thus

the same form; we understand (2) as specifying meaning, however, either because we happen to know already what "bicycle" means, or from the broader context of the statement ("Here is the difference between the bicycle and the tricycle; the bicycle has, etc."). (3), similarly, we will understand as going beyond *meaning* because of its broader context, or because we know what "bicycle" means, or perhaps because we know that the quality "popular" is unlikely to be part of the *meaning* of a term (at least in English). But consider this similar sentence:

(4) The bicycle is a rapid means of self-propulsion.

Now I have stated something about "bicycle" which is probably not contained in any dictionary definition for the term; yet we could still consider it to be so closely related to the meaning of "bicycle" that it is part of it. We may note that this statement is not necessarily true; it depends on the bicycle's gear ratio. But it is usually true, and we know this from our familiarity with bicycles. Nida's concept of "implicational" or "inferential" components of meaning, which are "implied by a particular meaning, though they do not form an essential part of the core meaning,"[14] may be helpful here. We shall return to "components" as a part of meaning below (at nn. 25-35); here the chief point to be observed is that the borders of meaning may be unclear, even to speakers of the language. Thus we might legitimately differ over whether an object appearing to conform to the dictionary definition of bicycle, but made out of a flexible plastic as a work of art and unusable as a means of travel, is a bicycle or not.[15]

A *fortiori*, greater difficulties may arise in analyzing the meaning of terms used in a different culture two thousand years ago. Thus we may take from Paul the sentence:

ὁ νόμος πνευματικός ἐστιν (Rom 7:14).

Is Paul here saying: (a) a particular νόμος is πνευματικός? or (b) νόμος in general is πνευματικός? or (c) it is part of the meaning of νόμος to be πνευματικός?

---

the two concluding chapters of Louw, *Semantics* (67-158) are titled "Semantics Is More Than the Meaning of Words" and "Semantics Is More Than the Meaning of Sentences."

[14] Nida, *Componential Analysis*, 38-39. Nida further distinguishes between "implicational" components, which follow necessarily from the core meaning, and "inferential" ones, which usually follow but in particular cases may be specifically denied.

[15] Note that such an object would not fit the Random House definition of "bicycle" (above, at n. 2), since that incorporates the term "vehicle," which in turn is defined in terms of "travel" or "convey[ance]"; the fantastic contraption I posited at n. 8, on the other hand, would fit that definition. But surely people would be far more likely to use "bicycle" for the art object ("See that plastic bike?") than for the fantastic vehicle ("What is *that*?").

There are two ways to answer these questions. First, we must explore as carefully as we can all other evidence about the meaning of νόμος in Paul's letters; if we establish that it means "law given by God," and further that πνευματικός means "caused by the divine Spirit,"[16] then it may be that πνευματικός is part of the meaning of νόμος here, at least as an implicational or inferential component.[17] Second, we can explore the context here for clues; the introductory word οἴδαμεν, which precedes the language I quote, implies that νόμος is generally agreed to be πνευματικός (but this could be an argument based on experience rather than the meaning of νόμος[18]).

The chief point is that while the sentence "νόμος is spiritual" tells us that the reality denoted by νόμος is spiritual, it does not tell us that the term νόμος means "spiritual"—on the whole, in fact, it rather implies that it does not. Inasmuch as I have defined *meaning* in terms of what is *implicit* in a term, I am entitled to operate with the assumption that whatever is *explicitly* affirmed is not part of the *meaning;* thus, if "bicycle" meant "a two-wheeled vehicle with one flat tire," there would ordinarily be no need to say, "The bicycle has a flat tire." There are exceptions; people do make meaning explicit, for clarity or for emphasis. But surely Paul's extended discussions of νόμος in Romans and Galatians were intended by and large to assert things about νόμος which were not simply true by definition. When Paul says something about νόμος, my starting assumption will be that his statement specifies neither *meaning* nor *reference,* but is simply *assertion.*

Yet this does not mean that an assertion will tell us nothing about meaning; it may inform us indirectly. Thus, while "the bicycle has a flat tire" does not mean that all bicycles have flat tires, but rather implies that ordinarily they do not, it does tell us that bicycles have (or may have) tires, and thus wheels. Likewise, ὁ νόμος πνευματικός ἐστιν tells us that νόμος is something which can be πνευματικός.[19]

---

16 BAGD, s.v. 2

17 See above, at n. 14.

18 Barrett (*Romans,* 146) implies the former view: "This [statement] was axiomatic in Judaism."

19 This example, however, serves to show the limitation of this kind of information, especially where a term (here πνευματικός) intersects the one under investigation (νόμος) only once. (The cognate πνεῦμα is associated with νόμος at Rom 7:6, 14: 8:2, 4; Gal 3:2, 5; 5:18, 22-23.) To begin with, it is not immediately obvious what classes of things may or may not be πνευματικός; to proceed, we would have to investigate the meaning of πνευματικός, and, taking into account the possibility that πνευματικός or νόμος is here used in some figurative or other special sense, the likelihood that this approach would tell us much about the meaning of νόμος is, in this instance, small.

Multiple Meanings: ?

I have referred above to the possibility that a single word may have multiple meanings. Dictionaries commonly organize their entries into discrete senses, and this is true, as we shall see, of the treatment of νόμος in Greek lexicons. Nevertheless there are problems with the idea of multiple distinct meanings, and these problems may also be seen with νόμος. Lyons discusses at length the difficulty of deciding whether a term has two distinct meanings, or rather one general meaning that in particular cases could be stated more particularly by other terms: as "red" may mean both "scarlet" and "crimson."[20] According to Lyons,

> distinctions of sense can be multiplied indefinitely. Does 'mouth' have the same meaning in 'the mouth of the river'. . . , for example, as it has in 'the mouth of the tunnel' or 'the mouth of the jar'? . . . It may well be that the whole notion of discrete lexical senses is ill-founded . . .[21]

When νόμος is used in one place of the law of Rome and in another of the law of Athens, we probably take these as examples of one general meaning. Should not the law of the Jews be considered as a further instance of this meaning? We shall see that the lexicons and exegetes all consider "Jewish law" as a separate meaning of νόμος; but has this judgment a semantic basis, or does it merely reflect the special theological interest which Jewish law has for most of those who write on νόμος? This difficulty is reflected in differences on how to define the meaning of "Jewish law."[22]

When one considers passages such as Gal 4:21b, where Paul seems to use νόμος to mean scripture, the distinction of a separate Jewish νόμος not analogous to the νόμος of Rome or Athens appears appropriate. But often, as with the phrase ὑπὸ νόμον (e.g., Gal 4:21a), νόμος in Paul seems to mean a law that is evidently Jewish but could also be analogous to any other law. A distinction between νόμος meaning Jewish law and νόμος meaning Jewish scripture is questionable precisely because in places such as Gal 4:21 we see the two together without apparent distinction.

It is sometimes said that the defining mark of νόμος in Paul's letters is not that it is Jewish, but that it comes from God.[23] If this is true, it may be sufficient justification for the separation of this meaning of νόμος from that which

---

[20] Lyons, *Semantics*, 2.406-9. "Red" is contrasted with "cry," meaning "weep" or "shout," which seem to be distinct meanings; but Lyons argues that this is uncertain.

[21] Lyons, *Semantics*, 2.554 (emphasis added).

[22] See Chapter 1.

[23] E.g., Burton; see Chapter 2 below, at n. 27.

refers to humanly instituted laws. But whether this is a true is a question which must be further considered.[24]

Methodology

The Analysis of Meaning

How shall we analyze meaning? Nida's account of meaning provides us with a starting point. I have referred to aspects of this account above;[25] now it will be profitable to elaborate. Nida, as I have noted, defines "meaning" in terms of sets of "distinctive features"[26] or "concepts";[27] these features or concepts he calls "semantic components."[28] Using the word "father" as an example, Nida divides such components into two classes. "Diagnostic components" distinguish the term from other similar ones;[29] in Lyons's terminology, they give the "sense" of a term.[30] Thus *male* distinguishes "father" from "mother," while *direct line of descent* distinguishes it from "uncle." For diagnostic components, contrast is critical; elsewhere Nida has written, "In fact, meaning exists only where systematic sets of contrasts exist."[31]

"Supplementary components" often appear in figurative expressions such as "he was like a father to the boy"; here there is no implication of kinship, but rather the speaker draws on such concepts as "e.g. (1) watchful care for and (2) companionship."[32] We can see from this example that supplementary

---

[24] It would not be enough to show that Paul and his audience believed νόμος to be divine; we would also have to show that this is part of the *meaning* of the term. Even then, a special sense of νόμος would not have been established. It was a common convention in the ancient world, not limited to Jews, that νόμος is divine—either in the sense of a single divine νόμος (e.g., Musonius Rufus [Lutz, *Roman Socrates*, 104.35]; Plutarch, *Uneducated Ruler*, 780C; Marcus Aurelius, *Meditations*, 7.9), or in the sense of human laws delivered by the gods (Diodorus Siculus, *Library of History*, 1.94.1-2).

[25] At nn. 4, 7, 14.

[26] Above, at n. 4.

[27] Above, at n. 7.

[28] Nida, *Semantic Structures*, 15.

[29] Or, more precisely, from other terms in the same "semantic domain." Nida, *Componential Analysis*, 33. A semantic domain is also defined by components: "A semantic domain consists essentially of a group of meanings . . . which share certain semantic components." The semantic domain of "father" is thus "kinship," defined by kinship relations.

[30] See above, at n. 10.

[31] Nida, *Semantic Structures*, 14.

[32] Nida, *Componential Analysis*, 35. One might suppose that "father" is here used with a different *meaning*; but, while Nida does not address this point, the presence of "like" tells against it. The speaker is making a comparison with biological fathers, but on the basis of

components will not necessarily attach to every member of the class identified by the term under investigation (fathers are not always caring). Nida also notes that

> One must not assume that any and all features of fathers are supplementary semantic components of *father*. Such components are restricted to precisely those features which occur in lexical contrasts.[33]

In other words, usage dictates. It may be, for instance, that fathers are generally larger than mothers and (at least until maturity) children; but size is not a supplementary component of "father" unless, in fact, there exist expressions such as "big as a father" which demonstrate this component.

Nida's example suggests that a term may be used without any implication of the supplementary components of meaning; thus, there is no contradiction in saying, "His father treated him brutally." Such a statement expressly denies the supplementary component (here, *watchful care*), but express denial is not necessary. One may use the term "father" in setting forth the genealogy of the Queen of England without suggesting anything about the relations her forbears had with their children. In such a case, *watchful care* is much like a separate meaning of "father" and, since nothing in the context suggests this meaning, the hearer will not think of it.

I have already referred to a further distinction relating to diagnostic components: that between "core," "implicational," and "inferential."[34] Little use will be made here of these precise terms, for it seems to me that in practice the distinctions are difficult to make. Nida's distinctions remain important, however, as a reminder that the delineation of core components is itself likely to be imprecise; instead of a definite catalog of what is essential to meaning, we may have components scaling off from "core" to "inferential" and beyond. This is surely especially likely when we deal with material as limited in quantity, and as remote from us in time and place, as Paul's letters.[35]

I noted above ("Meaning: Things or Concepts?") that viewing meaning as a matter of concepts (the sense of a term) may be complemented by viewing meaning as a matter of things (the denotation of a term). In itself, the use of

---

supplementary components of that meaning, not the diagnostic components related to blood relationship.

[33] Nida, *Componential Analysis*, 35.

[34] Ibid., 38-39; above, n. 14.

[35] So far as quantity is concerned, we will draw on other documents of Paul's approximate time and place in an investigation of νόμος. But we will still have far less material to work with than those analysts of contemporary language for whom Nida is principally writing.

components to describe meaning does not commit us to the former view against the latter, for even if *things* lie at the basis of meaning, *concepts* will ordinarily be essential for the identification of those things.[36] Still, in some cases concepts are much more clearly shorthand for specific things than in others, and the generally conceded meaning {νόμος = Pentateuch[37]} is such a case.[38] Ought we to regard νόμος, in this meaning, as simply a proper name for *these books,* in the sense described by Ryle?

> Using a proper name is not committing oneself to any further assertions whatso-ever. Proper names are appellations and not descriptions, and descriptions are descriptions and not appellations. . . . Proper names are arbitrary bestowals, and convey nothing true and nothing false, for they convey nothing at all.[39]

This is a real possibility for νόμος. When νόμος comes to function much like a name, as perhaps it does in Gal 4:21b where νόμος is said to tell of Abraham's two wives, we cannot assume that it still carries with it any elements of the general meaning of νόμος. But, neither can we assume that it functions only as a name. In Gal 4:21b, νόμος may be chosen deliberately because Paul wishes to use this story as a guide for the Galatians, or to connote some other idea associated with νόμος. In short, this meaning of νόμος, like other meanings, requires investigation.

Nida's terminology again is useful in delineating the problem. If νόμος simply equalled Pentateuch, it would seem that "Pentateuch" would be the sole diagnostic component of this meaning of νόμος; but the defining charac-teristic of diagnostic components "is that they serve to distinguish this mean-ing from others in the same domain,"[40] and "Pentateuch" is not sufficient to do this. Why does Paul say νόμος and not γράμμα, or γραφή, or βιβλίον, or Μωϋσῆς?[41] The meaning of νόμος as Pentateuch is not adequately specified until diagnostic components are stated that show how νόμος in this sense dif-

---

[36] There is no way to identify things verbally without using concepts. (One could, however, use pictures; cf. Lyons, *Semantics,* 1.209, on the definition of "cow.")

[37] BAGD, s.v. 4.a; Abbott-Smith, *Lexicon,* s.v. 5(a); Louw and Nida, *Lexicon,* 33.55; *TDNT* 4 (1967) 1070; Burton, *Galatians,* 459.

[38] Here I assume the validity of this as a separate meaning. I have noted above (at n. 22) that this is in fact uncertain.

[39] Ryle, "Meaning," 137. As Dr. Nida has pointed out to me in a letter dated August 17, 1988, names may nevertheless "carry strong associative meanings, e.g., Nero, Satan, and Hitler." Occasionally names may even pass into the language as general terms, as in "He's a regular Hitler," or "Caesar."

[40] Nida, *Componential Analysis,* 33.

[41] For identifying semantic domains, Louw and Nida, *Lexicon,* is extremely useful. The examples I give here are from ¶¶33.50, 52, 53, 55 and 59.

fers from these other terms, any of which could also be used to refer to the Pentateuch. Moreover, even if "Pentateuch" were the sole diagnostic component of one meaning of νόμος, this meaning might still incorporate supplementary components relevant to Paul's argument.

I want, therefore, to specify the meaning or meanings of νόμος in Paul's letters, by identifying both those diagnostic components which will distinguish νόμος from other similar terms, and such supplementary components as the evidence suggests.

Procedures for the Analysis of Meaning

How can this be done? According to Nida, "it is from observing the range of reference of a symbol that we normally determine its meaning."[42] Following this procedure, we could try to identify what νόμος refers to in each place where it appears in Paul's letters, and then analyze the components which this range of reference implies. This is on its face a reasonable procedure, and it might well be effective for the analysis of νόμος in Paul; but it seems to me that there would be sufficient difficulties in applying this method here that I prefer to proceed in a different way.[43]

In particular, specifying the referent of νόμος in Paul's writings is often difficult, especially when it is used in combinations like νόμος τῶν ἔργων and νόμος πίστεως (Rom 3:27) or ὁ νόμος τοῦ πνεύματος τῆς ζωῆς ἐν Χριστῷ Ἰησοῦ and ὁ νόμος τῆς ἁμαρτίας καὶ τοῦ θανάτου (Rom 8:2) or ὁ νόμος τοῦ Χριστοῦ (Gal 6:2). In some or all of these expressions Paul may or may not be referring to Jewish law; but even when it is apparent that νόμος refers to Jewish law in some sense, Paul employs expressions that raise some doubt as to what that sense is; see, e.g., Rom 2:14, 27, according to which uncircumcised Gentiles do νόμος,[44] or Rom 2:20, according to which νόμος provides ἡ μόρφωσις τῆς γνώσεως καὶ τῆς ἀληθείας. Even where Paul quotes νόμος, as in 1 Cor 9:8-9 (LXX Deut 25:4[45]), so that it would appear we have a precise referent, it is unclear whether the referent is the Pentateuch,[46] or Scripture generally,[47] or "the Mosaic code."[48]

---

[42] Nida, *Semantic Structures*, 15; cf. Nida, *Componential Analysis*, 64.

[43] Nida himself is writing principally for linguists analyzing languages in current use, who have far more material to work with than is available to us.

[44] Cf. Gal 5:14, according to which ὁ πᾶς νόμος has been fulfilled in one saying (λόγος).

[45] Paul either quotes or paraphrases Deuteronomy, depending on whether one reads φιμώσεις or κημώσεις in 1 Cor 9:9.

[46] So BAGD, s.v. 4.a.

[47] Since Scripture incorporates the Pentateuch, this cannot be excluded.

[48] So Burton, *Galatians*, 455 (meaning 2(a)); *TDNT*, 1070.

In such cases an understanding of what the term νόμος *means* might help us to fix the *referent*. Just as a range of referents will help to specify the meaning (or meanings) that encompass that range, so an understanding of meaning will suggest a range of referents; there is no reason in principle why investigation must proceed in one direction rather than the other. Or at any rate, the investigation can take up both aspects together; so I intend to proceed.

Thus, on the one hand, some things can be said about the referents for νόμος: for instance, 1 Cor 9:8-9 at least tells us that νόμος refers to something which says the words Paul quotes; Rom 2:14, 17 tell us that νόμος is connected in a special way to Jews. Any proposed meanings for νόμος must be consistent with such data.[49]

On the other hand, an analysis of the expressions in which νόμος is found in Paul's letters will reveal certain features implicit in νόμος which do not give us specific referents, but do "make possible certain types of reference"[50] and exclude others. For instance: we learn from Rom 3:19; 7:7; 1 Cor 9:8; 14:34 that νόμος speaks, and from Rom 2:13, 14, 25; Gal 5:3 that one does νόμος. These are features independent of the particular words νόμος says and the particular deeds by which it is done, and therefore these features do not specify referents for νόμος; but from Paul's use of such expressions as ὁ νόμος λέγει and ποιεῖν τὸν νόμον we learn that it *makes sense* to say such things of νόμος (as, presumably, it would not, except possibly in some figurative sense, to say them of θάλασσα). Thus this kind of analysis follows the suggestion of Ryle:

> To know what an expression means involves knowing what can (logically) be said with it, and what cannot (logically) be said with it. It involves knowing a set of bans, fiats and obligations, or, in a word, it is to know the rules of the employment of that expression.[51]

---

[49] That is, there must be a meaning consistent with these uses. There might, however, be other meanings of νόμος, found in other uses, which are unrelated to scripture or to Jews.

[50] Nida, *Semantic Structures*, 15. Nida's full statement is given above, at n. 4.

[51] Ryle, "Meaning," 143; cf. Silva, *Biblical Words*, 141-43 ("syntactic sense relations"), Lyons, *Semantics*, 1.261-66 ("syntactic lexical relations"). In this passage Ryle presents the "extensionalist" approach which Nida (*Componential Analysis*, 22-23) contrasts with his own "intensionalist" approach; the extensionalist approach "focusses on how words are used in contexts," while the intensionalist approach "focusses primarily upon the conceptual structures associated with certain linguistic units . . ." Nida (ibid., 23-24) allows that this approach is "complementary" to his own. Ullman (*Semantics*, 64-67) uses the term "operational" for Ryle's approach, contrasted to his own "referential" approach. Like Nida, Ullmann calls the two approaches "complementary"; he also suggests that in practice the approaches are the same (ibid., emphasis added):

But moreover, to the extent that expressions like ὁ νόμος λέγει and ποιεῖν τὸν νόμον are common in Paul's writings, we may infer that it is not only sensible to say that νόμος has a verbal content and that νόμος can be done, but, probably, that these propositions are taken for granted. This inference will be stronger if we also find the same or analogous expressions in related literature, such as other New Testament writings or the Septuagint.

On such a basis I will attempt to specify components of the meaning (or meanings) of νόμος. We may then compare such meanings of νόμος with those of other, related terms by comparing such terms' usage as categorized in these components of meaning: for example, do γραφή or δικαίωμα speak? and does one do them?

We shall see below that there are other important features of νόμος, besides those indicated by λέγειν and ποιεῖν; we shall likewise make comparisons with a variety of related terms in various domains, including: in the domain of writing, γραφή, γράμμα; in the domain of command, δικαίωμα, ἐντολή; in the domain of tradition, παράδοσις, ἔθος. By means of such comparisons I hope to specify the meaning of νόμος in Paul's letters.

If . . . the [operational] lexicographer tried, as he surely would, to identify some *typical uses* by extracting the *common feature or features* from a representative selection of contexts, then he would immediately relapse into a referential theory of meaning.

So it seems to me; but still I find the focus on "use" helpful. As Ullman says (63), "the operational definition . . . contains the salutary warning, which both the semanticist and the lexicographer would do well to heed, that the meaning of a word can be ascertained *only* by studying its use" (emphasis in the original). Likewise Nida (196): "The testing of conceptually determined meanings by noting the ways in which semantic units are used in the process of reference is absolutely essential."

Chapter Two

COMPONENTS OF MEANING IN Νόμος
AS USED BY PAUL

Existing analyses of νόμος do not clearly specify its meaning. A survey of the literature, in the first part of this chapter, will show the need for the new analysis which I undertake in the second part.

A Survey of Analyses of Νόμος

Lexicons and Dictionaries

For most readers of the New Testament in Greek, lexicography begins with Walter Bauer's lexicon, in German or English; as Silva remarks (in the course of discussing the lexicon's shortcomings), this is "the best specialized dictionary available for any ancient literature." But this is a tribute to Bauer's collection of materials to illustrate the usage of words found in early Christian literature; Bauer's classifications of meaning—and for νόμος, these are taken over without significant change by BAGD—are not the basis of his lexicon's pre-eminence, and they are not entitled to special deference.[1]

BAGD omits any general definition of νόμος and groups the term's meanings into five classes and two sub-classes. Each is illustrated with copious

---

[1] For criticisms of BAGD by semanticists, see Silva, *Biblical Words*, 172-74; Louw and Nida, *Lexicon*, viii-ix.

references to the New Testament and a range of other literature; in all, BAGD refers to 109 of Paul's 118 uses of νόμος. The classes are:

1. gener. of any law . . .[2]
2. a *rule* governing one's actions, *principle, norm* . . .[3]
3. esp. of the law which Moses received from God . . .[4]
4. of a collection of holy writings precious to the Jews—a. in the strict sense *the law* = the Pentateuch, the work of Moses the lawgiver . . . b. in the wider sense = Holy Scripture gener. . . .
5. fig. of Christianity as a "new law" . . .[5]

Of these, (1), "law," is scarcely a definition; BAGD surely does not mean that νόμος has every sense of "law"; and even if it did, it would be necessary to identify these senses. "Law" being left general, it is not clear how (1) differs from (2), especially with respect to Rom 3:27a, διὰ ποίου νόμου, which is BAGD's one unequivocal illustration of (1). As with (1), the terms used to define (2) are indistinct: would they include, for instance, an unconscious habit, or a self-imposed "norm" or "principle"?

The remaining three senses—to which BAGD assigns the vast majority of New Testament uses of νόμος—all describe specific entities to which νόμος refers. BAGD's descriptions of most of these senses use the term "law," which suggests elements of meaning common to senses 1 and 2. No such elements are specified, however. Thus BAGD generally treats νόμος as though it were simply a proper name;[6] but no analysis supports this treatment.[7]

---

[2] BAGD cites Rom 3:27a and possibly Rom 7:1f.

[3] Rom 7:21, 23a, b, c; 8:2b.

[4] Ninety-two uses in Paul are cited, classified according to the constructions in which they appear, but without distinction in meaning.

[5] Rom 3:27b; 8:2a; Gal 6:2.

[6] See the appendix to Chapter 1, at n. 39.

[7] Even as descriptions of *reference* and not *meaning*, BAGD's senses are not clear. Sense (3) implies that what is meant is the code delivered to Moses on Mt. Sinai, and hence the pertinent portions of Exodus, Leviticus, Numbers and Deuteronomy; but what of the oral law, also said to have been delivered to Moses? (m. Abot 1.1). Moreover, it is not clear that this precise sense would fit every text which BAGD lists under (3), such as Rom 2:26, according to which ἡ ἀκροβυστία may τὰ δικαιώματα τοῦ νόμου φυλάσσῃ. But if (3) does not mean the precise words found in the relevant portions of the Pentateuch, what does it mean?

(4a) and (4b) in contrast are precisely defined; but we should note that every case cited for (4a) would necessarily also fit (4b). Finally, (5) is really an instance of (1), since it is not νόμος itself but an associated term that supplies the reference to Christ (Rom 3:27b; 8:2a; Gal 6:2). As for the introductory note "fig.", that seems principally to express a theological qualm about referring to Christianity as a "law."

The other traditional Greek lexicons in common use do not give us much more help than BAGD. Like BAGD, LSJ uses the term "law" to give the general sense of νόμος; LSJ also uses the formulation "*that which is in habitual practice, use or possession,*" which clearly includes matters well beyond the actual scope of νόμος.[8] Thayer and Abbott-Smith likewise rely on "law"; their classifications of usage in the New Testament, like BAGD's, are lists of the different entities to which the term refers.[9] Abbott-Smith proposes the sense "a force or influence compelling to action," for which he cites Rom 7:21, 23a, 25; 8:2; although Abbott-Smith gives no other evidence that νόμος can bear this meaning, I have noted a similar sense in Epictetus and Josephus.[10]

The new *Greek-English Lexicon* of J. P. Louw and Eugene Nida, two semanticists whose work I cite in the appendix to Chapter 1, is somewhat different. Louw and Nida classify νόμος according to three senses in two distinct semantic fields:[11]

33.333: a formalized rule (or set of rules) prescribing what people must do . . . enforced by sanctions from a society . . .[12]

33.55: the first five books of the OT . . .

33.56: the sacred writings of the OT . . .

Each of these senses is in what Louw and Nida term semantic domain 33, "communication"; the first is in subdomain G', "Law, Regulation, Ordinance," with such other terms as δικαίωμα and κανών,[13] while the latter two are both in subdomain E, "Written Language," with such terms as γράμμα, βιβλίον, and γραφή. As one would expect with these authors, the definitions are clearer than we have seen before. In particular, they include in ¶33.333 the idea of enforcement by a society, which is at least a major step towards the

---

8 LSJ also specifies (s.v., I.b) a sense "of the *law* of God." But in each of the examples cited (from the LXX and New Testament), νόμος is specifically qualified by a term such as κυρίου (Ps 1:2) which actually supplies the reference to God, so it is not shown that this sense is in fact a separate meaning of νόμος. See Louw, *Semantics,* 51.

9 Thayer (s.v. 2), in contrast to BAGD and Abbott-Smith, treats the understandings {νόμος = law given to Moses} and {νόμος = Pentateuch} as equivalent; he thus avoids the considerable difficulty of deciding which uses fall in each category.

10 Chapter 1, n. 16. These examples do not support the limiting phrase "impelling to action."

11 They treat separately, in sections 33.58 and 33.341 respectively, the two idioms νόμος καὶ οἱ προφῆται (Rom 3:21) and ὁ νόμος τοῦ ἀνδρός (Rom 7:2). In each case the expression as a whole is taken to have a meaning which is not simply the sum of the meanings of the individual terms; see Nida, *Componential Analysis,* 113-14.

12 Δόγμα, as in Acts 16:4, is included in the same paragraph.

13 Cf. Subdomain F', "Command, Order," including ἐπιταγή and ἐντολή.

clarification of a major sense of νόμος. I think that this reliance on social enforcement as an element of the meaning of νόμος is questionable; this leads the authors to explain the use of νόμος for "the commands of God" on the basis that the people of Israel agreed to enforce these commands. But it is by no means clear that the use of νόμος for God's commands depends on this social element—especially for those Diaspora Jews who in fact used νόμος in this way. There still remains room for further analysis of the components of meaning of νόμος.

Louw and Nida include "Mosaic law" within the Pentateuch (¶33.55); in a forthcoming work they remark that although the law given on Mt. Sinai can be distinguished from the rest of the Pentateuch theologically, this distinction cannot be based on "specific, linguistic markers."[14] By making "Pentateuch" the designation of this meaning Louw and Nida tend to minimize the presence of elements of meaning common to ¶33.333, "formalized rule," which lies in a separate subdomain. But they do not expressly address this issue.

In the *Theological Dictionary of the New Testament* it is often difficult to separate the lexicography from the theology.[15] Two pages specifically on "The Usage in Paul"[16] appear in Gutbrod's lengthy *TDNT* essay on "The Law" in the Old Testament, Judaism, and the New Testament;[17] although Gutbrod's treatment is not aimed precisely at defining *meaning* in our terms, one can extract three basic senses of the νόμος, of which the principal one is:

> [Paul's] starting point is the traditional use of νόμος for the specific OT law. . . .
>
> In Paul νόμος is supremely that which demands action from man, a specific will. Hence one 'does' the law . . .
>
> . . . this will of the law may be seen esp. in the Mosaic Law of the OT.
> . . . [But Paul] attaches value to the Law as the living will of God in contrast to the Rabbinic stress on the fact that this will has been laid down once and for all. . . .
>
> The Law is one, the revealed will of the one God.[18]

---

[14] Louw and Nida, *Lexical Semantics*, Ch. 3. I am grateful to Dr. Nida for allowing me to see a draft of this work.

[15] This was one of the points made in James Barr's famous criticism of *TDNT* (*Semantics*, 206-62).

[16] *TDNT* 4 (1967) 1069-71.

[17] Ibid., 1036-85.

[18] Ibid., 1069-70. Two other specific senses are treated in the same paragraph: "the Decalogue . . . to some degree the law in a specific sense"; and "with a corresponding gen. .

Evidently "will" is the central term in this definition, and this indeed recurs when Gutbrod takes up "The Material Understanding of the Law in Paul."[19] We have then two thoughts: that νόμος is certain words, spoken at a certain time; that these words are the will of God.[20] Here *meaning, reference* and *assertion* are not easily separated. νόμος evidently refers to certain words; is it then Paul's *assertion* that these words are the will of God?[21] Or is "will of God" part of the *meaning* of νόμος? If so, what evidence have we that νόμος can bear such a meaning? If this is not the meaning of νόμος, what is?

Gutbrod also gives two other senses of νόμος in Paul, one that νόμος is Pentateuch, "even where its nature as command is not at issue," and the other, that it is used figuratively, "mostly . . . with a corresponding gen. or a word of distinction."[22] Gutbrod describes the figurative sense as, variously, "divine ordinance" (Rom 3:27), "the fact that . . ." (Rom 7:21), and "the claim or will . . . which controls my conduct."[23] Taken as meaning, "ordinance" suffers from the same imprecision as "law." Gutbrod's other two figurative meanings are suggestive, but he does not explain how they relate to the non-figurative meaning (or meanings) of νόμος.[24]

Other Systematic Treatments

E. D. Burton's commentary on Galatians includes an extended note on νόμος,[25] in which Burton divides New Testament usage into five meanings:

1. "statute or principle"

2. "divine law, the revealed will of God"

3. "the books that contain the law"

. . an individual law, e.g., R. 7:2." I do not know what is meant by the expression "to some degree"; it would seem that either νόμος refers to the Decalogue or it does not.

[19] *TDNT* 4 (1967) 1071-78; see 1072.

[20] This seems an odd way of speaking, for surely it would be more precise to say that God's will is that one do the law—not the law itself. But Gutbrod is quite consistent in his equation of νόμος and "will", even—as we shall see in a moment—where νόμος does not refer to the Old Testament law.

[21] Alternatively, it might be that νόμος *refers* to the will of God, and it is Paul's *assertion* that the will of God is these words.

[22] *TDNT* 4 (1967) 1071.

[23] Ibid. "Claim or will" is illustrated by Rom 7:25b; 8:2a and b; Gal 6:2 and Rom 13:8 (where Gutbrod takes ἕτερον to modify νόμου; against this view, see Cranfield, *Romans*, 2.675-76; Käsemann, *Romans*, 360-61).

[24] In the last of these figurative senses, the term "will" suggests a link to what Gutbrod describes as the principle sense of νόμος. But this would depend on a demonstration—which Gutbrod does not give—that "will" is in fact part of the meaning of νόμος.

[25] Burton, *Galatians*, 443-60.

4. "law as such"

5. "a force or tendency"[26]

For Burton the principal meaning is (2), to which he assigns 88 of Paul's uses of νόμος.[27] Thus the central point of νόμος is not a reference to Mosaic law, but rather a reference to "the revealed will of God," of which Mosaic law is only an instance. Such a classification implies that Paul (and his audience) thought in broader terms than "Mosaic law." Whereas most lexicographers would take the statement "νόμος was given on Mt. Sinai" to be a matter of definition, specifying one meaning of νόμος, for Burton this is an assertion, equivalent to "the words spoken on Mt. Sinai are the revealed will of God." So long as the connections between νόμος, Mt. Sinai and God are taken for granted, as I suppose they were by most Jews of Paul's time, it makes little difference whether they are regarded as matters of definition or of assertion. But there is a great difference if these connections come in doubt, as I shall argue they do for Paul;[28] for in that case one has to choose between either saying (if νόμος means "God's will") "νόμος was not given on Sinai," or (if νόμος means "law given at Sinai") "νόμος is not the will of God." In fact, as we shall see in Chapter 4, Paul is exceedingly careful not to make either of these statements; nevertheless, the logic of Paul's argument requires him to take one of these positions, and the choice—which depends on the meaning of νόμος— is important for understanding all that he says about νόμος.

Like other writers, Burton does not explore the relation between reference and meaning in Paul's use of νόμος.[29]

Like Burton, Heinrich Schlier includes in his commentary on the letter to the Galatians an excursus on νόμος.[30] His treatment of the term's meaning

---

[26] Ibid., 455-60.

[27] Two uses are assigned to meaning (1), one to meaning (3), three to (4) and five to (5). Nineteen uses are not mentioned.

[28] See Chapter 4, at nn. 49-60.

[29] Burton's scheme is also noteworthy for its subdivisions of meaning (2), "divine law"; there are four categories, according to how divine νόμος is "viewed" (whether as "concrete fact, . . . most frequently . . . the law of the O.T."; or "in general"; or "as a purely legalistic system"; or "as reduced to the ethical principle which constitutes its permanent element . . ."). These are not separate meanings and they cannot be distinguished by linguistic markers; rather, there are a series of propositions about one meaning, "will of God," and how that *should* be perceived.

Burton further subdivides each of these meanings by whether or not the definite article is present; if not, the term is "qualitative," that is, "thought of not specifically . . . but simply in its character as law . . ." (Burton, *Galatians*, 455). I shall take up this thesis below (at n. 107).

[30] Schlier, *Galater*, 176-88.

includes the familiar categories "Altes Testament," "Pentateuch," and "Regel, . . . Ordnung."³¹ To these Schlier adds νόμος as known to the Gentiles: not νόμος itself, but τὰ τοῦ νόμου (Rom 2:14), τὰ δικαιώματα τοῦ νόμου (Rom 2:26).³² This last sense, however, does not appear to be a separate meaning of νόμος itself, but rather to consist of two related idioms which actually depend for their meaning on νόμος in the sense of "Old Testament" or "Pentateuch."³³

Schlier also divides the meanings "Old Testament" and "Pentateuch" in a different way; he argues that since νόμος may refer to the entire Old Testament, including both the historical parts of the Pentateuch and the prophets, it may have the sense "Weisung" as well as the sense "Gesetz."³⁴ Part of the problem in understanding νόμος in Paul is, consequently, the presentation of the distinct senses "Gesetz" and "Weisung" by the single term νόμος, so that one can pass abruptly from νόμος as Gesetz in Gal 4:21a to νόμος as Weisung in 4:21b (οἱ ὑπὸ νόμον θέλοντες εἶναι, τὸν νόμον οὐκ ἀκούετε;).³⁵ This is a step forward, for with "Gesetz" and "Weisung" Schlier attempts to relate the meaning of νόμος to the specific references "Altes Testament" and "Pentateuch." But Schlier's treatment of "Gesetz" and "Weisung" as distinct senses is doubtful. In Paul's letters no clear distinction can be drawn, and indeed the example of Gal 4:21 suggests that we have here two *aspects* of a single *meaning*; for Paul's question loses its point if νόμος does not refer to the same thing in both places.

Finally among systematic presentations I note the recent treatment by Moo:³⁶

I.   "DEMAND OR BODY OF DEMANDS (USUALLY WITH SANCTIONS)"
     A.   "general" [Rom 2:14d, Gal 5:23]
     B.   "divine"

---

³¹ Ibid., 176-78 (senses 1, 2 and 4).

³² Ibid., 177 (sense 3).

³³ Schlier allows (ibid., 179) that Jewish "law" is the paradigm for the reference to Gentile "law"; but actually the refusal to use νόμος as such for Gentile "law" seems rather to deny that there is any separate "law" for which the Jewish can be a model. Thus Schlier's observation that Paul deals with both Jewish and Gentile "law", and thus with "law" in general, seems to rest on a dubious premise.

³⁴ Ibid., 178.

³⁵ Ibid., 179.

³⁶ Moo, "Law," 76. Moo presents his scheme in a chart; I have converted it to outline form, retaining Moo's descriptive terms. For each use Moo cites texts from Paul, putting question marks by those he considers doubtful. Here I omit the doubtful texts (including all those for I.B.2.a, "legalism") and give only illustrative ones where (as in I.B.2.c and d) the number is large.

    1. "general; the basic demand" [Gal 3:21b]

    2. "in its Mosaic form"

        a. "legalism"[37]

        b. "single command" [Rom 7:2b, 3]

        c. "body of commands" [Rom 2:13a, b, etc.]

        d. "system or economy" [Rom 2:12a, b, etc.]

    3. "in its NT form" [Gal 6:2]

II. "NON-'LEGAL' USES"

    A. "with reference to the canon" [Rom 3:19a, 21b, etc.]

    B. "'principle,' 'force,' 'authority'" [Rom 7:21]

Much of Moo's analysis is suggestive for our understanding of Paul. As a general matter, however, it may be doubted whether a single term will be used in eight or nine distinct senses by the same author—six senses in a single letter,[38] even three within three verses.[39] If νόμος were in fact so protean, the possibility of Paul having ever been understood is slim. It seems far more likely that much of what is noted are nuances dependent on immediate context rather than distinct meanings; moreover, like most other writers on the subject, Moo does not distinguish questions of reference and questions of meaning.[40]

Non-systematic Treatments

Every scholar who has written on Paul's view of νόμος has had to touch on the meaning of that term. These treatments are not the systematic treatment at which I aim, and in particular the question of meaning is rarely separated from the question of reference. Nevertheless some suggestive points are found in certain writers.

First, there is occasional discussion of the relation between the νόμος of Jews and other νόμοι, although with differing conclusions. On the one hand,

---

[37] Moo (ibid., 86-87) thinks this is a doubtful sense.

[38] In Romans, I.A; I.B.2.b, c and d; II.A and B; in Galatians, I.A; I.B.1; I.B.2.c and d; I.B.3; II.A.

[39] Rom 2:12a, 13a, 14d: I.B.2.d; I.B.2.c; I.A. In addition, Moo gives I.B.1 as a possible sense for Rom 2:15.

[40] Various particular distinctions are, I think, particularly suspect: for instance, "general demand" (I.A.) against "general divine demand" (I.B.1); "general divine demand" against "Mosaic divine demand" (I.B.2) (did Paul really think that there was a divine νόμος that was neither of Moses nor of Christ?); and especially "body of commands" (I.B.2.c) against "system or economy" (I.B.2.d). It is also a weakness of this classification that it so sharply separates Mosaic commands and system (I.B.2.c and d) from scripture (II.A); here again Gal 4:21 illustrates the close connection in which Paul held ideas that we sometimes attempt to separate (Moo puts Gal 4:21a in I.B.2.d and 4:21b in II.A.).

Bläser considers that while νόμος is the norm of Israelite society, it is radically distinguished from the laws of other peoples;[41] thus, when νόμος refers to something other than Old Testament νόμος, one should not assume that such a νόμος is similar to Old Testament νόμος on any essential point.[42] On the other hand, van Dülmen argues that Paul's use of νόμος with both Jewish and non-Jewish referents is deliberate, and means that everything which makes a total demand on humans—whether the will of God, or sin—is called νόμος.[43] Other writers have variously described senses of νόμος which apparently apply to both Jewish and non-Jewish νόμος; Grafe sees νόμος as not only "Norm" but "Gewalt" and "Macht";[44] Bultmann sees it as "compulsion, constraint."[45] Räisänen finds that νόμος means "order" or "rule" (both in the sense of "realm," not "command") in Rom 3:27b; 7:21; 8:2,[46] which resembles his view of Jewish νόμος as "the whole of Israel's sacred tradition."[47] E. P. Sanders considers that where νόμος does not refer to "the Jewish Torah" it means "rule," "norm," or "principle,"[48] descriptions that might very generally apply to Jewish νόμος as well.

These differences must be resolved on semantic and not on theological grounds; no doubt there is a major theological distinction between Jewish νόμος and (for instance) the νόμος of Rome, but this does not mean that the term itself has entirely distinct meanings in its different uses. Bläser's vehemence on the point reflects theology, not semantics. I shall pursue this question in my own analysis, later in this chapter.

A somewhat different treatment of the relation between Jewish νόμος and other νόμοι appears in C. H. Dodd's seminal essay on the relation between νόμος and תּוֹרָה. Dodd identifies three different senses of νόμος in Paul: (a) νόμος used "to denote the law of a community";[49] (b) νόμος "in the sense of

---

41 Bläser, Gesetz, 64.

42 Ibid., 70-71. Bläser notes such other νόμοι at Rom 3:27; 7:14-25; 8:2; Gal 6:2 (ibid., 24-28).

43 van Dülmen, Theologie, 118. She refers particularly to Rom 7:22-23. Note that on this reading it appears that Paul's understanding of Mosaic νόμος (which is the source of the idea of "total demand") governs his other uses of the term, and not that some general meaning of νόμος is also included when Mosaic νόμος is referred to.

44 Grafe, Lehre, 11.

45 Bultmann, Theology, 1.259. Here Bultmann speaks specifically of passages which he says do not refer to Jewish νόμος (Rom 7:2f, 22 - 8:1), but the sense fits Jewish νόμος as well (ibid., 1.260: "the law is the totality of the historically given legal demands" [emphasis added]).

46 Räisänen, Paul, 52.

47 Ibid., 16.

48 E. P. Sanders, Paul, the Law, 3, 15n.

49 Dodd, "Law," 26, 34-35.

'principle'";[50] and (c) νόμος equivalent to Hebrew תּוֹרָה.[51] But Dodd recognizes that these senses are not sharply separated. After discussing the second he adds:

> In all these cases it is not denied that Paul had in the back of his mind the thought of νόμος = תּוֹרָה. But because he was using a Greek and not a Hebrew word he was able to use expressions which would have been impossible but for the fact that תּוֹרָה by becoming νόμος had entered into a new field of associated "ideas."[52]

Dodd thus leaves unresolved the relations among the senses to which he points.

Second, the treatment of Jewish νόμος is also disputed. Some, like Schlier,[53] see Jewish νόμος as the combination of disparate elements: for J. A. Sanders, "*muthos* and *ethos*, or story and laws";[54] for Westerholm, "sacred scriptures" and "specific divine requirements given to Israel."[55] These writers generally take Paul's positive remarks about νόμος to refer to one element of it, while his negative remarks refer to the other element. But this view, notwithstanding the apparent neatness of its solution to certain difficult passages, fails to account for passages like Gal 4:21,[56] where the two proposed senses appear side-by-side in a context which seems to require that νόμος have the *same* reference.[57] Other scholars, accordingly, have maintained the unity of Jewish νόμος: van Dülmen, who sees νόμος in Paul "als ganzheitliche Grösse" and "ein Institut, ein Zeichen, nicht aber eine Summe einzelner Vorschriften";[58] and Räisänen, who, as I have already noted, says that "the word nomos refers to the whole of Israel's sacred tradition, with special emphasis on its Mosaic center."[59] Most important is the judgment of the semanticists Louw and Nida that Mosaic code and scripture are not distinct

---

[50] Ibid., 25-26, 36-37. Dodd's examples are Rom 2:14-15; 3:27; 7:23, 25; and 8:2.

[51] Ibid., 35-36 (Rom 3:10-18; 1 Cor 14:21).

[52] Ibid., 37.

[53] Above, at nn. 30-35.

[54] J. A. Sanders, "Torah," 138.

[55] Westerholm, *Israel's Law*, 108. See also Westerholm, "*Torah*."

[56] Λέγετέ μοι, οἱ ὑπὸ νόμον θέλοντες εἶναι, τόν νόμον οὐκ ἀκούετε;

[57] See also Rom 2:26-27, where Paul speaks favorably of the uncircumcised keeping νόμος. What is the referent here?

[58] van Dülmen, *Theologie*, 130, 133. Cf. Bläser, *Gesetz*, 63: "Pls spricht vom Gesetz als einer bekannten und unbestrittenen Grösse."

[59] Räisänen, *Paul*, 16. He adds, "Whether the unwritten *Torah*, the oral tradition of the fathers, is included in this usage, is not clear; at least, Paul never distinguishes between the written and the unwritten Torah."

senses with "specific, linguistic markers."[60] I shall further investigate this question in Chapter 4.

A few other points are also of interest. van Dülmen makes a noteworthy attempt to connect νόμος with other terms; but the conclusion that νόμος is equivalent to both ἐντολή and γραφή seems suspect, since Paul appears to use the three terms in different ways.[61] Werner Kelber fastens on the written character of νόμος as decisive,[62] an argument significant for its identification of a particular component of νόμος; but Kelber's conclusion—based in part on his entire theory of distinctions between oral and written communication—goes well beyond what can be shown from Paul's texts. It may be that νόμος is written,[63] although, as a matter of fact, Paul rarely says so; it does not follow, however, that this is the decisive feature of law, even in those passages where its written character is referred to. Where Paul treats the Mosaic law specifically as written, he uses γράμμα rather than νόμος (2 Cor 3:4-11).[64]

Besides the work of Räisänen, E. P. Sanders and Westerholm, the other major recent treatment of νόμος in Paul is Hans Hübner's *Law in Paul's Thought*. Hübner speaks simply of "the Law" (das Gesetz);[65] but although he offers no explicit definition, he often uses "Mosaic Law" as equivalent.[66] For Hübner, νόμος almost always relates to תּוֹרָה, and perhaps always does so;[67] but the term "relates" is critical, for Hübner does not think that νόμος always is תּוֹרָה. He rather asks, rhetorically: "Is not [Rom 7:23] the place, if anywhere, that it is appropriate to take *nomos* as not in *any way* referring to Torah?" --and then asserts that here too such a reference is at least possible.[68] What Hübner means by "in [some] way referring to Torah" is illustrated by his understanding of νόμος . . . τῶν ἔργων (Rom 3:27): "the expression of a fundamentally misplaced human *attitude* towards the Torah . . ."[69] Νόμος then may mean "attitude"—"attitude to law" to be sure, but still "attitude" and not "law."[70] This tenuous link to "law" should not obscure the fundamental shift

---

60 Louw and Nida, *Lexical Semantics*, Ch.3; id., *Lexicon*, ¶33.55.

61 van Dülmen, *Theologie*, 130, 134. Her view also seems to imply that ἐντολή equals γραφή.

62 Kelber, *Gospel*, 151-64.

63 But it is also possible that oral interpretations are included; note Phil 3:5: κατὰ νόμον Φαρισαῖος. See further Räisänen's comment in n. 59 above.

64 Kelber discusses this passage without perceiving its inconsistency with his thesis. Ibid., 157-58.

65 Hübner, *Law*, 15.

66 Ibid., e.g., 17.

67 Ibid., 145.

68 Ibid., 145-46; emphasis added.

69 Ibid., 139; emphasis added.

70 See also ibid., 138; cf. 144-45.

which is thus claimed for the meaning of νόμος, into an entirely new semantic domain. For this shift Hübner presents no evidence at all.

All of these writers leave unanswered the questions with which I began: how can we describe the meaning (or meanings) of νόμος as that term is used in Paul's letters? Does the meaning of νόμος vary as its referent varies, and if so, how?

An Analysis of Νόμος Based on Patterns of Usage

I now turn to my own attempt to determine the meaning of νόμος through a survey of patterns in its usage, and an analysis of what these patterns imply about the meaning of the term.[71] Out of these patterns I will attempt to identify aspects or components of meaning. These components of meaning will be used to compare νόμος to other, related terms.

Primarily, I will consider the usage of νόμος in Paul's letters; but I will also look at its usage elsewhere in the New Testament and in the Septuagint to determine whether the patterns identified in Paul's letters are consistent with usage in these other related documents. Such consistency is not essential to my results, for Paul and his audience could have used νόμος in ways distinct from its usage by other Christians and Jews; but if the patterns found in Paul also appear elsewhere that will be some evidence of the plausibility of what is proposed for Paul.

Patterns of Usage in Paul

To begin with, I will not distinguish between Paul's usage in Romans and his usage in Galatians. Whether Paul's view of νόμος differs in these two letters has not been settled;[72] but no one, to my knowledge, has argued that the *meaning* of the term differs. Although lexical meanings do change, ordinarily that is a gradual process. My survey will not offer any evidence that the meaning of νόμος changed for Paul.

In the Nestle-Aland[26] text, νόμος is found in four of the unquestioned letters of Paul, in 118 places.[73] Aland's concordance[74] discloses in addition

---

[71] For an elaboration of the basis for this approach, see "Procedures for the Analysis of Meaning" in the appendix to Chapter 1.

[72] See the summary of the discussion in Räisänen, *Paul*, 7-10. Hübner, *Law*, presents the most thorough recent argument for a systematic difference between the two letters, which Räisänen denies.

[73] It also appears at Eph 2:15 and 1 Tim 1:8 and 9. Since the relation of these letters to Paul is uncertain, I have excluded them from my survey of Paul's usage.

[74] Aland, *Vollständige Konkordanz*, s.v.

two passages within these letters in which other editions of the New Testament have read νόμος: Rom 9:32 (οὐκ ἐκ πίστεως ἀλλ᾽ ὡς ἐξ ἔργων νόμου) and 1 Cor 7:39 (γυνὴ δέδεται νόμῳ ἐφ᾽ ὅσον χρόνον ζῇ ὁ ἀνὴρ αὐτῆς). These variations are not significant for my investigation, since Paul certainly uses the phrases ἐξ ἔργων νόμου and δέδεται νόμῳ elsewhere even if he does not do so in these passages.[75]

In no case does Nestle-Aland[26] record significant manuscript support for the omission of any occurance of νόμος found in Nestle-Aland[26].[76] In some cases the omission of a passage containing νόμος has been proposed on non-textual grounds (generally unrelated to νόμος);[77] I have not attempted to consider such proposals. As will be seen, my analysis of the components of meaning of νόμος does not at any point turn on a single occurrence of νόμος; it is rather based on patterns exhibited in multiple identical or similar usages.

In my analysis I will look principally to the syntagmatic connections of νόμος: the words Paul links syntactically to νόμος. From this we can learn, in Gilbert Ryle's words, "what can (logically) be said with [a term]"; this is the heart of meaning.[78] But some paratactic relations—words used in parallel with νόμος—are also significant, and I will begin by noting these.

Paratactic Patterns. Paul uses three terms in evident parallel to νόμος, and four in evident opposition to it. First, at Rom 3:21 he speaks of δικαιοσύνη θεοῦ . . . μαρτυρουμένη ὑπὸ τοῦ νόμου καὶ τῶν προφητῶν . . . Here νόμος and προφῆται are parallel; but because this is an idiomatic expression (seen also in Matt 5:17; 7:12; 11:13; 22:40; Luke 16:16; 24:44; cf. John 1:45; Acts 13:15) which may have a meaning beyond that of its components taken separately,[79] this is an uncertain guide to the meaning of νόμος in other uses.

Second, in two passages νόμος appears in parallel with ἐντολή. In Rom 13:8-10 ἐντολή evidently refers to the separate commandments, οὐ μοιχεύσεις

---

[75] For ἔργων νόμου, see Rom 3:20, 28; Gal 2:16a, b, c; 3:2, 5, 10; for δέδεται νόμῳ, see Rom 7:2. Probably these parallels have led to the insertion of νόμος in Rom 9:32 and 1 Cor 7:39; the insertions are accepted in the Textus Receptus, but not in any of the principal modern editions (Aland, *Vollständige Konkordanz*, s.v.).

[76] In Rom 2:12, one manuscript has ἐννόμως for ἐν νόμῳ; in 1 Cor 9:20 the third ὑπὸ νόμον is omitted by a number of manuscripts, but the other three occurrences in that verse are unchallenged, as are those at Rom 6:15; Gal 3:23; 4:4, 5, 21; 5:18.

[77] For example, on 1 Cor 14:34-35 see Murphy-O'Connor, "Interpolations," 90-92. Here too the usage, ὁ νόμος λέγει, is found elsewhere in Paul (Rom 3:19, 7:7; 1 Cor 9:8).

[78] Ryle, "Meaning," 143; the full passage appears in the appendix to Chapter 1, at n. 51.

[79] Ὁ νόμος καὶ οἱ προφῆται may refer to the whole of scripture, and not just to the Pentateuch and the Prophets (so Louw and Nida, *Lexicon*, ¶33.58); it does not follow that νόμος or οἱ προφῆται taken alone includes the writings.

κ.τ.λ. (13:9), which together make up νόμος; in Rom 7:7-13, however, νόμος and ἐντολή appear to be used interchangeably.

Third, at Rom 7:6 some parallel relation between νόμος and γράμμα is implied. I note, however, that in 2 Cor 3:5-6, the other passage where Paul uses γράμμα as an apparent term for the Mosaic law, νόμος does not appear; we cannot assume that these terms are synonyms. I shall further explore the relations between νόμος, ἐντολή and γράμμα below.

The contrasting terms do not help us much. While contrasts are sometimes semantically linked, so that two terms help to define each other—as do "left" and "right", or "up" and "down"—others belong to the realm of what I have called *assertion*. νόμος and χάρις illustrate this; Paul opposes the two terms at Rom 6:14, 15; Gal 5:4, and implies an opposition at Gal 2:21; but I will argue in my treatment of Gal 2:21 in Chapter 5 that others in Galatia were probably saying that νόμος is χάρις. The disagreement between Paul and these others is not over semantics, but over the relations between actual entities.

Similarly, contrasts between νόμος and πίστις (Rom 4:16; 10:5; Gal 3:11; Phil 3:9[80]) and νόμος and δικαιοσύνη (Rom 4:13; Gal 2:21) do not explicate the meaning of νόμος. The contrast between νόμος and πνεῦμα in Gal 5:18 is more promising, for the proposition εἰ δὲ πνεύματι ἄγεσθε, οὐκ ἐστὲ ὑπὸ νόμον implies by its logical form a logical opposition between πνεῦμα and νόμος. Nevertheless, in Rom 7:14 and 8:2 Paul links νόμος and πνεῦμα:

Οἴδαμεν γὰρ ὅτι ὁ νόμος πνευματικός ἐστιν . . .

ὁ γὰρ νόμος τοῦ πνεύματος τῆς ζωῆς ἐν Χριστῷ Ἰησοῦ . . .[81]

In light of these passages, the clearest contrasts of πνεῦμα are not with νόμος but with γράμμα (Rom 7:6; 2 Cor 3:5-6) and σάρξ (Rom 8:4; Gal 5:16-26). We have already noted that γράμμα may itself be parallel to νόμος, and there is evidently also some connection between νόμος and σάρξ (e.g., Rom 7:5; Gal 5:16-26). Whether either of these terms is *semantically* linked to νόμος is a topic for consideration after we have examined the syntagmatic patterns in Paul's use of νόμος.

Syntagmatic Patterns. The Pauline usage of νόμος displays a number of significant syntagmatic patterns. One of these deserves special attention, which I will defer for the moment; this is the use of νόμος with an accompanying noun in the genitive case, such as νόμος πίστεως (Rom 3:27)

---

[80] In addition, ἔργα νόμου and ἀκοὴ πίστεως are contrasted at Gal 3:2, 5.

[81] The contrast between these verses and Gal 5:18 may reflect different meanings of πνεῦμα. I will take up Rom 7:14 and 8:2 in Chapter 6.

and ὁ νόμος τῆς ἁμαρτίας (Rom 7:23). This usage occurs in most of the passages where νόμος is said to be used "metaphorically,"[82] or in "a play on the term νόμος";[83] that is, not referring to Jewish law. I will consider this usage below, at nn. 103-6.

Here I wish rather to look at the variety of other syntagmatic patterns associated with νόμος. I have grouped these patterns into seven categories;[84] described for convenience in English, these patterns and categories (with their frequencies of occurrence in Paul[85]) are:

1a. νόμος is *verbal* (10):
It speaks (4), testifies (1), is written (3), is read (0), is heard (2).

1b. νόμος is *perceived* (3):
It is known (1), is seen (1), is found (1).

2. νόμος is a standard for *judgment* (17):
It is (not) against (2), judges (1), brings wrath (1), curses (1), (could not) condemn (1), (does not) justify (6); people transgress (3), sin (1), are blameless (1) with respect to νόμος.

3. νόμος is a *guide to conduct* (23):
It characterizes work (9), is the form of knowledge and truth (1), teaches (1); people do (4), keep (1), are guided by (1), fulfill (6) νόμος.

4. νόμος *controls* (31):
It commands (2), rules (2), frees (2), captures (1), (does not) nullify (1), excludes (2), wars (1); people serve (2), are bound by (2), are under (11), are free from (2), are released from (2), die with respect to (2) νόμος.

5. νόμος is tied to *particular people* (17):
People (do not) have (2), are from (2), are in (1), are under (11), rely on (1) νόμος.

6. νόμος has a *source* (6):
It comes to be (4), is given (2), is commanded (1), is received (0), is changed (0).

---

82 Räisänen, *Paul*, 16.
83 Bultmann, *Theology*, 259.
84 One pattern, ὑπὸ νόμου, is placed in two different categories (4 and 5).
85 In a few places "0" appears for a usage which is not found in Paul but is included because it is found elsewhere in the New Testament, and appears to be similar to usages which are found in Paul. The totals for components 4 and 6 are one less than the sums of the figures for constructions displaying those components, because Gal 3:23 employs two different constructions displaying component 4, as does Gal 3:19 for component 6.

7. *People put themselves under νόμος* (6):
They (do not) subject themselves to (1), pursue (2), (do not)
destroy (1), establish (1), can be ἑαυτοῖς (1) νόμος.[86]

The actual Pauline passages in question are set out in an appendix to this
chapter, grouped as above; parallel texts from elsewhere in the New
Testament are cited in the appendix but not reproduced.[87] An index to the
occurences of νόμος in Paul's letters appears at the end of the appendix.

Category 1b (νόμος is perceptible) should be especially noted; I have
included this because it is a pattern of usage, and seems to be analogous to the
patterns in 1a (νόμος is verbal). In itself, however, perceptibility is a quality so
general, and so nearly universal, as to be of little use. I will refer to this
category only rarely.

In this survey the primary evidence is the accumulation of syntagmatic
patterns; the grouping of these into seven groups is secondary. Other group-
ings would be possible. I have sought to group the patterns into large categories, for the purpose of revealing components of meaning as basic as possible, but at the same time I have wanted to note some distinctions. One could
group 2, 3 and 4 together under a rubric such as "command," but it seems to
me that the ideas of *judgment, guide* and *control* are sufficiently distinct to be
worth noting separately.

Now a basic question presents itself, which was introduced in the discussion of terminology in the appendix to Chapter 1. Do these various components of meaning relate to distinct meanings of νόμος, or to a common meaning? Is there, for example, one sense of νόμος in which it is verbal, a guide and
a control (components 1, 3 and 4), and a separate sense in which it is a
standard for judgment, defines people and has a source?[88]

These questions are difficult to answer conclusively, since in most cases a
single use of νόμος displays only one of these syntagmatic patterns, and
therefore only one of these components. In Rom 2:12, for example, we have
καὶ ὅσοι ἐν νόμῳ ἥμαρτον, διὰ νόμου κριθήσονται, two usages which I treat as

---

[86] I have placed all negatives in parentheses on the supposition that whatever is
explicitly denied of νόμος is something that might have been asserted of it; otherwise the
denial would be unnecessary. In Ryle's terminology (appendix to Chapter 1, at n. 51), what
is denied of νόμος is still within the realm of "what can (logically) be said with it. . ."

[87] In all, 104 of the Pauline uses of νόμος will be found in this appendix, including two
cited as comparable uses. The remaining uses do not appear to me to display a particular
syntagmatic pattern. 1 Cor 15:56 illustrates these: ἡ δὲ δύναμις τῆς ἁμαρτίας ὁ νόμος. Here
we have an assertion about νόμος, but nothing, so far as I can see, that is useful for establishing its meaning.

[88] Or perhaps components 1, 2, 3 and 4 are common to every sense of νόμος, while
components 5, 6 and 7 mark distinct senses.

exhibiting component 2, νόμος as a standard for judgment. But by the same token, the syntagmatic patterns exhibiting the other six components of νόμος are not present here. No one component, however, is sufficient by itself to establish a meaning; if there is direct evidence of only one at a particular point, others must nevertheless be assumed.[89] Moreover, if we look at passages with multiple occurrences of νόμος then we do find associations among various patterns and various components. Although we cannot assume that the meaning of νόμος is consistent throughout a passage, ordinarily a term's meaning does not change arbitrarily, nor does it change within a continuous discourse unless some sign is given that it changes. I will not pause here to consider exhaustively every possible such sign; this would require a full exegesis of every text in which νόμος appears. But if we make only the modest assumption that each occurrence of νόμος within a single verse has the same meaning as other occurrences within that verse, we find interconnections among most of the seven components.

TABLE 1
Different Components of Νόμος Found Within the Same Verse[90]

COMPONENT:	1	2	3	4	5	6
7			R2:14		R2:14	
6		R4:15 G3:21				
5	R3:19		R2:14			
4	R7:1,23 G4:21					
3	R2:13	R2:25, 27				
2						

Table 1 illustrates the connections. In Rom 2:14, for example, the three phrases ἔθνη τὰ μὴ νόμον ἔχοντα, τὰ τοῦ νόμου ποιῶσιν and ἑαυτοῖς εἰσιν νόμος show syntagmatic patterns that I have associated with components 5, 3 and 7, respectively. Assuming that νόμος has the same meaning (although not necessarily the same reference) throughout 2:14, this verse shows that

---

[89] These other components would not necessarily be among those I have specified. I cannot exclude the possibility that there are additional components of the meaning of νόμος, not suggested by syntagmatic patterns.

[90] Here "R" refers to Romans, and "G" to Galatians.

components 3, 5 and 7 are found together. Table 1 illustrates this by putting "R2:14" at each point where the columns and rows for components 3, 5 and 7 intersect.[91] While only eight out of the 21 cells in Table 1 are occupied, this is sufficient to interconnect every one of the seven components, as Figure 1 illustrates.

FIGURE 1

Links Between Different Components of
Νόμος Based Upon Display Within the Same Verse

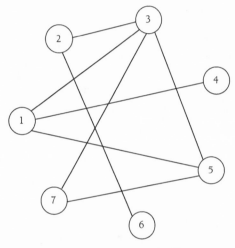

In this figure each line matches an occupied cell in Table 1; thus the evidence of Rom 2:14, as recorded in three cells of Table 1, requires the three lines connecting 3, 5 and 7 on Figure 1. The other cells of Table 1 are similarly matched by lines on Figure 1. Figure 1 indicates that there is no discrete group of components separate from other components. Moreover, if we look beyond single verses to paragraphs (taking the paragraph divisions shown in Nestle-Aland[26]), sixteen of the 21 possible connections now appear, as Table 2 shows; Figure 2 illustrates these connections.

---

91 Although the total of seven components implies 49 (seven times seven) combinations of two components, seven of these combinations are tautological (1 and 1, 2 and 2, etc.); the remaining 42 duplicate each other, since they include both (1 and 2) and (2 and 1), etc. Only 21 cells are needed to show distinct combinations; thus Table 1 is constructed with the bottom-right half blank; "R2:14" appears when Row 5 meets Column 3, but not where Row 3 meets Column 5.

TABLE 2
Different Components of νόμος
Found Within the Same Paragraph

COMPONENT:	1	2	3	4	5	6
7	R2B	R2B,C	R2B,3D	R8A	R2B	
6		R4C, G3E			R4C	
5	R2B,3B	R2B,C, 4C	R2B,C			
4	R7A,C G4D	R2D,8A G2B,5C	R2D,3D G2B,5C			
3	R2B, G3C	R2B,C, D,10A, G2B,3C, 5A,C Ph3B				
2	R2B G3C					

Key to Citations

R2B =	Rom 2:12-16	R7A =	Rom 7: 1- 6	G3E =	Gal 3:19-22
R2C =	2:17-24	R7C =	7:14-25	G4D =	4:21-31
R2D =	2:25-29	R8A =	8: 1-11	G5A =	5: 1- 6
R3B =	3: 9-20	R10A =	10: 1-13	G5C =	5:13-26
R3D =	3:27-31	G2B =	Gal 2:11-21	Ph3B =	Phil 3: 2-11
R4C =	4:13-25	G3C =	3:10-14		

FIGURE 2
Links Between Different Components of Νόμος
Based Upon Display Within the Same Paragraph

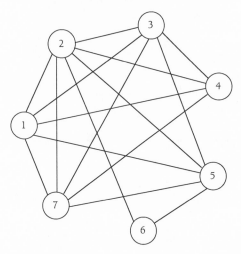

Such data do not conclusively settle the question of whether the meaning of νόμος varies within Paul's letters. In Chapter 4 I shall re-examine the possibility that Paul uses νόμος with different meanings by testing whether the components of meaning vary when the referent varies: that is, are the components of meaning found with Jewish νόμος different from those found with other νόμοι?[92] Although a term's meaning need not change when its referents change, there has been (as I have noted) a tendency to assume that this happens with νόμος; but my survey in Chapter 4 will not support this view, nor will my studies of selected passages in Chapters 5 and 6.

I conclude that all seven of these components belong together, and together constitute a single meaning of νόμος as it is used in Paul's letters. To further analyze the contrasts presented by these components we need to identify terms similar to νόμος, or, as is sometimes said, terms in the same semantic field. We will then be able to see how these components establish contrasts between νόμος and related terms, thus serving to mark out the semantic field of νόμος.

Ordinarily a term is located within a single semantic field, but it may be useful to think of νόμος as occupying the intersection of several overlapping fields, suggested by the various aspects of its meaning. Aspect 1, that νόμος is

---

[92] This examination will depend on an identification of the different referents for νόμος, which I will undertake in Chapter 3.

verbal, suggests the domain of communication, and particularly written communication; even where Paul hints at an unwritten νόμος he uses the imagery of writing to describe it: thus Gentiles show τὸ ἔργον τοῦ νόμου γραπτὸν ἐν ταῖς καρδίαις αὐτῶν (Rom 2:15; cf. Jer 31 [LXX 38]:33).[93] In this domain, γραφή and, especially for Paul, γράμμα suggest themselves as related terms. Aspects 2 and 4 each suggest the domain of command, in which we may compare νόμος with δικαίωμα and ἐντολή. Aspect 5 suggests the domain of custom, in which we may compare νόμος with ἔθος and παράδοσις. Aspects 3, 6 and 7, on the other hand, seem to me to suggest no particular domain, but rather qualities which might attach to (among other things) either command or custom. Various relationships suggest themselves; one would expect both command and custom to be guides (aspect 3), and command but not necessarily custom to have a source (aspect 6); while either might or might not be perceived as something to which one subjected oneself (aspect 7).

These a priori judgments can be tested by looking at the usage of the related terms. γραφή displays syntagmatic patterns falling within aspect 1, verbal communication: see Rom 1:2; 4:3; 9:17; 10:11; 11:2; Gal 3:8; 4:30;[94] it displays aspect 4, command, at Gal 3:22: συνέκλεισεν ἡ γραφὴ τὰ πάντα . . . (cf., for νόμος, Gal 3:23 and Rom 7:2). The other five aspects do not appear in Paul's use of γραφή.[95]

With γράμμα, in contrast, we do not see any syntagmatic patterns similar to those Paul uses with νόμος.[96] This is a particularly striking result; we could easily suppose both νόμος and γράμμα to refer to the Mosaic law, and thus to be identical in meaning;[97] but this would be a confusion of meaning and reference. Even if both terms refer to the same thing (and this is not at all certain), their meanings are quite distinct; the syntagmatic patterns demonstrate this.

Also important with γράμμα is the paratactic contrast with πνεῦμα (Rom 2:29; 7:6; 2 Cor 3:6a, b, 7-8). We have noted above[98] that the relationship between νόμος and πνεῦμα is ambiguous.

---

[93] This suggests that writing may be a supplementary component of νόμος: strongly associated, but not necessary. (See the appendix to Chapter 1, at nn. 32-33.)

[94] That γραφή is written appears in the term's transparent relationship to γράφω. (On transparency, see Silva, Biblical Words, 48-51.)

[95] In a sense γραφή is a guide, for things happen κατὰ τὰς γραφάς (1 Cor 15:3, 4); but γραφή is not presented as a guide for an individual's conduct. These verses might better be taken to illustrate aspect 4, command.

[96] However, as with γραφή, the meaning "written" is transparent.

[97] Cf. Abbott-Smith, Manual Lexicon, s.v.

[98] At n. 81.

With δικαίωμα we can see aspect 1b, that it is perceptible (Rom 1:32), and aspect 3, that δικαιώματα are kept (Rom 2:26) and fulfilled (Rom 8:4).[99] In Luke 1:6 we see δικαίωμα and ἐντολή in parallel, as are νόμος and ἐντολή in Rom 7:7-13.

With ἐντολή we see aspects 3, that it is a guide to conduct (1 Cor 7:19), and 6, that it has a source (Rom 7:9); aspect 4, control (or command) is transparent. Outside Paul, ἐντολή appears under aspects 1, verbal (Mark 10:5, 1 John 2:7a, c [λόγος]), and 7, something under which one may put oneself (Matt 5:19 [λύω]; Mark 7:8 [ἀφίημι], 9 [ἀθετέω]).

TABLE 3
Components of Meaning Found in Νόμος
And Related Terms

COMPONENT:	νόμος	γραφή	γράμμα	δικαίωμα	ἐντολή	ἔθος	παράδοσις
1	X	X	{X}	X	(X)		{X}
2	X						(X)
3	X			X	X	(X)	(X)
4	X	X					
5	X					(X)	X
6	X				X	(X)	X
7	X				(X)		X

Key
( ) = Not in Paul, but elsewhere in the New Testament
{ } = Transparent meaning

Ἔθος does not appear in Paul. Elsewhere in the New Testament, however, it is found in patterns suggesting aspect 3, that it is a guide (e.g., Luke 1:9; 2:42; John 19:40; Heb 10:25); aspect 5, that it characterizes a people (Acts 16:21; 25:16; 26:3; 28:17); and aspect 6, that it has a source (Acts 6:14; 15:1; 16:21).[100]

Finally, παράδοσις displays aspects 5, that it characterizes a people (Gal 1:14); 6, that it has a source (1 Cor 11:2; this aspect is presumably also transparent); and probably 7, that one puts oneself under it (Gal 1:14: Paul is a

---

[99] At Rom 5:16, 18, Paul uses δικαίωμα in the distinct sense of acquittal (BAGD, s.v., 3).

[100] Note that for aspects 5 and 6 our only New Testament evidence comes from Luke. But these aspects can also be found in other Jewish authors writing in the Diaspora: Philo, De Iosepho 6 §29; Josephus, Ag.Ap. 1.35 §317; J.W. 5.9.4 §402.

ζηλωτής for the ancestral traditions).[101] Outside of Paul's undisputed letters we find aspect 1, that παράδοσις is verbal (2 Thess 2:15);[102] aspect 2, that it is a standard for judgment (Matt 15:2, 3, 6; Mark 7:3, 5); aspect 3, that it is a guide (Mark 7:5; Col 2:8; 2 Thess 3:6); and further evidence of aspect 7: one "establishes" παράδοσις (Mark 7:9: ἵστημι), or "holds fast" to it (Mark 7:3, 8; 2 Thess 2:15: κρατέω). In particular, παράδοσις is associated with humans (Gal 1:14; Col 2:8; Matt 15:3, 6; Mark 7:8, 9, 13), and in this it may be contrasted with ἐντολὴ θεοῦ (Mark 7:8, 9, 13), or with Christ (Col 2:8), or with ἀποκάλυψις [τοῦ υἱοῦ] (Gal 1:16).

These aspects of the meaning of these various terms are summarized in Table 3. This table does not necessarily give us a full picture of the meaning of these terms. First, I have only been interested in points of contrast or comparison with νόμος. Second, we have only a small number of New Testament texts for most of these terms, and these texts may not manifest every component which is properly part of the meaning of these terms. For my purposes, however, the chief point illustrated by Table 3 is the replication with terms comparable to νόμος of syntagmatic patterns comparable to those found with νόμος. Every component of the meaning of νόμος is found with at least one other term, and every component but 2 is found with at least two other terms. Together, they distinguish νόμος from each of these terms and constitute its meaning.

Νόμος With the Genitive. There remains for consideration here the important pattern of νόμος with an associated noun in the genitive case.[103] In Paul we find the following expressions:

[ὁ νόμος] τῶν ἔργων (Rom 3:27).

νόμος πίστεως (ibid.).

ὁ νόμος τοῦ ἀνδρός (Rom 7:2).

ὁ νόμος τοῦ θεοῦ (Rom 7:22; 8:7).

νόμος θεοῦ (Rom 7:25).

ὁ νόμος τοῦ νοός μου (Rom 7:23).

ὁ νόμος τῆς ἁμαρτίας (ibid.).

νόμος ἁμαρτίας (Rom 7:25).

---

[101] Cf. Rom 9:31, where Israel "pursues" (διώκω) νόμος.

[102] Note that according to this text παράδοσις may be written.

[103] These occurrences of νόμος are also included, as the Appendix shows, in the survey of syntagmatic patterns which yielded the seven components of meaning described above.

ὁ νόμος τῆς ἁμαρτίας καὶ τοῦ θανάτου (Rom 8:2).

ὁ ... νόμος τοῦ πνεύματος τῆς ζωῆς ἐν Χριστῳ Ἰησοῦ (ibid.).

νόμος δικαιοσύνης (Rom 9:31).

ὁ νόμος Μωϋσέως (1 Cor 9:9).

ὁ νόμος τοῦ Χριστοῦ (Gal 6:2).

The import of many of these genitives is not clear, but there may be at least two different relationships presented: ὁ νόμος τοῦ θεοῦ is evidently a genitive of source, and ὁ νόμος τοῦ ἀνδρός is usually thought to specify the realm in which the νόμος referred to operates—that is, in matters relating to an ἀνήρ (and γυνή).[104] Moreover, the parallels with ὁ νόμος τοῦ θεοῦ (Rom 7:22; 8:7) suggest that all of the genitival expressions with νόμος in Rom 7:22 to 8:7 are likewise genitives of source.[105] I shall consider this passage further in Chapter 6.

These genitival expressions thus imply a diversity of νόμοι, and further indicate that this diversity appears both in the sources of νόμος and in the realms which νόμος governs.[106] This implied diversity does not rule out the proposition that in truth νόμος is one, as other passages in Paul's letters (for example, Romans 2) may suggest. But in light of the diversity implied by the genitives, the idea that νόμος is one best taken, when it appears, as extrinsic to the meaning of the term.

Νόμος and the Article. One element of usage remains to be noted: the often-discussed question of whether by νόμος Paul means something different

---

[104] In Chapter 6 I will suggest that τοῦ ἀνδρός may be a genitive of source; but most commentators take the phrase to mean "of marriage" (so, e.g., Dodd, Romans, 119; Dunn, Romans, 1.368; Kuss, Römer, 2.435-36; Sanday and Headlam, Romans, 173; Schlier, Römer, 216; Zahn, Römer, 329). Both of these kinds of genitival expressions have many parallels in the roughly contemporary writings of Josephus, like Paul a Jew writing in the Diaspora. For genitive of source, note ὁ τοὐμοῦ δεσπότου νόμος (J.W. 2.10.4 §195 and ὁ νόμος τοῦ θεοῦ (Ant. 11.5.1 §§124, 130; for genitives specifying the realm of νόμος, see, e.g., ὁ νόμος τῆς γραφῆς (J.W. 5.1.3 §20); νόμος πολέμου (ibid., 2.6.2 §90; 3.8.5 §363; and six other places). Where the genitive specifies the realm of νόμος, νόμος evidently refers to what is customary.

[105] This does not rule out a double meaning; one might say that the law coming from ἁμαρτία (personified) is that which governs ἁμαρτία (one's sinful acts).

[106] Even if τοῦ ἀνδρός in Rom 7:2 is not a genitive of source, Rom 7:25 states that different νόμοι have different realms: Ἄρα οὖν αὐτὸς ἐγὼ τῷ μὲν νοΐ δουλεύω νόμῳ θεοῦ τῇ δὲ σαρκὶ νόμῳ ἁμαρτίας. The authenticity of this sentence is often questioned, but, I think, unnecessarily. See the treatment of this verse in Chapter 6.

than he does by ὁ νόμος.[107] I think the whole literature on this question can be summarized very briefly. The argument that anarthrous νόμος has a special meaning—usually called "qualitative" νόμος—rests on theoretical considerations as to the significance of the definite article; when one begins instead with Paul's texts, no distinction can be shown.[108] This difficulty with the texts means that the most sophisticated proponents of qualitative νόμος must concede, with Burton, that sometimes "the thing chiefly or even exclusively in the mind is the O.T. law . . .", and yet maintain that "it is *thought of* not specifically as the O.T. system but simply in its character as law . . ."[109]

I do not find this thesis persuasive. What is meant by asserting that in Rom 2:12 or 14—Burton's examples[110]—Paul is thinking *of* O.T. law, but not *as* O.T. law? Even if this distinction can be explained, it only disposes of the counter-texts; it provides no textual support for the theory of qualitative νόμος and indeed it renders textual support impossible, for it subordinates the textual evidence of Paul's meaning to the hypothetical reconstruction of what he *must* have meant.

Nor is the theoretical argument for qualitative νόμος persuasive in itself. The variations in the usage of the Greek article are too complex to allow sweeping generalizations about its significance; we may note, for example, the tendency to avoid the article after a preposition (as in ὑπὸ νόμον or ἐν νόμῳ)[111] and, when a noun in the genitive is associated with another noun, for both nouns to have or lack the article together (as in ἔργα νόμου or ὁ νόμος τοῦ θεοῦ).[112] As Robertson says:

---

[107] This is a feature in Burton's discussion of νόμος; see above, at nn. 25-29.

[108] See Grafe, *Paulinische Lehre*, 6-7; Thayer, *Lexicon*, s.v. νόμος; Moulton and Turner, *Grammar*, 177; Moule, *Idiom Book*, 113; and especially the detailed analysis in Bläser, *Gesetz*, 1-30.

[109] Burton, *Galatians*, 455 (emphasis added).

[110] Ibid., 456.

[111] There are variations. Of 47 usages of νόμος in Paul's letters with a preposition, 34 lack the article; with ὑπό (11 uses), νόμος is always anarthrous; with ἀπό (4 uses), never.

[112] In 32 cases in Paul there are three exceptions: Rom 2:13 (twice) and 27.

These usages with the genitive and with prepositions are both discussed by Bläser (*Gesetz*, 10, 13). They are only two of the most significant features in the usage of the article; Funk, in his dissertation on the syntax of the article in Paul ("Syntax," 41-71), devotes 41 pages to a survey of theories on the subject. In contrast, Burton (*Galatians*, 454n) cites for "qualitative" νόμος Slaten, "Qualitative Use"; Slaten in turn rests his thesis on Burton, *Notes*, 25-26, which itself rests entirely on (i) the citation of Matt 21:32 (presumably referring to ἐν ὁδῷ δικαιοσύνης) and (ii) the asserted contrast in Rom 8:24 between the two anarthrous uses there of ἐλπίς: ἐλπὶς δὲ βλεπομένη οὐκ ἔστιν ἐλπίς, understood as "a hope [indefinite] which is seen has not the *quality* of hope." This example does not make it clear to me how the qualitative sense differs from the indefinite; but if there is a difference in this particular text, it still remains a small point on which to erect a

The Greek article is not the only means of making words definite. Many words are definite from the nature of the case. The word itself may be definite, like γῆ, οὐρανός, Ἰησοῦς. The use of a preposition with definite anarthrous nouns is old, as in ἐν οἴκῳ. . . . The context itself often is clear enough. . . . Whenever the Greek article occurs, the object is certainly definite. When it is not used, the object may or may not be.[113]

One more consideration is suggested by the linguistic principle termed "the rule of maximal redundancy": according to this rule, when we are confronted with a term of uncertain meaning, we should define it

> in such fashion *as to make it contribute least to the total message derivable from the passage where it is at home,* rather than, e.g., defining it according to some presumed etymology or semantic history.[114]

Silva explains:

> When any piece of information is transmitted, considerable interference and distortion (*noise*) cannot be avoided; if the means of communication is one hundred percent efficient, the slightest interference will obliterate information. . . . In the vast majority of cases, the hearers do receive the information because of the built-in redundancy of the language. . . . [M]issing a complete word seldom bothers us because the sentence as a whole normally discloses that word. Even if we fail to hear a complete sentence when listening to a speech, we are unlikely to miss anything that is not automatically deducible from the rest of the speech.[115]

We may ask: will Paul have conveyed important nuances in the meaning of the term νόμος solely by the insertion or the omission of the single syllable ὁ (τοῦ, τῷ, τό)? Where such a possible nuance cannot be shown from any other evidence in the text, I think prudence requires us to dismiss it.

---

towering edifice. (One should also note that the phrase cited in Matt 21:32 can be explained by the two patterns I have noted in the text above: ὁδός lacks the article because of the preposition ἐν; δικαιοσύνη then lacks the article because of its relationship to ὁδός.)

[113] Robertson, *Grammar*, 756; cf. BAGD, §§249-76; Schwyzer, *Grammatik*, 2:24; Smyth, *Grammar*, ¶¶1126, 1128. Of νόμος in particular, Robertson remarks (*Grammar*, 796) that it "is used with a great deal of freedom by Paul. In general when νόμος is *anarthrous* in Paul it refers to the Mosaic law, as in ἐπαναπαύῃ νόμῳ . . ." (emphasis added).

[114] Joos, "Semantic Axiom," 257. While Joos formulated the rule for dealing with hapax legomena, it is applicable generally to terms of uncertain meaning in a particular context; see Silva, *Biblical Words*, 153-56.

[115] Silva, *Biblical Words*, 154 (emphasis in the original).

Usage Elsewhere in the New Testament

The syntagmatic patterns associated with νόμος in the New Testament outside of Paul's undisputed letters are summarized in the appendix to this chapter, and they fit easily into the seven categories developed from Paul's usage. This evidence from other early Christian writers thus tends to confirm my analysis of the meaning of νόμος in Paul.

Usage in Other Literature

Although I have not attempted a comprehensive survey of νόμος in other Greek literature, three of the four senses of νόμος which I noted in Chapter 1 relate easily to my components of meaning. νόμος of a city or people[116] and νόμος as custom[117] call special attention to component 5; νόμος as force[118] calls special attention to component 4. νόμος as reason[119] is a thought not found in Paul's patterns of usage; but if the point of identifying νόμος with reason is simply to say that reason ought to rule,[120] then this meaning is essentially a metaphor which depends especially on component 4.[121]

I have given special attention to the Septuagint. There the usage is more diverse than in the New Testament. For the most part it fits within my seven categories; but there are also, especially outside the Pentateuch, other syntagmatic patterns, often found only once or twice, that are difficult to classify. Category 1, verbal νόμος, can be illustrated by γράψεις . . . πάντας τοὺς λόγους τοῦ νόμου τούτου, or πάντα τὸν νόμον τοῦτον (Deut 27:3, 8, and many similar passages); by τό βιβλίον τοῦ νόμου τούτου (Deut 28:61; 29:20; 31:26; Josh 23:6; 4 Kgdms 14:6 [without articles]; and many similar passages); and in other ways, principally found in the Deuteronomistic history.[122]

---

116 Chapter 1, n. 13.

117 Chapter 1, n. 15.

118 Chapter 1, n. 16.

119 Chapter 1, n. 14.

120 See especially Dio Chrysostom's account (*Orations* 1.75):

ὁ δ' ἐγγὺς οὗτος ἑστηκὼς τῆς βασιλείας παρ' αὐτὸ τὸ σκῆπτρον ἔμπροσθεν ἰσχυρὸς ἀνήρ, πολιὸς καὶ μεγαλόφρων, οὗτος δὴ καλεῖται Νόμος, ὁ δὲ αὐτὸς καὶ Λόγος Ὀρθὸς κέκληται Σύμβουλος καὶ Πάρεδρος, οὗ χωρὶς οὐδὲν ἐκείναις πρᾶξαι θέμις οὐδὲ διανοηθῆναι.

And this one standing by Royal Rule, just before her very sceptre, a man strong, gray and noble: he is called Law; but he has also been called Right Reason, Counselor and Coadjutor. Without him none of the others may act or think.

121 Components 1, 2 and 3 may also be involved.

122 Category 1b, perceptible νόμος, is illustrated by, e.g., ἐπιστῆσαι πρὸς πάντας τοὺς λόγους τοῦ νόμου (2 Esdr 18:13; cf. Prov 9:10; 13:15 [γνῶναι]).

Category 2, νόμος as a standard for judgment, is illustrated by τὰς κρίσεις αὐτοῦ τὰς γεγραμμένας ἐν τῷ βιβλίῳ τοῦ νόμου (Deut 30:10; cf. 3 Kgdms 2:3 [κρίματα]); by πᾶσαν πληγην . . . τὴν γεγραμμένην ἐν τῷ βιβλίῳ τοῦ νόμου τούτου (Deut 28:61; cf. 29:20, 21, 27; Josh 8:34); and κατὰ τοῦ νόμου μου ἠσέβησαν (Hos 8:1; cf. Dan 9:11).

Category 3, νόμος as a guide, is illustrated by a number of standard expressions, including φυλάσσειν τὸν νόμον (e.g., Exod 13:10; Lev 19:19, 37; Ps 118:44, 55); ποιεῖν τὸν νόμον (e.g., Num 5:30; Josh 22:5; cf. Deut 27:26; 28:58 [ποιεῖν τοὺς λόγους τοῦ νόμου]); πορεύεσθαι τῷ νόμῳ (e.g., Exod 16:4; Neh 10:29; Ps 77:10); to do things κατά νόμον (e.g., Num 6:21; Deut 4:8); and, within legal codes, οὗτος ὁ νόμος followed by a verb in the future indicative (e.g., Exod 12:43; Lev 6:9; generally a noun in the genitive case specifies the realm of the particular law in question).

Category 4, law as command, is illustrated by ἐνετείλετο Μωϋσῆς . . . καθὰ γέγραπται ἐν τῷ νόμῳ (Josh 8:31; cf. Neh 8:14; 9:14), and perhaps also by the usage with the future tense described under category 3 above.

Category 5, that νόμος defines a people, I do not find in the Septuagint.

Category 6, that νόμος has a source, is illustrated by δώσω σοι . . . τὸν νόμον (Exod 24:12; cf. Lev 26:46; Isa 8:20), and, conversely, by οὐκ ἔστι νόμος (Lam 2:9), which in context means that νόμος has not been given.

Category 7, that people put themselves under νόμος, is illustrated by ἡμέραι πολλαὶ τῷ Ἰσραήλ . . . ἐν οὐ νόμῳ (2 Chr 15:3); by ζητῆσαι τὸν νόμον (2 Esr 7:10; cf. Ps 104:45 [ἐκζητεῖν]); by ἔρριψαν τὸν νόμον (2 Esr 19:26; cf. Isa 24:17 [ἀθετεῖν]; Ps 88:30 [ἐγκαταλείπειν]; Am 2:4 [ἀπωθεῖν]); by οἱ ἀντεχόμενοι τοῦ νόμου (Jer 2:8); and by ἠγαπασα τὸν νόμον (Ps 118:97, 113, 163, 165; cf. Prov 28:4).

So far I think the LXX usage supports my analysis of Paul; it indicates that the features I identified contribute to a meaning attested in Jewish as well as Christian literature. But other usages found in the Septuagint indicate a greater freedom with νόμος than Paul takes; for example, νόμους ἀληθείας (Neh 9:13); ὁ νόμος . . . ἐν καρδίᾳ (Pss 36:31; 39:8; Isa 51:7);[123] τὰ θαυμάσια ἐκ τοῦ νόμου (Ps 118:18); and ἐμπλησθήσονται τοῦ νόμου (Sir 2:16).

Summary

With a definition of the meaning of νόμος as it is used in Paul's letters, I am now in a position to look at the individual occurrences of νόμος in those letters and attempt to identify the referents of the term: Jewish νόμος? νόμος

---

123 In Rom 2:15, τὸ ἔργον τοῦ νόμου is written in the heart.

in general? or some particular νόμος which is not Jewish? In Chapter 3 I will survey all of the occurrences of νόμος in Paul's undisputed letters and try to identify, from the evidence of the immediate context, what references are possible in each case. When that survey is completed I shall use its results (i) to re-examine the thesis that νόμος in Paul's letters has a constant meaning, irrespective of shifts in its reference, and (ii), to analyze what is denoted by Jewish νόμος: Mosaic code, scripture, or something else. These projects will occupy Chapter 4; at the conclusion of that chapter I shall select two passages for the more thorough investigation that will occupy Chapters 5 and 6.

Appendix To Chapter 2

Syntactic Patterns in the Usage of Νόμος In the Undisputed Letters of Paul; Grouped According to Implied Components of Meaning

Summary

1a. νόμος is *verbal* (10):[1]

It speaks (4), testifies (1), is written (3), is read (0), is heard.

1b. νόμος is *perceived* (3):

It is known (1), is seen (1), is found (1).

2. νόμος is a standard for *judgment* (17):

It is (not) against (2), judges (1), brings wrath (1), curses (1), (could not) condemn (1), (does not) justify (6); people transgress (3), sin (1), are blameless (1) with respect to νόμος.

3. νόμος is a *guide to conduct* (23):

It characterizes work (9), is the form of knowledge and truth (1), teaches (1); people do (4), keep (1), are guided by (1), fulfill (6) νόμος.

4. νόμος *controls* (31):

---

[1] Numbers in parentheses indicate the number of times a pattern is found in Paul's seven undisputed letters (text according to Nestle-Aland[26]). The totals for components 4 and 6 are one less than the sums of the figures for constructions displaying those components, because Gal 3:23 employs two different constructions displaying component 4, as does Gal 3:19 for component 6. Zero appears for usages found not in Paul's letters but elsewhere in the New Testament.

It commands (2), rules (2), frees (2), captures (1), (does not) nullify (1), excludes (2), wars (1); people serve (2), are bound by (2), are under (11),[2] are free from (2), are released from (2), die with respect to (2) νόμος.

5. νόμος is tied to *particular people* (17):
    People (do not) have (2), are from (2), are in (1), are under (11), rely on (1) νόμος.

6. νόμος has a *source* (6):
    It comes to be (4), is given (2), is commanded (1), is received (0), is changed (0).

7. People *put themselves under* νόμος (6):
    They (do not) subject themselves to (1), pursue (2), (do not) destroy (1), establish (1), can be ἑαυτοῖς (1) νόμος.

---

[2] ὑπὸ νόμον appears in both category 4 and category 5.

TEXTS

Pattern	In Paul	Other NT
1a. νόμος is verbal: It speaks	... ἢ καὶ ὁ νόμος ταῦτα οὐ λέγει; (1 Cor 9:8) ... καθὼς καὶ ὁ νόμος λέγει (1 Cor 14:34) οἴδαμεν δὲ ὅτι ὅσα ὁ νόμος λέγει τοῖς ἐν τῷ νόμῳ λαλεῖ... (Rom 3:19) ... εἰ μὴ ὁ νόμος ἔλεγεν... (Rom 7:7)	
testifies	... δικαιοσύνη θεοῦ... μαρτυρουμένη ὑπὸ τοῦ νόμου καὶ τῶν προφητῶν ... (Rom 3:21)	
is written	ἐν γὰρ τῷ Μωϋσέως νόμῳ γέγραπται ... (1 Cor 9:9) ἐν τῷ νόμῳ γέγραπται ὅτι ... (1 Cor 14:21) ... ὃς οὐκ ἐμμένει πᾶσιν τοῖς γεγραμμένοις ἐν τῷ βιβλίῳ τοῦ νόμου ... (Gal 3:10) [cf. ... τὸ ἔργον τοῦ νόμου γραπτὸν ἐν ταῖς καρδίαις αὐτῶν ... (Rom 2:15)]	Luke 2:23, 10:26, 24:44; Acts 24:14; John 1:45, 8:17, 10:34, 15:25
is read	———————	Matt 12:5; Acts 13:15
is heard	... τὸν νόμον οὐκ ἀκούετε; (Gal 4:21) οὐ γὰρ οἱ ἀκροαταὶ νόμου δίκαιοι παρὰ τῷ θεῷ ... (Rom 2:13)	John 12:34

Pattern	In Paul	Other NT
1b. νόμος is perceived: It is known	... γινώσκουσιν γὰρ νόμον λαλῶ ... (Rom 7:1) [cf. οἴδαμεν δὲ ὅτι ὅσα ὁ νόμος λέγει τοῖς ἐν τῷ νόμῳ λαλεῖ ... (Rom 3:19) Οἴδαμεν γὰρ ὅτι ὁ νόμος πνευματικός ἐστιν ... (Rom 7:14)]	John 7:49
is seen	βλέπω δὲ ἕτερον νόμον ἐν τοῖς μέλεσίν μου ... (Rom 7:23)	James 1:25
is found	εὑρίσκω ἄρα τὸν νόμον ... ὅτι ... (Rom 7:21)	

2. νόμος is a standard for judgment: It is (not) against	ὁ οὖν νόμος κατὰ τῶν ἐπαγγελιῶν τοῦ θεοῦ; (Gal 3:21) κατὰ τῶν τοιούτων οὐκ ἔστιν νόμος. (Gal 5:23)	
judges	... καὶ ὅσοι ἐν νόμῳ ἥμαρτον, διὰ νόμου κριθήσονται (Rom 2:12)	John 7:51, Acts 23:3, James 2:9, 12
brings wrath	ὁ γὰρ νόμος ὀργὴν κατεργάζεται (Rom 4:15)	
curses	Χριστὸς ἡμᾶς ἐξηγόρασεν ἐκ τῆς κατάρας τοῦ νόμου ... (Gal 3:13)	

Pattern	In Paul	Other NT
(could not) condemn	Τὸ γὰρ ἀδύνατον τοῦ νόμου ... ὁ θεός ... κατέκρινεν τὴν ἁμαρτίαν ἐν τῇ σαρκί ... (Rom 8:3)	
(does not) justify	... μὴ ἔχων ἐμὴν δικαιοσύνην τὴν ἐκ νόμου ἀλλὰ τὴν διὰ πίστεως Χριστοῦ ... (Phil 3:9) εἰ γὰρ διὰ νόμου δικαιοσύνη, ἄρα Χριστὸς δωρεὰν ἀπέθανεν (Gal 2:21) ὅτι δὲ ἐν νόμῳ οὐδεὶς δικαιοῦται παρὰ θεῷ δῆλον ... (Gal 3:11) ... ὄντως ἐκ νόμου ἂν ἦν ἡ δικαιοσύνη (Gal 3:21) κατηργήθητε ἀπὸ Χριστοῦ, οἵτινες ἐν νόμῳ δικαιοῦσθε, τῆς χάριτος ἐξεπέσατε (Gal 5:4) Μωϋσῆς γὰρ γράφει τὴν δικαιοσύνην τὴν ἐκ τοῦ νόμου ... (Rom 10:5)	Acts 13:38
People		
transgress	... διὰ τῆς παραβάσεως τοῦ νόμου τὸν θεὸν ἀτιμάζεις (Rom 2:23) ... ἐὰν δὲ παραβάτης νόμου ἦς ... (Rom 2:25) καὶ κρινεῖ ... σὲ τὸν ... παραβάτην νόμου (Rom 2:27)	Heb 10:28, James 2:9, 11; cf. Acts 18:13 (παρὰ τὸν νόμου); Acts 6:13; 21:28 (κατὰ ... τοῦ νόμου)
sin	... ὅσοι ἐν νόμῳ ἥμαρτον ... (Rom 2:12)	Acts 25:8
are blameless	... κατὰ δικαιοσύνην τὴν ἐν νόμῳ γενόμενος ἄμεμπτος (Phil 3:6)	

Pattern with respect to νόμος	*In Paul*	*Other NT*
3. νόμος is a *guide* to conduct:		
It		
characterizes work	... εἰδότες δὲ ὅτι οὐ δικαιοῦται ἄνθρωπος ἐξ ἔργων νόμου ... (Gal 2:16)	

ἵνα δικαιωθῶμεν ... οὐκ ἐξ ἔργων νόμου ...
(Gal 2:16)

ὅτι ἐξ ἔργων νόμου οὐ δικαιωθήσεται πᾶσα σάρξ.
(Gal 2:16)

ἐξ ἔργων νόμου τὸ πνεῦμα ἐλάβετε ἢ ἐξ ἀκοῆς πίστεως;
(Gal 3:2)

ὁ οὖν ἐπιχορηγῶν ὑμῖν τὸ πνεῦμα καὶ ἐνεργῶν δυνάμεις ἐν ὑμῖν, ἐξ ἔργων νόμου ἢ ἐξ ἀκοῆς πίστεως;
(Gal 3:5)

Ὅσοι γὰρ ἐξ ἔργων νόμου εἰσίν ...
(Gal 3:10)

... τὸ ἔργον τοῦ νόμου γραπτὸν ἐν ταῖς καρδίαις αὐτῶν ...
(Rom 2:15)

... ἐξ ἔργων νόμου οὐ δικαιωθήσεται πᾶσα σάρξ ...
(Rom 3:20)

... δικαιοῦσθαι πίστει ἄνθρωπον χωρὶς ἔργων νόμου.
(Rom 3:28)

{cf. ... [διὰ νόμου] τῶν ἔργων; (Rom 3:27)}

Pattern	In Paul	Other NT
is the form of knowledge and truth	... ἔχοντες τὴν μόρφωσιν τῆς γνώσεως καὶ τῆς ἀληθείας ἐν τῷ νόμῳ· (Rom 2:20)	
teaches	καὶ γινώσκεις τὸ θέλημα καὶ δοκιμάζεις τὰ διαφέροντα κατηχούμενος ἐκ τοῦ νόμου ... (Rom 2:18)	
People		
do	... ὅτι ὀφειλέτης ἐστὶν ὅλον τὸν νόμον ποιῆσαι. (Gal 5:3) ... οἱ ποιηταὶ νόμου δικαιωθήσονται. (Rom 2:13) ... ἔθνη τὰ μὴ νόμον ἔχοντας φύσει τὰ τοῦ νόμου ποιῶσιν ... (Rom 2:14) Περιτομὴ μὲν γὰρ ὠφελεῖ ἐὰν νόμον πράσσῃς· (Rom 2:25) [cf. ἐπικατάρατος πᾶς ὃς οὐκ ἐμμένει πᾶσιν τοῖς γεγραμμένοις ἐν τῷ βιβλίῳ τοῦ νόμου τοῦ ποιῆσαι αὐτά. (Gal 3:10) ὁ δὲ νόμος οὐκ ἔστιν ἐκ πίστεως, ἀλλ᾽ ὁ ποιήσας αὐτὰ ζήσεται ἐν αὐτοῖς. (Gal 3:12)]	
keep	οὐδὲ γὰρ οἱ περιτεμνόμενοι αὐτοὶ νόμον φυλάσσουσιν ... (Gal 6:13) [cf. ... τὰ δικαιώματα τοῦ νόμου φυλάσσῃ ... (Rom 2:26)	Acts 7:53; 21:24 (φυλάσσειν); Acts 15:5; James 2:10 (τηρεῖν)
are guided by	... κατὰ νόμον Φαρισαῖος ... (Phil 3:5)	Luke 2:22, 24, 27, 39; Acts 22:12; 23:3; 24:19; John 18:31; 19:7; Heb 7:5, 16; 8:4; 9:19, 22; 10:8

Pattern	In Paul	Other NT
fulfill	ὁ γὰρ πᾶς νόμος ἐν ἑνὶ λόγῳ πεπλήρωται ... (Gal 5:14)	
	... οὕτως ἀναπληρώσετε τόν νόμον τοῦ Χριστοῦ. (Gal 6:2)	
	... ἡ ἐκ φύσεως ἀκροβυστία τόν νόμον τελοῦσα ... (Rom 2:27)	
	... τέλος γὰρ νόμου Χριστὸς ... (Rom 10:4)	
	ὁ γὰρ ἀγαπῶν τὸν ἕτερον νόμον πεπλήρωκεν. (Rom 13:8)	
	πλήρωμα οὖν νόμου ἡ ἀγάπη. (Rom 13:10)	

νόμος

4
νόμος controls:
It

commands	ἐὰν οὖν ἡ ἀκροβυστία τὰ δικαιώματα τοῦ νόμου φυλάσσῃ ... (Rom 2:26)	Eph 2:15; cf. Matt 22:36, 40
	... ἵνα τὸ δικαίωμα τοῦ νόμου πληρωθῇ ἐν ἡμῖν ... (Rom 8:4)	
rules	... ὥστε ὁ νόμος παιδαγωγὸς ἡμῶν γέγονεν εἰς Χριστόν ... (Gal 3:24)	
	... ὁ νόμος κυριεύει τοῦ ἀνθρώπου ἐφ ὅσον χρόνον ζῇ (Rom 7:1)	
frees	ἐγὼ γὰρ διὰ νόμου νόμῳ ἀπέθανον ... (Gal 2:19)	
	ὁ γὰρ νόμος τοῦ πνεύματος τῆς ζωῆς ἐν Χριστῷ Ἰησοῦ ἠλευθέρωσεν σε ἀπὸ τοῦ νόμου τῆς ἁμαρτίας καὶ τοῦ θανάτου. (Rom 8:2)	

Pattern	In Paul	Other NT
captures	βλέπω δὲ ἕτερον νόμον ἐν τοῖς μέλεσίν μου ... αἰχμαλωτίζοντά με ἐν τῷ νόμῳ τῆς ἁμαρτίας τῷ ὄντι ἐν τοῖς μέλεσίν μου. (Rom 7:23)	
(does not) nullify	... νόμος οὐκ ἀκυροῖ εἰς τὸ καταργῆσαι τὴν ἐπαγγελίαν. (Gal 3:17)	
excludes	ἡ καύχησις ... ἐξεκλείσθη ... διὰ ποίου νόμου; ... διὰ νόμου πίστεως. (Rom 3:27)	
wars	βλέπω δὲ ἕτερον νόμον ἐν τοῖς μέλεσίν μου ἀντιστρατευόμενον τῷ νόμῳ τοῦ νοός μου ... (Rom 7:23)	
People		
serve	Ἄρα οὖν αὐτὸς ἐγὼ τῷ μὲν νοΐ δουλεύω νόμῳ θεοῦ τῇ δὲ σαρκὶ νόμῳ ἁμαρτίας. (Rom 7:25)	
are bound by	... ὑπὸ νόμον ἐφρουρούμεθα συγκλειόμενοι ... (Gal 3:23) ἡ γὰρ ὕπανδρος γυνὴ τῷ ζῶντι ἀνδρὶ δέδεται νόμῳ· (Rom 7:2)	
are under	... τοῖς ὑπὸ νόμον ὡς ὑπὸ νόμον, μὴ ὢν αὐτὸς ὑπὸ νόμον, ἵνα τοὺς ὑπὸ νόμον κερδήσω· (1 Cor 9:20) ... ὑπὸ νόμον ἐφρουρούμεθα ... (Gal 3:23) ... γενόμενον ὑπὸ νόμον ... (Gal 4:4) ... ἵνα τοὺς ὑπὸ νόμον ἐξαγοράσῃ ... (Gal 4:5) ... οἱ ὑπὸ νόμον θέλοντες εἶναι ... (Gal 4:21) ... οὐκ ἐστὲ ὑπὸ νόμον. (Gal 5:18)	

οὐ γάρ ἐστε ὑπὸ νόμον ἀλλὰ
ὑπὸ χάριν.
(Rom 6:14)

... οὐκ ἐσμὲν ὑπὸ νόμον ἀλλὰ ὑπὸ
χάριν.
(Rom 6:15)

are free from   ... ἐλευθέρα ἐστιν ἀπὸ τοῦ νόμου ...
(Rom 7:3)

... ἠλευθέρωσέν σε ἀπὸ τοῦ νόμου τῆς
ἁμαρτίας καί τοῦ θανάτου.
(Rom 8:2)

are released   ... κατήργηται ἀπὸ τοῦ νόμου τοῦ
from   ἀνδρός.
(Rom 7:2)

νυνὶ δὲ κατηργήθημεν ἀπὸ τοῦ νόμου ...
(Rom 7:6)

die with   ... νόμῳ ἀπέθανον ...
respect to   (Gal 2:19)

... καί ὑμεῖς ἐθανατώθητε τῷ νόμῳ ...
(Rom 7:4)

[cf. ... κατηργήθημεν ἀπὸ τοῦ νόμου
ἀποθανόντες ἐν ᾧ κατειχόμεθα ...
(Rom 7:6)]

νόμος

5.
νόμος is tied to
particular people:

People

(do not) have   ... ἔθνη τὰ μὴ νόμον ἔχοντα (φύσει) ...   John 19:7; Acts 7:53
(Rom 2:14)

... οὗτοι νόμον μὴ ἔχοντες ...
(Rom 2:14)

are from   εἰ γὰρ οἱ ἐκ νόμου κληρονόμοι ...
(Rom 4:14)

... οὐ τῷ ἐκ τοῦ νόμου μόνον ἀλλὰ
καὶ τῷ ἐκ πίστεως Ἀβραάμ ...
(Rom 4:16)

Pattern	In Paul	Other NT
are in	… ὅσα ὁ νόμος λέγει τοῖς ἐν τῷ νόμῳ λαλεῖ … (Rom 3:19)	
are under	… τοῖς ὑπὸ νόμον ὡς ὑπὸ νόμον, μὴ ὢν αὐτὸς ὑπὸ νόμον, ἵνα τοὺς ὑπὸ νόμον κερδήσω· (1 Cor 9:20)	
	… ὑπὸ νόμον ἐφρουρούμεθα … (Gal 3:23)	
	… γενόμενον ὑπὸ νόμον … (Gal 4:4)	
	… ἵνα τοὺς ὑπὸ νόμον ἐξαγοράσῃ … (Gal 4:5)	
	… οἱ ὑπὸ νόμον θέλοντες εἶναι … (Gal 4:21)	
	… οὐκ ἐστὲ ὑπὸ νόμον. (Gal 5:18)	
	οὐ γάρ ἐστε ὑπὸ νόμον ἀλλὰ ὑπὸ χάριν. (Rom 6:14)	
	… οὐκ ἐσμὲν ὑπὸ νόμον ἀλλὰ ὑπὸ χάριν. (Rom 6:15)	
rely on	Εἰ δὲ σύ … ἐπαναπαύῃ νόμῳ … (Rom 2:17)	

νόμος

6.
νόμος has a
source:

It

comes to be	οὗ δὲ οὐκ ἔστιν νόμος … (Rom 4:15)	cf. Matt 5:18, Luke 16:17
	ἄχρι γὰρ νόμου … (Rom 5:13)	
	… μὴ ὄντος νόμου … (Rom 5:13)	
	νόμος δὲ παρεισῆλθεν … (Rom 5:20)	

Pattern	In Paul	Other NT
is given	... ὁ νόμος ... προσετέθη ... (Gal 3:19) εἰ γὰρ ἐδόθη νόμος ὁ δυνάμενος ζῳοποιῆσαι ... (Gal 3:21)	John 1:17; 7:19; Heb 8:10 (LXX); 10:16 (LXX)
is commanded	... ὁ νόμος ... διαταγεὶς δι᾽ ἀγγέλων ἐν χειρὶ μεσίτου. (Gal 3:19)	
is received	——————	Acts 7:53
is changed	——————	Heb 7:12

7.
People put
themselves under
νόμος:

They

(do not) subject themselves to	... τῷ γὰρ νόμῳ τοῦ θεοῦ οὐχ ὑποτάσσεται ... (Rom 8:7)	
pursue	Ἰσραὴλ δὲ διώκων νόμον δικαιοσύνης ... (Rom 9:31) ... νόμον οὐκ ἔφθασεν. (Rom 9:31)	
(do not) destroy	νόμον οὖν καταργοῦμεν ...; (Rom 3:31) [cf. ... εἰ γὰρ ἃ κατέλυσα ... (Gal 2:18)]	Matt 5:17; 15:6 (some mss.)
establish	... νόμον ἱστάνομεν. (Rom 3:31) [cf. ... ταῦτα πάλιν οἰκοδομῶ ... (Gal 2:18)]	
can be ἑαυτοῖς	... (ἑαυτοῖς) εἰσιν νόμος· (Rom 2:14)	

νόμος

INDEX TO APPENDIX

[Gal 2:18	cf. 7]		Gal 2:23	4,4,5
19a	4		24	4
b	4		4: 4	4,5
21	2		5	4,5
3: 2	3		21a	4,5
5	3		b	1a
10a	3, cf. 3		5: 3	3
10b	1a		4	2
11	2		14	3
12	cf. 3		18	4,5
13	2		23	2
17	4		6: 2	3
18			13	3
19	6, 6			
21a	2		Phil 3: 5	3
b	6		6	2
c	2		9	2

Chapter 3

REFERENTS FOR Νόμος: BASIC CATEGORIES

I now proceed with the working hypothesis, developed in Chapter 2, that νόμος in Paul's letters has always the same meaning, defined by seven components.[1] These components are general, and neither separately nor together do they specify any particular νόμος; although I have drawn my evidence for these components largely from Jewish and Christian sources, nothing in them limits their application to Jewish or Christian objects. How they *are* applied—to what νόμος in fact refers—thus awaits investigation.

There are some preliminary issues to be addressed before we turn again to Paul's letters.

Kinds of Reference

We might begin by asking simply whether νόμος in Paul's letters always refers to Jewish νόμος, and if not, to what else it refers. But there are more variations here than these questions imply. First, as we saw in Chapter 1, to say that νόμος as Paul uses it refers to Jewish νόμος begs the question, what is Jewish νόμος: Mosaic law? Scripture? Sacred tradition?

Second, not only may νόμος have different referents—for example, Jewish νόμος, Roman νόμος or Greek νόμος; but referents may be of different kinds. We shall see that Paul uses νόμος with different kinds of referents, and these

---

[1] These are set out in the appendix to Chapter 2.

variations will clarify Paul's understanding of νόμος, and thus help to clarify his argument concerning the term.

Lyons classifies references into seven types, which will be useful in showing the variety of ways in which Paul uses νόμος. Two distinctions provide a starting point:

> Among referring expressions we can distinguish those that refer to individuals from those that refer to classes of individuals: we will call these singular and general expressions, respectively. We can also distinguish those which refer to some specific individual (or class of individuals) from those which (granted that they do have reference) do not refer to a specific individual or class; and these we will call definite and indefinite expressions, respectively.[2]

Note, first, that Lyons speaks of "referring expressions," not terms; thus "the president of France" is considered to refer,[3] not the separate word "president."[4] I shall return to this point below, in connection with expressions like ὁ νόμος τοῦ θεοῦ.

When Lyons's two distinctions are combined, they give us these four classes (1) *definite singular*: e.g., "the man who was here yesterday"; (2) *definite general*: "the men who were here yesterday"; (3) *indefinite singular*: "a man who was here yesterday"; and (4) *indefinite general*: "some men who were here yesterday."[5] Lyons notes, however, that classes (3) and (4) each allow a variation: they are *specific* if they refer to particular men who were here yesterday, and *non-specific* if they do not, as in "I wish I could find a man (some men) who was (were) here yesterday"—that is, any would do.[6] Therefore I

---

[2] Lyons, *Semantics*, 1.178. (Lyons marks certain defined terms, such as the four he defines here, with an *; I omit these *s).

[3] Ibid., 185.

[4] The word "President" does, however, *denote*, and this is analogous to reference. *Denotation* is the relation between the term "president" and the kind of non-linguistic entity—namely, presidents—identified by "president"; denotation is thus an aspect of *meaning*, independent of context where *reference* depends on context. See "Meaning and Reference" in the appendix to Chapter 1; Lyons, *Semantics*, 1.177-97, 206-15.

In a particular context the word "president" with no modifier may refer, as in "the President left the White House this morning . . ."

[5] Example (1) comes from Lyons, *Semantics*, 1.181; the rest I derive from his discussion.

[6] Ibid., 187-88; the example is mine. Lyons says that when an "indefinite noun-phrase is being used non-specifically . . . . it is far from clear that it is correctly regarded as a referring expression" (ibid., 188; * omitted). I will nevertheless speak of such expressions as referring, for they do identify possible referents and exclude the rest of the universe; the peculiarity of this kind of reference seems to me to be sufficiently signalled by calling it "non-specific."

will modify (3) and (4) to *indefinite singular specific* and *indefinite general specific* reference, and add classes (5) *indefinite singular non-specific*; and (6) *indefinite general non-specific.*

There is finally (7), *generic* reference, as in "lions are friendly beasts," provided this is understood as asserting something "about the class of lions as such."[7]

In these English examples, singular and general references are indicated by singular and plural forms, and definite and indefinite are indicated by the definite and indefinite articles. But only context will distinguish between specific and non-specific reference, and this is also true for generic reference; as Lyons observes, "a lion," "the lion" and "lions" may all be generic.[8]

In Greek formal distinctions will not necessarily be decisive; singular nouns may be used collectively or distributively to indicate a number of persons or things,[9] and these usages cannot be excluded for νόμος *a priori.* More important for my purposes are the absence of an indefinite article in Greek, and the peculiarities in the use of the Greek definite article. The matter is summarized thus by Robertson:

> The Greek article is not the only means of making words definite. Many words are definite from the nature of the case. . . . The use of a preposition with definite anarthrous nouns is old . . . The context itself often is clear enough. . . . Whenever the Greek article occurs, the object is certainly definite. When it is not used, the object may or may not be.[10]

Between specific and non-specific indefinite reference, in Greek as in English there does not appear to be a formal distinguishing mark. τις does not help; it may have either the sense "any" (which would be non-specific) or the

---

[7] Ibid., 194. Lyons also distinguishes between generic *propositions* which are "essential" or "analytic" and those (like "lions are friendly beasts") which are not; but in either case the *reference* is generic.

Note that generic reference need not include every member of the class marked by this term; we can say "lions are four-footed" even though an occasional lion, through mishap or genetic anomaly, has only three feet.

[8] Lyons, *Semantics*, 1.194.

[9] Smyth, *Grammar*, 269 (¶¶996, 998); Smyth illustrates the collective with ἵππον in ἵππον ἔχω εἰς χιλίαν, "I have about a thousand horse," and the distributive with βίῳ in ὅσοι δίκαιοι ἐγένοντο ἐν τῷ ἑαυτῶν βίῳ, "all who proved themselves just in their lives." Cf. BDF, 77 (¶¶139, 140); Robertson, *Grammar*, 409; Kühner-Gerth, *Grammatik*, 2.2.13-15. The plural may also be used for the singular, but this does not concern us; νόμος is always singular in Paul.

[10] Robertson, *Grammar*, 756; see also Smyth, *Grammar*, 288-89; Schwyzer, *Grammatik*, 2.24.

sense "some" (which would be specific).[11] A good example is Gal 1:9, where εἴ τις ὑμᾶς εὐαγγελίζεται παρ' ὃ παρελάβετε would seem to refer to a specific person (or persons) actually among the Galatians; but only the context tells us this. Likewise generic reference is not formally marked; although grammarians speak of a "generic" article, the article is often not generic, and generic use allows but does not require the article.[12]

In all, I see only one reliable formal guide to reference, namely that the article appears to exclude indefinite reference.[13] Beyond this, while singular νόμος does not rule out a general or plural reference, it certainly points us away from it; in the examples of collective and distributive use I quoted above,[14] the plural reference of the singular noun was unmistakable in the context. But at this stage, all of the seven kinds of reference described by Lyons are possible for νόμος in Paul's letters. To recapitulate, with examples closer to my subject, these are:

(1) Definite singular: e.g., νόμος may refer to ὁ νόμος τῶν Ἰουδαίων.

(2) Definite general: e.g., οἱ νόμοι τῶν Ἰουδαίων καὶ τῶν Ῥωμαίων.

(3) Indefinite singular specific: e.g., νόμος ὁ δυνάμενος ζῳοποιῆσαι.

(4) Indefinite general specific: e.g., νόμοι οἱ δυναμένοι ζῳοποιῆσαι.

(5) Indefinite singular non-specific: e.g., νόμος ὁ δυνάμενος ζῳοποιῆσαι.[15]

(6) Indefinite general non-specific: e.g., νόμοι οἱ δυναμένοι ζῳοποιῆσαι.

(7) Generic: e.g., ὁ νόμος κρίνει.[16]

The first of these examples, ὁ νόμος τῶν Ἰουδαίων, raises a point I noted earlier: that *expressions* refer. My interest, however, focuses on the single term νόμος. When νόμος is accompanied by a noun in the genitive, as it is fourteen times in Paul's letters, the entire phrase clearly refers; but what of νόμος itself,

---

[11] LSJ, s.v.; BAGD, s.v.

[12] Smyth, *Grammar*, 286-87 (¶1118); BDF, 131-32 (¶252); Schwyzer, *Grammatik*, 2.24-25; Robertson, *Grammar*, 757.

[13] See above, at n. 10.

[14] N. 9.

[15] Form alone, as I have said, cannot tell us whether this phrase from Gal 3:21 is specific or non-specific. I shall take up this verse again in relation to its context; see below, at nn. 43-46.

[16] This is generic when, in context, it is a statement about νόμος as such; that is how I use it in describing component 2 of the meaning of νόμος. In another context it might be a statement about a particular νόμος.

as employed in such expressions? Again "denotation"[17] might be used to describe the contribution of νόμος to the expression: that is, the term *denotes* a kind of entity, the expression as a whole *refers* to an entity (or entities) of this kind. This is the usage employed by Lyons; but it will be useful for my purposes to modify this usage somewhat. Denotation in this case is very close to general reference. If I say, "Now I shall discuss νόμοι—in particular, the νόμος of the Jews," "νόμοι" and "the νόμος of the Jews" are both referring expressions, each of which could exist independently; the first expression refers generally to some group or class of νόμοι, and the second specifies a νόμος from that group or class. I shall say that "νόμος of the Jews," occurring by itself, collapses this pair of referring expressions into one, and therefore that it contains an *implicit general reference* to a group or class of νόμοι: the reference that would be made by the first part of the expression if it were expanded in the way I have just described.

I adopt this non-standard use of the term "reference" because it facilitates comparison of Paul's different uses of the term νόμος, particularly of those uses in genitival phrases like ὁ νόμος τοῦ θεοῦ. I can now say that every occurrence of νόμος refers to some νόμος or νόμοι, usually explicitly but sometimes implicitly; in ὁ νόμος τοῦ θεοῦ the implicit reference of νόμος is to some class of νόμοι,[18] and τοῦ θεοῦ specifies that member of the class which comes from God.[19] Specifying a reference for every use of νόμος allows me to build a comprehensive picture of what Paul can invoke the term for. From a linguist's point of view it might be preferable to say that sometimes in Paul's letters νόμος refers (as in expressions like ὁ νόμος λέγει), while at other times it only denotes (as in expressions like ὁ νόμος τοῦ θεοῦ),[20] but from my point of view

---

[17] See n. 4 above.

[18] Even if the general class is as large as the class of all νόμοι, implicit reference will not be generic. The point of generic reference is to allow assertions about objects identified by a term "as such"; but implicit reference as I use that term does not involve any assertions about the class referred to.

But it may be difficult to tell what the general class is; it might be "those things within the meaning of νόμος," or it might be some sub-class of those things, or it might be a special class not in fact within the meaning of νόμος when that term is used without τοῦ θεοῦ. Thus ὁ νόμος τῆς ἱστορίας (Josephus, *J.W.* 1.1.4 §11) appears to refer to the customary practices of historians; it does not follow that νόμος absolute can mean "customary practices of a craft."

[19] Taking τοῦ θεοῦ to be a genitive of source.

[20] Lyons (*Semantics*, 1.208) explains the difference between denotation and reference thus:

How does denotation differ from reference? . . . reference is an utterance-bound relation and does not hold of lexemes as such, but of expressions in context. Denotation, on the other hand, like sense, is a relation that applies

this introduces an unnecessary complexity.[21] For me the chief questions are: when Paul says νόμος, does he always refer to Jewish νόμος? And if not, to what else does he refer? My use of "implied general reference" allows me to employ "reference" consistently for the relation between νόμος and the extra-linguistic entities for which it stands, without having to shift to "denotation" or "sense."

On this view, the implicit reference of νόμος in such expressions will be definite general; I think it must be definite if the reference of the whole expression is,[22] and this will at least be so in the majority of cases where the expression is articular.[23]

References in Paul's Letters

I shall treat each of Paul's letters in turn, beginning with the two (1 Corinthians and Philippians) in which νόμος appears only incidentally, proceeding to Galatians, and concluding with Romans.

---

in the first instance to lexemes and holds independently of particular occasions of utterance.

But Lyons also notes (ibid., 1.206) that some writers use "reference" for what he calls "denotation," and others use "denotation" for what he calls "reference."

[21] Linguistically, the notion of "sense" is also pertinent with an expression like ὁ νόμος τοῦ θεοῦ, for the significance of νόμος may lie more in its relation to other terms (its "sense"), along the lines of my analysis in Chapter 2, than in its relation to non-linguistic entities (its "denotation"). What "entities" does νόμος in this expression denote?

[22] I do not see how one can select a definite member out of an indefinite class.

[23] Hübner (Law, 144; cf. 138-39) suggests another view of these genitival expressions. "According to our reflections on [Rom] 3.27, the genitives occurring there, 'of works' and 'of faith', define the Law in regard to the perspective of the moment from which it is regarded." But it is not clear from Hübner's discussion whether he considers each genitival expression in its entirety to refer to (as he says) "Torah," or νόμος by itself to do so. If the former is his view, then νόμος itself has, as I have suggested, an implicit general referent; if the latter, then Hübner has interpreted the genitive case in a way (as specifying "the perspective of the moment from which [the nomen regens] is regarded") for which I can see no grammatical basis.

I find the same lack of clarity in Lohse, "ὁ νόμος"; Lohse argues (p. 285) "dass Paulus in der Tat am Anfang von Röm 8 durchgehend den Begriff νόμος in prägnanten Sinn als das alttestamentliche Gesetz versteht," but I think the better understanding is that it is the phrases νόμος + genitive which refer to "Old Testament law."

Note on Verse References

In citing texts from Paul's letters I shall generally use lower-case Roman letters only when νόμος occurs more than once in a verse; then a will refer to the first occurrence of νόμος, b to the second, and so forth.

1 Corinthians

Here νόμος appears nine times, once (14:34) in the disputed passage 14:34-35.[24] In two of these passages νόμος is identified as containing the written words of Jewish Scripture[25]—including the prophets: Deut 25:4 and Isai 28:11.[26] The references in these passages are definite and singular, but we cannot assume that they are simply to Scripture. Rather, here νόμος includes Scripture without necessarily being limited to it; I shall simply call it "Jewish νόμος".

In 1 Cor 9:9 Paul speaks of ὁ Μωϋσέως νόμος, evidently as identical to ὁ νόμος of 9:8. In line with my discussion above, we may accordingly take the former νόμος to refer implicitly to a larger class of νόμοι of which ὁ Μωϋσέως νόμος is a member. This larger class is not otherwise identified.

Beyond these passages relating νόμος to Scripture, we have the more problematic 14:34: αἱ γυναῖκες . . . ὑποτασσέσθωσαν, καθὼς καὶ ὁ νόμος λέγει. Here no text is cited; if we examine the text usually suggested,[27] Gen 3:16, we find a completely different kind of statement—future indicative against the third-person imperative of 1 Cor 14:34—and no verbal parallels at all: αὐτός σου κυριεύσει. It has thus been suggested that the reference here is not to Scripture but to oral law;[28] whether or not this is so, the reference is to

---

[24] On the textual question presented by 14:34-35, see Fee, *First Corinthians*, 699-705; Murphy-O'Connor, "Interpolations," 90-92.

[25] That is, the Septuagint, or another Greek text if Paul had another. I use the term "scripture" because it cannot be demonstrated that Paul used the Septuagint as we have it (see the following note).

[26] 1 Cor 9:8; 14:21. In neither case does Paul quote precisely from the Septuagint as we have it. At 9:8 he says οὐ κημώσεις βοῦν ἀλοῶντα, against οὐ φιμώσεις βοῦν ἀλοῶντα (Deut 25:4), but the two different verbs are evidently close equivalents (LSJ, s.v.). In 14:21 Paul takes greater liberties: ἐν ἑτερογλώσσαις καὶ ἐν χείλεσιν ἑτέρων λαλήσω τῷ λαῷ τούτῳ, καὶ οὐδ᾽ οὕτως εἰσακούσονταί μου contrasts with διὰ φαυλισμὸν χειλέων διὰ γλώσσης ἑτέρας, ὅτι λαλήσουσιν τῷ λαῷ τούτῳ . . . καὶ οὐκ ἠθέλησαν ἀκούειν (Isa 28:11-12 [LXX]). Here the one phrase appearing verbatim in both Paul and the Septuagint is underscored; words appearing in both passages but in different form are bold-face. Despite the differences—which could stem from Paul's use of a text form no longer extant (Fee, *First Corinthians*, 679 n. 20)—the resemblances are sufficient to identify the text which Paul cites.

[27] E.g., by Barrett, *First Corinthians*, 330; Nestle-Aland[26], margin.

[28] Fee, *First Corinthians*, 707; Fee regards 1 Cor 14:34-35 as a gloss.

something verbal, and must be definite and singular. It cannot be shown to be a reference to Jewish νόμος,[29] but no other νόμος is suggested. Next comes the four-fold ὑπὸ νόμον of 1 Cor 9:20. To be ὑπὸ νόμον is evidently to be under a definite νόμος,[30] and Paul's argument requires that each νόμος here have the same referent.[31] It is conceivable that the reference is indefinite ("to those under a law I became as under [the same] law"); but nothing suggests this. It is far more likely that the reference is singular, definite, and to Jewish νόμος, as the three-fold Ἰουδαῖος of the first part of the verse implies.

Finally we have 15:56: ἡ δὲ δύναμις τῆς ἁμαρτίας ὁ νόμος. The only thing clear from the immediate context of this statement is that Paul considers his reference to be so clear as to require no explanation; but this itself is of the greatest importance, for it indicates that Paul can use the term standing alone without any ambiguity as to its reference.[32] The other uses of νόμος in this letter imply strongly that this ordinary, unspecified reference is to Jewish νόμος, often meaning specifically the words written in Scripture.[33]

Philippians

In Philippians νόμος appears three times in close succession: 3:5, 6, 9. None of these uses is associated with the citation of Scripture, but the reference to Jewish νόμος is nevertheless clear, especially in 3:5 where νόμος first appears. In this verse κατὰ νόμον Φαρισαῖος is presented in series with περιτομῇ ὀκταήμερος, ἐκ γένους Ἰσραήλ, φυλῆς Βενιαμίν and Ἑβραῖος ἐξ Ἑβραίων—each a marker of Jewish identity—and Φαρισαῖος is itself a reference to a Jewish group marked at least in part by its approach to Jewish νόμος as a guide to conduct.[34] This term thus suggests that Paul here refers particularly to νόμος as comprising specific standards of conduct for Jews

---

[29] Note, however, the parallel from Josephus, *Ag.Ap.* 2.24 §§200-1 (cited by Fee, *First Corinthians*, 707 n. 35).

[30] Or possibly νόμοι; I see nothing to suggest a plural sense, however, or to explain the use of the singular if νόμοι are meant.

[31] One will not gain those under Jewish νόμος by being under Roman νόμος.

[32] This conclusion is not certain. It might be that Paul's reference is made clear by something in the context of his audience—for example, he could be quoting a sentence known to the Corinthians.

[33] 1 Cor 9:9 suggests, however, that Paul thinks his audience may (on his first use of νόμος) require a reminder. I shall consider this point further in Chapter 4, nn. 43-46.

[34] Matt 23:2; Mark 7:3 par.; Josephus, *J.W.* 2.8.14 §162, *Ant.* 17.2.4 §41.

(component 3 of the meaning of νόμος);[35] but this does not rule out a broader view of νόμος.[36]

The clarity of the reference for νόμος in Phil 3:5 settles the matter for 3:6 and 9 as well; there is nothing to suggest that the reference changes here, in mid-argument. As in 3:5, the focus in 3:6 and 9 is on νόμος as a guide by which conduct is judged; thus in 3:6 Paul is ἄμεμπτος . . . κατὰ δικαιοσύνην τὴν ἐν νόμῳ, and in 3:9 δικαιοσύνη is not ἐκ νόμου.

Galatians

We have seen in 1 Corinthians and Philippians, where νόμος does not appear to be the focus of any dispute, that Paul uses the term with definite singular reference to Jewish νόμος—sometimes specifically including words drawn or paraphrased from Scripture. The casual appearance of these references in non-polemical contexts suggests that this is the normal reference of νόμος for Paul.

Now we turn to Galatians. Here νόμος occurs 32 times, from 2:16 to 6:13. As elsewhere, the term enters the discussion without introduction or explanation; here it appears initially in the three-fold ἔργα νόμου of Gal 2:16. But instead of taking all these passages in order, I will begin with those where the reference is clearest.

Definite Singular References (Jewish νόμος). In Gal 3:17 Paul refers to the νόμος coming into existence 430 years after the διαθήκη given to Abraham; this obviously is a definite singular reference, and 430 years is the period given in Exod 12:40 (LXX) for the dwelling of the Israelites in Egypt and in Canaan—thus, plausibly, from Abraham to the giving of the law at Mt. Sinai.[37] Again, the giving of νόμος is referred to in Gal 3:19 (διαταγεὶς δι' ἀγγέλων ἐν χειρὶ μεσίτου); whatever the source of the details of this account,[38] the definite singular reference must be to the same νόμος just specified in 3:17: that given at Mt. Sinai. The argument equally requires that the νόμος of 3:21a be the same, for it is the argument of 3:17-20 which

---

[35] Burton (*Galatians*, 458) groups Phil 3:5 among texts where νόμος "refers to the legalistic element in the O. T., or to the O. T. or any part of it, looked at as Paul's opponents looked at it . . ." This last phrase, based presumably on the polemical context of Galatians and perhaps Romans, illustrates the value for my purposes of 1 Corinthians and Philippians, where there is no polemic about νόμος. I see no reason to think that Paul is here adopting someone else's use of the term.

[36] For example, Scripture, since Scripture contains standards of conduct.

[37] Betz, *Galatians*, 158 n. 49; Burton, *Galatians*, 184; Schlier, *Galaterbrief*, 147-48. (In Codex B the period is 435 years; in Gen 15:13, 400 years.)

[38] See, e.g., Betz, *Galatians*, 168-70.

prompts the question posed in 3:21: ὁ οὖν νόμος κατὰ τῶν ἐπαγγελιῶν τοῦ θεοῦ;

All of these references are particularly striking because the 430 years of 3:17 seem not only to specify the νόμος given at Sinai but to exclude any broader reference (for example, to Scripture as a whole). These passages must then be contrasted with the equally specific Gal 4:21b: τὸν νόμον οὐκ ἀκούετε; This question is followed by a discussion of the two sons of Abraham, a story told in Scripture. Thus νόμος here, while certainly Jewish, is not presented as commandments.[39] But the reference in 4:21b also establishes the reference in 4:21a (Λέγετέ μοι, οἱ ὑπὸ νόμον θέλοντες εἶναι . . .), for the argument here makes no sense unless νόμος refers to the same thing in both clauses.[40]

Definite singular references are implicit in 5:3 (. . . ὅλον τὸν νόμον ποιῆσαι), 14 (ὁ γὰρ πᾶς νόμος ἐν ἑνὶ λόγῳ πεπλήρωται) and 6:13 (οὐδέ . . . νόμον φυλάσσουσιν), for only a specific νόμος can be done, fulfilled or kept. Moreover, the specific νόμος here is evidently Jewish: in 5:3 and 6:13 νόμος is specifically associated with περιτομή, and in 5:14 with the text ἀγαπήσεις τὸν πλησίον σου ὡς σεαυτόν (Lev 19:18 [LXX]).

In 4:4, γενόμενον ὑπὸ νόμον must refer to a specific law because it refers to the actual state of a specific individual, Christ; one cannot be ὑπὸ νόμον generically or indefinitely. Again, the reference here is necessarily to Jewish νόμος.[41] The same argument applies to ὑπὸ νόμον in 3:23.

Next, on the strength of the rule that the article makes a noun definite even though the absence of the article does not make the noun indefinite, νόμος in 3:12 (ὁ δὲ νόμος οὐκ ἔστιν ἐκ πίστεως) and 24 (ὁ νόμος παιδαγωγὸς ἡμῶν γέγονεν) has specific reference, evidently to Jewish νόμος.[42]

Definite General Reference. Like νόμος in 5:3, 14; 6:13, the phrase ὁ νόμος τοῦ Χριστοῦ in 6:2 has definite singular reference, for this νόμος too is to be fulfilled (ἀναπληρόω); but the precise referent for the phrase is uncertain. According to the argument I make above (text following n. 16), νόμος as used

---

[39] Paul may however have chosen the term νόμος here because of the idea that νόμος commands; at any rate, he uses the story of Abraham as authority for his argument.

[40] An indefinite reference for 4:21a is implausible in any event; no one is suggesting that the Galatians ought to be under *some* νόμος, but rather under *the* νόμος.

[41] It is natural to infer that the same νόμος is referred to by ὑπὸ νόμον in 4:5 also; but while I think this is probable I do not think it is inevitable.

[42] See above, at n. 10; although the article does not exclude generic reference, neither 3:12 nor 3:24 seems open to a generic interpretation.

Νόμος is also articular in 3:19, 21a; 4:21b; 5:3, 14; 6:2. All of these have been identified as having specific reference on other grounds, as have 4:4 and 6:13, where νόμος is anarthrous.

in 6:2 makes an implicit general reference to some class of νόμοι; but it is unclear what this class is.

Indefinite Singular Non-Specific Reference. Probably there are other definite references in Galatians, but before turning to them I note an evident indefinite singular reference: εἰ γὰρ ἐδόθη νόμος ὁ δυνάμενος ζῳοποιῆσαι ... (Gal 3:21b). We know—most directly from the unreal form of the following apodosis[43]—that there is no νόμος ὁ δυνάμενος ζῳοποιῆσαι; we might then say that this expression refers to nothing. But this would seem to miss Paul's point. Although nothing fits this description, something might fit it, and Paul invites us to suppose—only momentarily, to be sure—that something does fit it. In the moment that this condition (εἰ γὰρ ἐδόθη ...) is before us, Paul's expression does refer, and its referent is indefinite, singular, and non-specific: to any νόμος that is able to make alive.[44]

Moreover, when we look inside Paul's expression to the separate term νόμος, here too there appears (implicitly) an indefinite, singular, non-specific reference. Paul has not said, εἰ γὰρ ἦν ὁ νόμος δυνάμενος ζῳοποιῆσαι, "if the law were able to make alive," in which case ὁ νόμος would be the referring expression and its reference definite and singular;[45] by saying rather εἰ γὰρ ἐδόθη νόμος Paul supposes that another νόμος might have been given, and refers to that νόμος—whatever it might be.[46] This is also the reference of 3:21c, ὄντως ἐκ νόμου ἂν ἦν ἡ δικαιοσύνη.[47]

---

[43] ὄντως ἐκ νόμου ἂν ἦν ἡ δικαιοσύνη. Moreover, this apodosis is virtually identical to the refuted protasis of Gal 2:21 (see Winger, "Unreal Conditions").

[44] It may be recalled that Lyons does not think "non-specific reference" is actually reference; I have allowed that it is different from other kinds of reference, but maintained that the term is still useful in such cases (above, n. 6).

[45] In this case "able to make alive" would be attributive rather than referential; see Lyons, *Semantics*, 1.185-86.

[46] But Paul does not have in mind any νόμος at all—as if the νόμος of Rome, or of Tarsus, might have been able to do this. He means a νόμος *given*, and by *given* he evidently means *given in the way the Mosaic law was given* (whether by God or by angels is an issue he leaves open.)

[47] Alternatively, we could say that the reference in 3:21c is definite on the ground that in 3:21c we presume (contrary to fact) that a νόμος fitting the indefinite description of 3:21b was given, and refer to that particular νόμος. On this view the hypothetical νόμος presumably exists *in place of* the actual, Jewish νόμος known to Paul; or rather, this hypothetical νόμος *would be* Jewish νόμος. Lyons suggests this treatment in an analogous case; as he puts it, when a phrase refers to a previous indefinite reference, the second reference is to "'that unique though hypothetical entity which would be crucially involved in actualizing the possible world characterized in the first part of the sentence'" (*Semantics*, 1.192-93).

This construction would probably be the correct one for analyzing the relation between the proposition of 3:21c and that of 2:21b: διὰ νόμου δικαιοσύνη. If we construe

At one more point in Galatians νόμος is usually translated as having indefinite, non-specific reference: κατὰ τῶν τοιούτων οὐκ ἔστιν νόμος (Gal 5:23),
"against such things there is no law,"[48] rather than "the law is not against such
things."[49] So far as I can see only the absence of the article accounts for the
general acceptance of the former interpretation.[50] This is anarthrous νόμος
thus taken to be indefinite rather than (in Burton's terminology) qualitative;[51]
nevertheless, the cautions adduced in the last chapter against relying on the
article's absence still apply.

We may compare νόμος in 5:23 with its use earlier in the same passage, at
5:14 and 18. The first of these I have already noted as a definite reference to
Jewish νόμος.[52] Gal 5:18 well illustrates the uncertainty of the article as a
guide: εἰ δὲ πνεύματι ἄγεσθε, οὐκ ἐστὲ ὑπὸ νόμον, in which both πνεῦμα and
νόμος are anarthrous. Some translate both as definite,[53] and others translate
πνεῦμα as definite but νόμος as indefinite;[54] but I have not seen any translation which treats πνεῦμα as indefinite. Everyone agrees, then, that the absence
of the article is not controlling, especially in prepositional phrases; but what
the context implies about νόμος is variously interpreted.

I do not see that the context for 5:23 is any clearer. The question may be
put thus: for Paul and his audience, was the thought of different νόμοι so

---

the reference of 3:21c to be indefinite, to any νόμος, and that of 2:21b to be definite, to
Jewish νόμος, then it would follow that the refutation of 2:21b would not entail the refutation of 3:21c; for perhaps δικαιοσύνη could come through some non-Jewish νόμος. But I do
not think that Paul has any thought of this; the possibility he raises is rather that the Jewish
νόμος—in Paul's terminology, the νόμος δεδωκώς—might have been different.

    Nevertheless, I think that for my purposes it will be best to keep our attention on
what is said or presumed about what νόμος exists. From this perspective, in both 3:21b and
c Paul refers indefinitely and non-specifically to a kind of thing which (Paul implies) could
exist, although actually it does not.

    [48] So AV, RV, RSV, NAB; with variations in wording but the same sense are NASB,
NEB, JB, NJB and the commentaries of Betz (271), Bruce (251), Burton (318), Mussner
(384) and Schlier (247).

    [49] So the two recent German translations appearing in Nestle-Aland, Das Neue
Testament (revidierte Fassung der Lutherbibel von 1984; Einheitsübersetzung der Heiligen
Schrift [1979]): "das Gesetz nicht," rather then "kein Gesetz." The same view is apparently
taken by Räisänen (Paul, 114-15) and Sanders (Paul, the Law, 49 n. 6); neither discusses
the point.

    [50] This is Burton's ground (Galatians, 318); Betz, Bruce, Mussner and Schlier do not
discuss the point.

    [51] That is, "having the qualities for which the term stands" (Burton, Galatians, 454; see
also Slaten, "Qualitative Νόμος"). See Chapter 2, n. 29.

    [52] See following n. 40.

    [53] AV, RV, NASB, RSV, NAB, Betz (Galatians, 271; he brackets "the" in his translation).

    [54] NEB, JB, Burton (Galatians, 302), Bruce (Galatians, 242).

readily present that it could be suggested simply by the omission of the article? Or was the reference of νόμος to Jewish νόμος rather so ordinary that it would be presumed unless, as in Gal 3:21b, either Paul's expression or the context required another understanding?

At this stage of my examination the question of Gal 5:18 and 23 must be left open; although νόμος in these verses follows a specific reference in 5:14 to Jewish νόμος, a non-specific reference ("any law") remains possible in 5:18 and 23.

Other Passages: Possible Ambiguities. There remain to be considered fifteen occurrences of νόμος in Galatians. In each of them, as in 5:18 and 23, an indefinite reference is possible, but there is very little to suggest that this possibility is realized. Thus in Gal 2:16, where νόμος first appears in this letter, ἔργα νόμου are things of which Jews have special knowledge (Ἡμεῖς φύσει Ἰουδαῖοι . . . εἰδότες . . . [2:15-16]); it is a natural inference that Jewish νόμος is meant, not only in 2:16 but in 2:19a, b and 21, and then in 3:2, 5, 10b, where ἔργα νόμου again appear. Moreover, διὰ νόμου in 2:19, obscure though it is, is much easier to understand as a definite reference than as an indefinite one; for it implies either a personal experience of νόμος[55] or an action of νόμος,[56] both of which require a specific νόμος; and if a specific νόμος is meant, it is surely Jewish.

Despite these considerations, however, I will not rule out the possibility that νόμος in some or all of its nine occurrences from Gal 2:16 to 3:10a refers to something other or more than Jewish νόμος. The obscurity of the phrases ἔργα νόμου and πίστις Χριστοῦ, the puzzling opposition between the two and their uncertain relation to δικαιοσύνη, the curious expression διὰ νόμου νόμῳ ἀπέθανον, in which νόμος is opposed to νόμος—all these difficulties should make us cautious. Gal 2:15-21 in particular is one of the two texts which I will examine more carefully in Chapters 5 and 6 of this dissertation; conclusions can await that examination.

What has been said for Gal 2:16 through 3:10a applies also to the six occurrences of νόμος in Galatians which I have not yet mentioned: 3:10b, 11, 13, 18; 4:5; 5:4. Gal 3:10b is a special case, for while τὸ βιβλίον τοῦ νόμου clearly has a specific reference, that specificity might be supplied by either τὸ

---

[55] So Burton, *Galatians*, 132.

[56] So, in different ways, Schlier (*Galaterbrief*, 101), referring to the role of νόμος in the death of Christ; Betz (*Galatians*, 122), referring to "3:19-25 . . . attributing to the Torah an active role in salvation (3:22) . . ."

βιβλίον or τοῦ νόμου.[57] But in general, 3:10b, 11, 13 and 18 appear next to the clear references to Jewish νόμος in 3:12, 17 and 19, and *prima facie*, the case for their reference to Jewish νόμος is very strong. Likewise, ὑπὸ νόμον in 4:5 follows immediately on ὑπὸ νόμον in 4:4, which—because it is describing Christ—plainly refers to Jewish law; so, presumably, does 4:5. Finally, 5:4 follows the reference to Jewish νόμος in 5:3.

Results. We have thus found in Galatians: (1) twelve definite singular references to Jewish νόμος;[58] (2) seventeen probable definite singular references to Jewish νόμος;[59] (3) one definite general reference;[60] and (4) two indefinite, singular non-specific references.[61] Thus in 29 of 32 places, νόμος in Galatians probably or certainly refers to Jewish νόμος. But the scope of this Jewish νόμος is not specified. In three associated verses (3:17, 19, 21a) it is apparently the law given to Moses at Mt. Sinai, and once (4:21b) it is Scripture; elsewhere we have no more to go on than the general meaning of νόμος as developed in Chapter 2.

Romans

Finally we come to the greatest body of Paul's uses of νόμος, the 74 appearing in the letter to the Romans. νόμος appears in every chapter from 2 through 10, and then again in 13; the greatest concentrations, however, are in chapters 2 (19 uses) and 7 (23 uses).

Definite Singular References (Jewish νόμος). Here as in Galatians we may begin with passages where it is clear that νόμος refers definitely to Jewish νόμος. In 3:19a, ὁ νόμος λέγει evidently refers to the collection of scriptural quotations found in 3:10-18;[62] thus νόμος refers to (or includes) Scripture in 3:19a (ὅσα ὁ νόμος λέγει . . .). 3:19b (. . . τοῖς ἐν νόμῳ λαλεῖ) is less clear; evidently νόμος here is associated with νόμος in 3:19a, but the expression τοῖς

---

[57] The Septuagint, which Paul seems to be paraphrasing, is clearer: οἱ λόγοι τοῦ νόμου τούτου (Deut 27:26). Here the specificity is supplied by οὗτος; νόμος itself, then, has implicitly a general reference.

[58] Gal 3:12, 17, 19, 21a, 23, 24; 4:4, 21a, b; 5:3, 14; 6:13.

[59] Gal 2:16a, b, c, 19a, b, 21; 3:2, 5, 10a, b, 11, 13, 18; 4:5; 5:4, 18, 23.

[60] Gal 6:2; this is an implicit reference for νόμος as embedded in ὁ νόμος τοῦ Χριστοῦ.

[61] Gal 3:21b, c.

[62] With minor changes, Paul follows the LXX text of Psalms 13:1-3 (= Rom 3:10-12); 5:10 (= Rom 3:13a, b); 139:4 (= Rom 3:13c); 9:28 (= Rom 3:14); Isai 59:7-8 (= Rom 3:15-17); and Psalm 35:2 (= Rom 3:18); in addition, οὐκ ἔστιν δίκαιος in Rom 3:10 is found in Eccl 7:20 (LXX), but this phrase (in contrast to the others) is so short that an allusion remains uncertain. The texts are set forth, and the variations discussed, in Cranfield, *Romans*, 1.192-94.

ἐν νόμῳ suggests that νόμος is broader than the words of Scripture; nevertheless, this is evidently Jewish νόμος. Then in 3:21b, ὁ νόμος καὶ οἱ προφῆται evidently also refers to Scripture; as this is an idiom we cannot extract a specific reference for νόμος by itself, but at least the relation to Jewish νόμος is clear.

Rom 5:13a refers to a time when there was no νόμος, and 5:14 relates this to the time from Adam to Moses; thus νόμος here evidently refers to the law given to Moses. The following νόμος, which "enters" (νόμος δὲ παρεισῆλθεν [5:20]), evidently has the same referent.

Rom 7:7c refers specifically to a νόμος which says οὐκ ἐπιθυμήσεις; this evidently is (or includes) the Mosaic law.[63] Moreover, 7:7c is so closely linked (γὰρ) to the immediately preceding and parallel 7:7b that νόμος is evidently the same in both clauses. Then, in Rom 10:5 we have Μωϋσῆς γὰρ γράφει τὴν δικαιοσύνην τὴν ἐκ τοῦ νόμου ὅτι ὁ ποιήσας αὐτὰ ἄνθρωπος ζήσεται ἐν αὐτοῖς, where ὁ ποιήσας . . . αὐτοῖς is a close approximation of Lev 18:5 (LXX);[64] νόμος here evidently refers to the commandments of God (προστάγματά μου) which are the antecedent for ἅ in Lev 18:5.

Rom 13:8 and 10 are analogous to Gal 5:3, 14; 6:13; they tell how one may "fulfill" (πληρόω, πλήρωμα) νόμος, which must thus be definite, and the quotations in 13:9 from Exod 20:13-15 [= Deut 5:17-19, 21], Lev 19:18 (LXX) show that this definite νόμος is Jewish.

In all of these passages the referent for νόμος is more-or-less specifically identified. In many others νόμος evidently has a definite referent and that is evidently Jewish; but, as was often the case in Galatians, that referent cannot be more particularly identified. Thus in Rom 2:14a and c we have ἔθνη τὰ μὴ νόμον ἔχοντα, and this Jewish νόμος is evidently the one which, according to 2:14b, Gentiles nevertheless perform (τὰ τοῦ νόμου ποιῶσιν).[65] Then, τὸ ἔργον τοῦ νόμου written in the Gentile hearts (2:15) is evidently the work of a definite νόμος; so this also is Jewish.[66]

Rom 2:13, which relates νόμος to justification παρὰ θεῷ, necessarily refers to a definite νόμος, and undoubtedly that is Jewish. In 2:12, which introduces νόμος, the link to Judaism is less obvious; but the division there presumed between those ἄνομος and those ἐν νόμῳ requires us to think of the division

---

[63] Exod 20:17 [= Deut 5:21] (LXX).

[64] ἃ ποιήσας ἄνθρωπος ζήσεται ἐν αὐτοῖς. Nestle-Aland[26] records a number of variations to Rom 10:5, but only the relatively rare omission of ἄνθρωπος affects the parallel to Lev 18:5, and this is probably to be explained as harmonization with Gal 3:12.

[65] But note that it is not νόμος itself which the Gentiles do, but rather τὰ τοῦ νόμου.

[66] For Rom 2:14d, see below, at n. 84.

between Jews and Gentiles, already referred to in 2:9-10 and specifically tied to νόμος in 2:14.

Rom 2:17-24 addresses σὺ 'Ιουδαῖος, and all five of the occurrences of νόμος in these verses are thereby specifically associated with Judaism. In 2:25-27 we have not only the already-established association of νόμος with Judaism, but the specific links to περιτομή and ἀκροβυστία; here again, νόμος refers to Jewish νόμος.

But Rom 2 raises acutely the difficulty of specifying what I am calling "Jewish νόμος" more precisely. According to 2:14, Gentiles νόμον μὴ ἔχοντες nevertheless τὰ τοῦ νόμου ποιῶσιν; the concluding phrase of the verse (οὗτοι . . . εἰσιν νόμος) then implies that they do not need νόμος in the written form which the term characteristically implies.[67] According to 2:26, there are Gentiles—here identified specifically as the uncircumcised—who keep τὰ δικαιώματα τοῦ νόμου, and according to Rom 2:27, there are uncircumcised people (now qualified as uncircumcised ἐκ φύσεως) τὸν νόμον τελοῦσα. These expressions create a puzzle which I will not attempt to solve here;[68] I will examine Romans 2 more fully in Chapter 4.

Romans 3:19a, b and 21b I have already noted as definite references to Jewish νόμος; I pass over 3:20a, b, 21a, 27a, b and 28 for the moment,[69] and come to 3:31: νόμον οὖν καταργοῦμεν . . .; . . . νόμον ἱστάνομεν. Although it might be possible to speak of destroying νόμος non-specifically ("some νόμος," "any νόμος") or generically, I do not know how any νόμος can be established but a specific one. If this is so, then the parallel between the two clauses of 3:31 suggests that the two νόμοι are the same;[70] and there is no

---

[67] This idea is of course at home in Judaism; see especially Jer 38:33 (LXX), an expression recalled by Rom 2:15. But it is not exclusively Jewish; see, e.g., ἄγραπτα κἀσφαλῆ θεῶν νόμιμα, "the unwritten immutable laws of the Gods," in Sophocles (Antigone, 454-55), and the very common idea of ἔθος as νόμος ἄγραφος (see Chapter 4, at n. 65).

[68] A possible solution is that νόμος here refers to only part of the Mosaic law (so Räisänen, Paul, 28; Sanders, Paul, the Law, 101-3). But note the difficulty: in Rom 2 Paul uses precisely the term ἀκροβυστία to describe Gentiles without νόμος; is it really likely that Paul can have chosen this term if he does not mean νόμος to include the commandment to circumcise? Räisänen (28) concludes that Paul employs a "looseness of speech" of which he himself is not aware; but this is a desperate expedient.

Another approach is to treat Paul's references to Gentile law-observance as "rein hypothetisch" (van Dülmen, Theologie, 82); but I do not think this solves the problem. As hypothetical cases they can still advance the argument; they cannot do this if they are self-contradictory.

[69] See below, under "Possible Ambiguities."

[70] This is disputed by Barrett (Romans, 84), who takes the second νόμος to refer to "the full meaning of religion . . . found and understood in the gospel . . ." I cannot recon-

question here of destroying any specific νόμος except the Jewish. Likewise, when 9:31b speaks of (not) attaining νόμος (εἰς νόμον οὐκ ἔφθασεν) a specific reference is implied, and this is evidently to the νόμος δικαιοσύνης of 9:31a which, because it is pursued by the Jews, is evidently Jewish.[71] Finally, a definite reference to Jewish νόμος is sometimes suggested by the definite article.

As I noted above in discussing Galatians,[72] the article may be present with a generic reference, and for this reason I will defer discussion of most of the articular uses not already treated.[73] But in at least five places the possibility of generic reference may be dismissed summarily. First, in 4:16, οἱ ἐκ τοῦ νόμου are clearly not those characterized by any νόμος, but by Jewish νόμος. Next, in 7:12, 14, Paul is surely not saying that all νόμος is ἅγιος or πνευμάτικος; rather, the reference is definite, and to Jewish νόμος. Then 8:4: τὸ δικαίωμα τοῦ νόμου cannot mean the requirement of all νόμος, or of νόμος as such; it must rather be a specific νόμος, and none is presented except the Jewish.

Definite Singular References (Not Jewish νόμος). Next, 7:21 is in a class by itself: εὑρίσκω ἄρα τὸν νόμον, τῷ θέλοντι ἐμοὶ ποιεῖν τὸ καλόν, ὅτι ἐμοὶ τὸ κακὸν παράκειται. This is certainly a definite reference, and the νόμος referred to is set out explicitly as an association between wishing to do good and finding evil close at hand.[74] Similarly, νόμος in 7:3 evidently refers to the ὁ νόμος τοῦ ἀνδρός of 7:2b.[75]

---

cile any change in the meaning of νόμος with the μὴ γένοιτο· ἀλλά . . ., by which Paul indicates that the concluding sentence of 3:31 refutes the opening sentence.

There is one alternative: if the first νόμος is generic, then its destruction can be refuted by the establishment of a single νόμος. But I see no hint of a generic reference to νόμος up to this point, while the definite references to Jewish νόμος in Rom 2 and at 3:19a, b, 21 are abundant.

[71] Because of the negative, one could take 9:31b as indefinite ("did not attain *any* νόμος"); only I see nothing to suggest that the attainment of *some* or *any* νόμος is of interest to Paul.

[72] Above, n. 42.

[73] Articular uses with a noun in the genitive will be treated separately below.

[74] That is, the passage is to be understood: "I find it to be a νόμος that, just as I wish to do good, evil is close at hand." Here I take the ὅτι clause to be direct discourse dependent on εὑρίσκω (Robertson, *Grammar*, 1035), in apposition to τὸν νόμον; similarly, Barrett, *Romans*, 149; Cranfield, *Romans*, 1.362; Käsemann, *Romans*, 205; Sanday and Headlam, *Romans*, 182-83; Wilckens, *Römer*, 2.89; Kuss, *Römer*, 2.456; Räisänen, *Paul*, 50 n.34; Schlier, *Römer*, 233; Mussner, *Römer*, 264-65.

It may be that this association has something to do with Jewish νόμος, but that does not mean that it is Jewish νόμος. In a footnote (*Romans*, 1.362 n.1), Cranfield cites some interpretations according to which νόμος refers to Jewish νόμος, but these paraphrases are unacceptably violent to the Greek (see Sanday and Headlam, *Romans*, 182-83). For exam-

Definite General References. Each of the genitival phrases with νόμος[76] evidently has a definite reference; all are articular except νόμος θεοῦ and νόμος ἁμαρτίας of 7:25a, b, but the references for these two anarthrous expressions are presumably the same as those for ὁ νόμος τοῦ θεοῦ in 7:22 and ὁ νόμος τῆς ἁμαρτίας in 7:23c.[77] Likewise, ἕτερος νόμος in 7:23a is given a definite reference by what follows: this is the νόμος . . . ἀντιστρατευόμενος κ.τ.λ. But what these definite references are has long been disputed,[78] and (except for 9:31a, where the νόμος δικαιοσύνης pursued by Jews is evidently Jewish) cannot be settled in this survey.[79] As I have argued,[80] in each of these expressions νόμος itself has an implied general reference to some category of νόμος from which a member is identified by the genitival expression.[81]

Indefinite Singular References. One might infer from the references to Jewish νόμος in 2:14a, b, and c[82] that 2:14d (ἔθνη . . . εἰσιν νόμος) also refers to Jewish νόμος. But here I draw back; could Paul have said that Gentiles *are*

ple, Dunn (*Romans*, 1.393) gives: "the law *as I encounter it in the reality of the situation just described* is that evil has a stronger say in my actions" (emphasis added). But this is not in fact "the [Jewish] law"; it is at most an effect of that "law." If Paul wishes to discuss effects he has appropriate terminology close at hand; see ἡ ἁμαρτία . . . in 7:13. Here he is not discussing effects, but saying what the νόμος in question is; so far as Jewish νόμος is concerned, the thrust of Rom 7:14-20 is not to say what it does but what it is unable to do.

Wilckens (*Römer*, 2.89) objects that the general sense "Regel" is not found in Hellenistic literature. Räisänen (*Paul*, 50-51 n.34) supplies illustrations of this sense, but Wilckens is in any event too demanding; νόμος here is used metaphorically, and metaphorical usages do not depend on the previous existence of the same metaphor.

Lohse, who generally takes νόμος in 7:21 to 8:4 to refer to Jewish νόμος, allows that "Paulus das Wort νόμος gelegentlich auch im weiteren Sinn gebrauchen kann, um eine allgemeine Ordnung oder Regel zu bezeichnen," and construes 7:21 in this way ("νόμος," 285).

On this passage, see further in Chapter 6, below.

[75] Note that while ὁ νόμος τοῦ ἀνδρός may be Jewish, it is evidently not the whole of Jewish νόμος; thus neither does νόμος in 7:3 refer simply to Jewish νόμος. (On 7:2b, see further in n. 81 below).

[76] Rom 3:27a, b; 7:2b, 22, 23b, c, 25a, b; 8:2a, b; 9:31a.

[77] So Bläser (*Gesetz*, 12), noting especially the ἄρα οὖν of 7:25.

[78] Hübner, for example (*Law*, 144-46), takes most of them to be to Jewish νόμος. while Räisänen (*Paul*, 52) calls these uses of νόμος "word-play," and takes only the negative expressions to refer to Jewish νόμος.

[79] In Chapter 6 I will examine the genitival expressions in 7:22-25.

[80] Above, at n. 22.

[81] Note that in 7:2b, ὁ νόμος τοῦ ἀνδρός, the general category may be Jewish νόμος, from which τοῦ ἀνδρός singles out that part of the νόμος which relates to husbands and wives; in 7:3 νόμος is then applied to this part of νόμος. I discuss Rom 7:2b further in Chapter 6, n. 178; there I suggest a more general sense for νόμος.

[82] See above, at n. 65.

Jewish νόμος?[83] This seems rather to be an indefinite reference: doing *the* νόμος, they are *a* νόμος[84] (to themselves[85]); we saw in Gal 3:21b and c that Paul can make such an indefinite reference.[86] At 7:2a, similarly, the νόμος which binds wife to husband turns out in 7:2b to be ὁ νόμος τοῦ ἀνδρός; but while this explanation makes the reference of 7:2a definite,[87] I take the reference as it appears, in advance of that which makes it definite, to be specific but indefinite.[88]

Generic References. I have alluded to the possibility of generic reference; this emerges most clearly at 4:15b: οὗ δὲ οὐκ ἔστιν νόμος οὐδὲ παράβασις. Here the generic understanding ("where there is no νόμος there is no transgression" = "transgression by definition requires a νόμος to be transgressed") is natural, and is suggested particularly by the present tense.[89]

Wilckens denies the generic reference, preferring to see a reference directly to Jewish νόμος and thus to the time of Abraham when that νόμος did not exist;[90] but there is no real antithesis here. We may grant that Abraham's time, before Jewish νόμος, is at issue; but does 4:15b merely assert the absence of transgressions at that time, or does it assert a generic proposition which explains this absence? Generic references will ordinarily be associated with definite references. If one says (to borrow Lyons's example[91]), "lions are friendly beasts," that will usually be because one wants to assert that some particular lion is friendly. If Paul had intended a definite reference he could

---

83 So *JB*, but with qualms: "they can be said to 'be' the law."

84 So *AV, RV, RSV, NASB, NAB, NJB*; cf. *NEB*: "they are their own law."

85 It is not clear whether ἑαυτοῖς modifies ἔχοντες or εἰσιν.

86 In Gal 3:21 the indefinite reference appeared to be non-specific. Here it is difficult to tell.

87 But not necessarily singular. There may be various οἱ νόμοι τοῦ ἀνδρός (Jewish, Roman, Greek, etc.); but this distinction is immaterial to Paul's argument.

88 Thus *RV, RSV, NASB, NEB* and *NAB* all render νόμος in 7:2a without the definite article (but contrast *AV*: "bound by the law"). But perhaps there is no real distinction between an indefinite reference which is immediately made definite, and one which is simply definite.

89 Most modern translations suggest the generic interpretation: *NEB* and *JB* directly, *AV, RV, RSV, NASB* and *NAB* by use of the present tense. Among the commentators, see Käsemann, *Romans*, 121; less explicitly, Cranfield, *Romans*, 1.241.

90 Wilckens, *Römer*, 1.271: "Denn als allgemeine Sentenz im Sinne von «nulla poena sine lege» wäre der Satz kraftlos und fast entbehrlich . . ." (Nevertheless Wilckens translates 4:15b with a present tense; ibid., 268).

91 Above, at n. 7.

have used the imperfect tense; but the present tense surely expresses a general truth.[92] From 4:15b it is only a small step to 5:13b: ἁμαρτία δὲ οὐκ ἐλλογεῖται μὴ ὄντος νόμου. Nevertheless Käsemann distinguishes the two propositions,[93] translating 5:13b with a past tense.[94] But I think the argument for generic reference in 4:15b applies equally to 5:13b, or becomes even stronger with the precedent of 4:15b. We should not be deterred by the explicit reference to Jewish νόμος in 5:13a, any more than by the evident connection of 5:13b to Jewish νόμος in particular; it is normal, as I have said, for generic propositions to be offered because of their implications for particular cases. As with 4:15b, the present tense of 5:13b is decisive.

Other Passages: Possible Ambiguities. Twenty uses of νόμος in Romans remain to be considered. A definite reference to Jewish νόμος is probable in these cases, but other possibilities can be noted.

As in Galatians, the expression ἔργα νόμου can be interpreted indefinitely ("works of any νόμος"); but in each of the places where it is found in Romans there are clear definite references to Jewish νόμος close at hand, and this is far more likely for ἔργα νόμου as well.[95] In several places phrases reminiscent of Rom 4:15b or 5:13b suggest a generic reference; but these phrases lack the present tense that was decisive for 4:15b and 5:13b.[96] While the present tense is found at 4:15a, ὁ γὰρ νόμος ὀργὴν κατεργάζεται, this can be simply continuative: at all times [Jewish] νόμος brings wrath. A generic reference in Rom 7:4, 5, 6, where only the phrase τῶν ἁμαρτιῶν in 7:5 recalls 5:13b, is still less likely; but it cannot be ruled out by the immediate context.

At Rom 7:1a, b (. . . γινώσκουσιν γὰρ νόμον λαλῶ . . . ὁ νόμος κυριεύει τοῦ ἀνθρώπου ἐφ᾽ ὅσον χρόνον ζῇ . . .) the reference could be definite and to Jewish νόμος,[97] or definite but not to Jewish νόμος,[98] or generic;[99] nothing in the immediate context requires one of these understandings over the others,

---

[92] Smyth, *Grammar*, ¶1877; Burton, *Syntax*, 8; Robertson, *Grammar*, 866. A historical present would be most unusual for Paul, and in such an argument; I cannot see that anything suggests it.

[93] Käsemann, *Romans*, 121.

[94] Ibid., 189.

[95] For Rom 3:20a and 28, see 3:19a, b, 21b, 31a, b; for 9:32 (where νόμου is found in some mss.), see 9:31a.

[96] Rom 3:20b; 7:7a, 8, 9.

[97] So Cranfield, *Romans*, 1.333.

[98] So Käsemann, *Romans*, 187.

[99] So Sanday and Headlam, *Romans*, 172.

and the argument works with any of them,[100] so we are left with the bare question of what νόμος will have suggested to Paul and his audience in a neutral context; all our evidence indicates that this is Jewish νόμος.

In 7:16, σύμφημι τῷ νόμῳ ὅτι καλός could be generic, but coming on the heels of 7:12 and 14 where νόμος is also said to be πνευματικός and ἅγιος, a definite reference to Jewish νόμος is more likely. Similarly, τὸ . . . ἀδύνατον τοῦ νόμου ἐν ᾧ ἠσθένει διὰ τῆς σαρκός (8:3) could be generic, but, because this is presented as the background for God's sending of his son, a definite reference to Jewish νόμος is strongly suggested. In 10:4 the famous τέλος γὰρ νόμου Χριστός is conceivably generic, but there is no reason to think that it is unless generic νόμος has been a major topic heretofore in the letter.[101]

There remain five verses in which an indefinite reference to νόμος is possible but unlikely. Only in Rom 7-8 and 3:27 have we noted references which may be to a νόμος other than Jewish νόμος;[102] the predominance of definite reference to Jewish νόμος almost surely governs 3:21a;[103] 4:13, 14;[104] and 6:14, 15, in each of which such a definite reference fits well.

Results. We have thus the following categories: (1) 35 references to Jewish νόμος;[105] (2) twenty probable references to Jewish νόμος;[106] (3) two definite references to a νόμος which is not Jewish, or at least not the whole of Jewish νόμος;[107] (4) two indefinite references;[108] (5) thirteen implicit general references to a category of νόμος;[109] and (6) two references to νόμος generically.[110] Thus, in 55 out of 74 places νόμος in Romans probably or certainly refers to Jewish νόμος, usually of unspecified scope. But nineteen other uses of νόμος show the term applied in a more general way—whether generically, or generally, or indefinitely, or definitely but not to Jewish νόμος.

---

[100] That is, the argument of 7:1 works on each understanding. The following illustration (7:2-3) depends on Jewish νόμος, not Roman νόμος or νόμος as such; see Chapter 6, n. 43.

[101] In the immediate context, I have already noted that νόμος δικαιοσύνης in 9:31a and νόμος in 10:5 are definite references to Jewish νόμος.

[102] Rom 7:3, 21; and the various genitival expressions.

[103] Note especially 3:19a, b, 21b.

[104] Note especially 4:16.

[105] Rom 2:12a, b, 13a, b, 14a, b, c, 15, 17, 18, 20, 23a, b, 25a, b, 26, 27a, b; 3:19a, b, 21b, 31a, b; 4:16; 5:13a, 20; 7:7b, c, 12, 14; 8:4; 9:31b; 10:5; 13:8, 10.

[106] Rom 3:20a, b, 21a, 28; 4:13, 14, 15a; 6:14, 15; 7:1a, b, 4, 5, 6, 7a, 8, 9, 16; 8:3; 10:4.

[107] Rom 7:3, 21.

[108] Rom 2:14d (specificity uncertain); 7:2a (specific).

[109] Rom 3:27a, b; 7:2b, 22, 23a, b, c, 25a, b; 8:2a, b, 7; 9:31a.

[110] Rom 4:15b; 5:13b.

Conclusions

This now completes my survey of references for νόμος in Paul's undisputed letters. Several points have emerged:

(1) νόμος most often refers definitely to Jewish νόμος; this is especially evident when, as in 1 Corinthians and Philippians, νόμος does not appear to be the subject of controversy.

(2) While this Jewish νόμος can occasionally be identified more precisely as including (a) laws given at Mt. Sinai, or (b) Scripture,[111] usually there is no such specification.

(3) Sometimes, especially in Romans, Paul uses compound expressions (usually νόμος plus a noun in the genitive) to specify a definite νόμος. What these definite referents are is unclear.

(4) These same expressions also imply a use of νόμος to refer to a general category of νόμος, from which the rest of the expression specifies one member. What these categories of νόμος are is not clear.

(5) In at least two places Paul uses νόμος itself to refer definitely to a νόμος other than Jewish νόμος.

(6) In at least three places Paul refers to νόμος indefinitely, and in at least one non-specifically: a (any) νόμος.

(7) In at least two places Paul uses νόμος with a generic referent: νόμος as such.

From this survey it follows that, despite the preponderance of references to Jewish νόμος, Paul understands and uses the term νόμος in a broader sense, to refer to things other than Jewish νόμος. All of the variant references which I have noted—generic, general, indefinite and definite—refer to something other than Jewish νόμος.[112] It does not necessarily follow from this that Jewish νόμος is of the same kind as these other νόμοι; but the frequency with which Paul refers to other νόμοι in the course of his treatment of Jewish νόμος[113] suggests that he does regard them as all of the same kind—certainly distinct, yet sharing common features.

I identified seven such features of νόμος in Chapter 2, and moreover concluded that all seven features seem to attach to a single meaning of νόμος used consistently throughout Paul's letters. From my surveys of the meaning and references of νόμος as used in Paul's letters I therefore draw this hypothe-

---

[111] It is often supposed, for example by most of the lexicons, that in such cases νόμος is *only* the Sinaitic code, or *only* Scripture. But the texts do not show this.

[112] With the possible exception of ὁ νόμος τοῦ ἀνδρός in Rom 7:2b, which may mean that part of Jewish νόμος governing marriage. See Chapter 6, n. 178; there I propose a different interpretation.

[113] And *only* in his treatment of Jewish νόμος.

sis: that Paul's understanding of Jewish νόμος is shaped in part by his understanding of νόμος in general. If this be so, it invites further inquiry into
whether Paul draws on this understanding of νόμος as part of his critique of
Jewish νόμος. That is, Paul's varied uses of νόμος may be not simply "plays[s]
on the term νόμος,"[114] but deliberate development of his thought.

Two areas now present themselves for immediate investigation. First,
when I identified seven apparent components of the meaning of νόμος in
Chapter 2, I concluded that these components all relate to a single meaning of
νόμος used throughout Paul's letters, irrespective of the particular νόμος
referred to. Now that I have made a rough division between references to
Jewish νόμος and references to some other νόμος (or νόμοι), these components must be re-examined. Do they apply irrespective of reference? Or must
we distinguish between the meaning of νόμος when it refers to Jewish νόμος,
and its meaning when it refers to another νόμος?

Second, I want to examine further the referent for what I have called
"Jewish νόμος." We have seen that sometimes the context specifies this νόμος,
or at any rate elements of this νόμος, more precisely; usually it does not. I
wish now to consider how these elements of Jewish νόμος relate to one
another. Do they suggest separate νόμοι within the general rubric of Jewish
νόμος? Do Paul's other references to Jewish νόμος fit within these categories,
or must there be other categories as well? Or does Paul's usage as a whole
rather suggest an over-arching concept of Jewish νόμος which includes all of
these elements? If so, how may this concept be defined? How does it relate to
other, non-Jewish νόμος?

These topics will occupy Chapter 4. When they have been examined I will
be prepared to move, in Chapters 5 and 6, to the testing of my hypothesis
about the relation of Jewish and non-Jewish νόμος against specific passages of
Paul's letters.

---

[114] Bultmann, *Theology*, 1.259.

Chapter 4

REFERENTS FOR Νόμος: FURTHER EXPLORATIONS

Distinctions in Reference Compared
With Distinctions in Meaning

In Chapter 2 I tried to define the meaning of νόμος by grouping the syntactic patterns in which νόμος occurs in Paul's letters into seven categories, each of which suggested a general concept associated with νόμος;[1] in Chapter 3 I tried to identify the various νόμοι to which Paul refers in each particular place where he uses νόμος. Now I wish to consider how the patterns identified in Chapter 2 relate to the references identified in Chapter 3. Are certain syntactic patterns associated with certain references?

For this purpose I divide the references found in Paul's use of νόμος into six categories:

    (A) References to Jewish νόμος (58 references).[2]

    (B) Probable references to Jewish νόμος (37 references).[3]

---

[1] These are summarized in Chapter 2, at nn. 85-86, and set out in full in the appendix to Chapter 2.

[2] Rom 2:12a, b, 13a, b, 14a, b, c, 15, 17, 18, 20, 23a, b, 25a, b, 26, 27a, b; 3:19a, b, 21b, 31a, b; 4:16; 5:13a, 20; 7:7b, c, 12, 14; 8:4; 9:31b; 10:5; 13:8, 10; 1 Cor 9:8, 20a, b, c, d; 14:21, 34; 15:56; Gal 3:12, 17, 19, 21a, 23, 24; 4:4, 21a, b, 5:3, 14; 6:13; Phil 3:5, 6, 9.

[3] Rom 3:20a, b, 21a, 28; 4:13, 14, 15a; 6:14, 15; 7:1a, b, 4, 5, 6, 7a, 8, 9, 16; 8:3; 10:4; Gal 2:16a, b, c, 19a, b, 21; 3:2, 5, 10a, b, 11, 13, 18; 4:5; 5:4, 18, 23.

(C) What we might call references to Jewish νόμος, but to a (hypothetical) *different* Jewish νόμος (two references).[4]

(D) References to a specific νόμος which may or may not be Jewish (two references).[5]

(E) Referring expressions in which νόμος is qualified (usually by a term in the genitive); I have argued that νόμος in these expressions has an implicit general reference to a class (or classes) of νόμος (15 references).[6]

(F) References to non-Jewish νόμος (four references).[7]

These categories are ranged over a continuum from plain references to Jewish νόμος to plain references to non-Jewish νόμος. In Table 4 I show which components of meaning are associated with the occurrences of νόμος in each of these six categories of reference.

TABLE 4
Components of Meaning Correlated
To Categories of Reference

Component of Meaning[8]	1	1b	2	3	4	5	6	7	None	Sum[9]
Category of Reference A	8	0	9	13	11	12	3	3	6	58
B	1	1	7	9	9	5	0	0	9	37
C	0	0	1	0	0	0	1	0	0	2
D	0	0	0	0	2	0	0	0	0	2
E	1	1	0	1	9	0	0	2	1	15
F	0	1	0	0	0	0	2	1	0	4
Sum	10	3	17	23	31	17	6	6	16	118

---

[4] Gal 3:21b, c: εἰ γὰρ ἐδόθη νόμος κ.τ.λ.

[5] Rom 7:2a, 3, both of which refer to the νόμος τοῦ ἄνδρος of Rom 7:2b; Rom 7:2b itself I treat in category E below.

[6] Rom 3:27a, b; 7:2b, 22, 23a, b, c, 25a, b; 8:2a, b, 7; 9:31a; 1 Cor 9:9; Gal 6:2.

[7] Rom 2:14d refers to such νόμος indefinitely; Rom 4:15b and 5:13b, generically; and Rom 7:21, definitely.

[8] These components, as fully outlined in the appendix to Chapter 2, are that νόμος (1) is verbal, (2) is perceived, (3) is a standard for judgment, (4) is a guide to conduct, (5) controls, and (6) is tied to particular people; and that (7) people put themselves under νόμος.

[9] A total of eleven references (seven in category A and four in category B) involve the expression ὑπὸ νόμου, which I have interpreted as displaying both component 4 and component 5. The figures in the "sum" column eliminate this duplication.

From Table 4 we can see that νόμος as applied to Jewish νόμος is associated with every component of the meaning of νόμος but 1b. For non-Jewish νόμος the evidence is more equivocal. Category F is so small that it gives only limited information about the meaning of νόμος as applied to non-Jewish νόμος; only components 1b, 6 and 7 are attested. Nevertheless I see nothing to suggest that such *references* are associated with a peculiar *meaning* for νόμος.

In the first place, three of these four references appear in close proximity to references to Jewish νόμος: for Rom 2:14d, compare 2:14a, b, c, 15; for Rom 4:15b, compare Rom 4:13, 14, 15a; for Rom 5:13b, compare 5:13a. In each of these cases Paul's argument requires that non-Jewish νόμος be viewed as analogous to Jewish νόμος.

Second, we may inquire whether, a priori, it is likely that Paul would have supposed that non-Jewish νόμος lacks the components of meaning—1, 2, 3, 4, and 5—which happen not to be attested. Was non-Jewish νόμος not verbal? Was it not related to judgment, did it not guide or control, was it not the property of a people? In default of any evidence supporting such hypotheses, I judge each of them to be improbable.

Third, we may turn to category E. So far I have not attempted to identify what class of νόμος is implicitly referred to by the term νόμος in such expressions as ὁ νόμος τοῦ θεοῦ. At this point the issue is somewhat narrower: is this νόμος Jewish or not? It is often argued that such expressions as a whole refer to Jewish νόμος;[10] but this implies that νόμος by itself has a broader reference to νόμος in some more general sense; the qualifying genitive then limits this class to Jewish νόμος, while νόμος itself is non-Jewish.

There are two other possible understandings, both unlikely. First, νόμος could refer to Jewish νόμος, and the qualifying expressions designate some portion of that νόμος; but I can see nothing in the texts to support or elucidate the division of Jewish νόμος into (for example) that part which is "of God" and that part which is "of sin and death." Or second, the genitive expressions might do something other than specify a particular νόμος; in Hübner's terms, they might "define the Law in regard to the perspective of the moment from which it is regarded."[11] Grammatically this is far-fetched; indeed, Hübner makes no attempt to show that the genitive case can convey such a sense.[12] I

---

[10] But there is no agreement on this. In recent literature, compare Räisänen (*Paul*, 52) who takes *negative* expressions of this kind (such as ὁ νόμος τῆς ἁμαρτίας) to refer to Jewish νόμος, with Sanders (*Paul, the Law*, e.g. 99), who takes the *positive* expressions to have that reference.

[11] Hübner, *Law*, 144.

[12] Contrast Smyth (*Grammar*, ¶1290): "A substantive in the genitive limits the meaning of the substantive on which it depends." Cf. Robertson, *Grammar*, 493.

think the thesis rests principally on the premise that Paul simply must mean Jewish νόμος whenever he says νόμος. But this cannot be a premise; it must be demonstrated; and in a number of cases—these expressions in which νόμος is qualified among them—the probabilities are strongly against it. The regularity with which Paul uses νόμος standing alone to refer to Jewish νόμος does not mean that the same reference is made when νόμος is linked to a qualifying genitive. To the contrary, these modifying expressions may be used precisely because Paul does not intend the same reference as when νόμος stands alone.[13]

If category E be taken for non-Jewish νόμος, then, as Table 4 shows, components 1, 3, 4, 6 and 7 are all attested for non-Jewish νόμος, and only components 2 and 5 are not. These omissions are noteworthy, but I think they tell us more about the argument Paul is making than about the meaning of νόμος. Component 2 is that νόμος is a standard for judgment; one would suppose this to be true for any νόμος, but Paul is not interested in any judgment. The relation of Jewish νόμος to God's judgment is an issue in Romans, Galatians, and Philippians; the relation of other νόμοι to other judgments is not an issue.

The case of component 5 is similar: νόμος as something possessed by peoples. This idea will have been a commonplace for νόμος in the ordinary, political sense; we can see it even under the Roman empire in the opening lines of Gaius's Institutes, "Omnes populi qui legibus et moribus regentur partim suo proprio, partim communi omnium hominum iure utuntur." ("Every people that is governed by statutes and customs observes partly its own peculiar law and partly the common law of humankind").[14] Jews writing in the Diaspora used νόμος in this sense even while applying the same term to their own sacred writings; thus Josephus remarks, Οὐκοῦν ἄπειροι μὲν αἱ κατὰ μέρος τῶν ἐθῶν καὶ τῶν νόμων παρὰ τοῖς ἅπασιν ἀνθρώποις διαφοραί ("Surely there are endless distinctions in the details of customs and laws among all people"); he then proceeds to expound the particular merits of Jewish νόμος.[15]

---

[13] No doubt it is true that Jewish νόμος is the only νόμος which is of particular interest to Paul when writing to his congregations; but this does not establish the point at issue here. It is equally a matter of course that Paul is familiar with νόμος in other senses, and there is nothing implausible in supposing that he might refer to νόμος in some other sense in order to make a point about Jewish νόμος. This is precisely what he does in Rom 4:15b and 5:13b.

[14] Gaius, Institutes, I.1.

[15] Ag.Ap. 2.16 §164; cf. Philo, De Iosepho 6 §29, 9 §42 (speaking of νόμιμα rather that νόμοι).

The association of a νόμος with a people is thus standard, and so is the specific application of this association to Jewish νόμος.[16] This application is, at any rate, what Paul is interested in; he has no concern with the character of other νόμος except as that illuminates Jewish νόμος, and while occasionally (Rom 4:15b; 5:13b) he refers explicitly to the character of νόμος as such in order to make some point about Jewish νόμος, on the question of its association with particular peoples he prefers to make his point obliquely. But certainly Paul is not drawing any distinction between Jewish νόμος and other νόμοι in this matter.

In this Paul follows Philo and Josephus, although his point is different. Philo asserts that Jewish νόμοι[17] are the best νόμοι, taking it for granted that they are comparable to other νόμοι. Thus Philo says of other nations that, if they could start again,

κὰταλιπόντας ἂν οἶμαι τὰ ἴδια καὶ πολλὰ χαίρειν φθάσαντας τοῖς πατρίοις ἑκάστους μεταβαλεῖν ἐπὶ τὴν τούτων μόνων τιμήν.

I think that, leaving behind its peculiar practices and bidding a full-hearted farewell to its ancestral ways, each would turn to the honor of these [laws] alone.[18]

Josephus is more ecumenical; he praises Jewish νόμοι,[19] and even reports that the Romans partly adopted them;[20] but he also maintains:

δεῖ γὰρ τοὺς εὖ φρονοῦντας τοῖς μὲν οἰκείοις νόμοις περὶ τὴν εὐσέβειαν ἀκριβῶς ἐμμένειν, τοὺς δὲ τῶν ἄλλων μὴ λοιδορεῖν,

for it is necessary that one who thinks rightly keep strictly to his native laws concerning piety—without, however, reviling those of others.[21]

Here Josephus, like Philo, assumes the commensurability of different νόμοι. Elsewhere Josephus refers to Jewish νόμος with a variety of adjectives that imply its comparability to other νόμοι: πάτριος,[22] ἐπιχώριος,[23] ἴδιος,[24]

---

[16] I will develop this point further (at nn. 77-90) in considering Greek and Hellenistic evidence for the understanding I shall propose of Jewish νόμος in Paul's letters.

[17] Unlike Paul, both Philo and Josephus commonly use the plural.

[18] De Vita Mosis, 2.7 §44.

[19] E.g., Ag.Ap., 2.19 §§178, 183.

[20] J.W., 5.9.4 §402.

[21] Ag.Ap., 2.13 §144.

[22] E.g., Ant. 4.4.4 §71, 5.1.26 §108, 7.7.7 §130, 9.12.1 §243, 10.1.3 §11, 10.10.5 §214, 11.4.8 §§109, 110, 19.6.3 §301, 19.8.2 §349. (In many of these passages Josephus speaks of νόμοι rather than νόμος).

[23] Ibid., 4.6.9 §139.

[24] Ibid., 4.6.8 §138, 12.7.1 §291.

οἴκοθεν,[25] ἐγγενῆ.[26] Josephus also writes that Hannukah was instituted when Judas and the citizens "made" (θεῖναι) νόμον to celebrate this festival;[27] here Jewish νόμος—and specifically νόμος relating to divine worship—comes from humans, not from God.[28]

Paul is not (with Philo) claiming Jewish νόμος to be the best νόμος, nor even (with Josephus) claiming that it deserves the same respect as other νόμος. He is concerned only with Jewish νόμος, and principally with a critique of it. Nevertheless, like both Philo and Josephus, Paul uses the same term, νόμος, whether the referent is Jewish or something else. There is no evidence in his letters that the basic meaning of the term varies according to whether or not it refers to Jewish νόμος.[29]

Jewish νόμος: Identifying the Referent

Now we come to the second question left open by my general survey in Chapter 2 of the references for νόμος in Paul's letters: the precise referent, or referents, for Jewish νόμος. I will first note the usual analysis of this question, as presented in most lexicons and exegetical treatments; then I will set out the evidence from Paul's letters; then I will present my analysis of Jewish νόμος as found in Paul's letters, supporting this analysis with evidence from Greek and Hellenistic sources, and finally applying it to particular issues raised by Paul's letters.

The Usual Solution

I have already, in Chapter 2, surveyed the lexicographical and exegetical analyses of νόμος. Walter Bauer's lexicon gives a typical analysis of what I have termed Jewish νόμος, dividing it into three classes: in English translation, (a) "the law . . . which Moses received from God"; (b) "the Pentateuch"; and (c) "Holy Scripture gener."[30] BAGD treats the first of these as the usual sense, citing for it 92 passages in Paul; while some follow BAGD in this,[31] others

---

[25] Ibid., 11.6.5 §210.

[26] Ibid., 15.7.10 §260.

[27] Ibid., 12.7.7 §324.

[28] The significance of the institution of Jewish law by humans was pointed out to me in class by Professor Shaye J. D. Cohen.

[29] Besides the syntactic patterns which yield the seven components discussed here, I identified in Chapter 2 several paratactic patterns associated with νόμος. Each of these, however, is found only at points where νόμος clearly or probably refers to Jewish νόμος—categories A and B, as I have defined them in this chapter.

[30] BAGD, s.v. νόμος 3, 4.a, 4.b.

[31] E.g., Gutbrod, TDNT 4 (1967) 1069-70.

regard Scripture as the normal sense.[32] Another significant variation is presented by Burton; where BAGD focuses on Mosaic law, thus emphasizing a particular, concrete pronouncement, Burton takes the basic sense of νόμος to be "divine law, the revealed will of God in general"—however embodied.[33] On this view, the defining mark of the predominant meaning of νόμος in Paul's letters is not that it is Jewish but that it comes from God.

In contrast to all these writers, Räisänen treats all references to Jewish νόμος as reflecting a single sense resisting precise definition: "the whole of Israel's sacred tradition, with special emphasis on its Mosaic center."[34] Similarly, van Dülmen refers to νόμος in Paul "als ganzheitliche Grösse" and as "ein Institut, ein Zeichen, nicht aber eine Summe einzelner Vorschriften."[35] Now let us turn to Paul's letters themselves.

Paul's Own Identifications of Jewish νόμος

In Chapter 3 we saw that sometimes Paul's usage of νόμος implies a precise referent, but often it does not. Moreover, even when a precise referent is implied we cannot assume that the precise referent is the *whole* of the νόμος referred to. Thus in 1 Cor 9:8-9 we learn that ὁ νόμος says ὁ κημώσεις βοῦν ἀλοῶντα, evidently a variant of Deut 25:4.[36] Presumably Paul understands ὁ νόμος to include more than this verse; but this citation of ὁ νόμος does not tell us whether this νόμος is (a) the legal portion of the Pentateuch, or (b) the Pentateuch as a whole, or (c) all of Scripture, or (d) something else. We do not therefore have direct evidence for what the referents of νόμος in Paul's letters *are*, but only for what they *include*.

In noting these referents it will be useful not only to identify citations to Scripture, but to characterize them briefly. Thus we can say that νόμος at various points includes:

1. specific legal provisions (quoted from Exodus, Leviticus, Deuteronomy)	Rom 7:7c; 13:8, 10; 1 Cor 9:8; Gal 5:14[37]

---

[32] E.g., Louw and Nida, *Lexicon*, §§ 33.55, 56; Schlier, *Galater*, 176-78; Davies, "Paul and the Law," 92.

[33] Burton, *Galatians*, 455-58.

[34] Räisänen, *Paul*, 16. Cf. Thayer, *Lexicon*, s.v. 2.

[35] van Dülmen, *Theologie*, 130, 133.

[36] The LXX reads: οὐ φιμώσεις βοῦν ἀλοῶντα.

[37] Here Rom 2:21-22 also comes to mind, where three commandments from the Decalogue are alluded to: ὁ κηρύσσων μὴ κλέπτειν κλέπτεις; ὁ λέγων μὴ μοιχεύειν μοιχεύεις; ὁ βδελυσσόμενος τὰ εἴδωλα ἱεροσυλεῖς;

But these are different from the passages I cite, for the direct connection is not to νόμος but to Ἰουδαῖος. It is not said that νόμος says these things, and indeed the form of the

2. legal provisions (alluded to by quotation   Rom 10:5; Gal 3:12
   from Leviticus)

3. foretellings (quoted from Isaiah)   1 Cor 14:21

4. foretellings (alluded to without   Rom 3:21b; 1 Cor 14:34
   identification)

5. judgments (quoted from Psalms and Isaiah)   Rom 3:10-19a

6. a narrative (alluded to; found in Genesis)   Gal 4:21b

All of these could be identified with Scripture, as a kind of greatest common factor. But some other references are more recalcitrant to this kind of assimilation:

7. the commandments given to Moses at Mt.   Rom 5:13a, 20; Gal 3:17, 19, 21a
   Sinai (alluded to; found in Exodus,
   Leviticus, Numbers, Deuteronomy)

Among these, Gal 3:17 dates the giving of ὁ νόμος to 430 years after Abraham, a date fitting the time of the exodus;[38] strictly speaking, this description excludes all the material referred to in the passages noted in (3), (5), (6), and probably (4).

These are the most precise references to the content of something we can call Jewish νόμος. They number only seventeen out of the 58 clear references (95 clear and probable references) to Jewish νόμος which I list in note 2. Some of these other uses are adjacent to the seventeen I have just catalogued, and in such cases we might therefore assume the same referent: thus we might conclude that νόμος in Rom 7:7a, b, 8 and 9 has the same referent as in 7:7c (see category [1]); that Rom 10:4 and Gal 3:10a, b, 11 and 13, like Rom 10:5 and Gal 3:12, belong in category (2); that Rom 3:19b, 20a and 20b belong with 3:19a in category (5); and that Gal 3:18, 23 and 24 belong with 3:17, 19 and 21a in category (7).

Even so, we would have precise referents for only 32 uses of νόμος: less than one-third of Paul's clear and probable references to Jewish νόμος. The other 63 such references are not connected to Jewish νόμος through any specific identification of their referents, but—as we saw in Chapter 3—through the following factors:

---

first two clauses is altered from the legal form of Exod 19:13-14, Deut 5:18-19 (on the legal form, see Daube, *Jewish Law*, 74-93), while the third is not phrased as a command at all.

[38] Exod 12:40 (LXX) gives 430 years as the length of time the Israelites dwelt in Canaan and Egypt.

(a) a reference in the immediate context to Ἰουδαῖοι or (negatively) to ἔθνη (22 references).[39]

(b) a reference in the immediate context to circumcision (two references).[40]

(c) indications that the reference is to a definite νόμος, which from the general context of the letter is evidently Jewish νόμος (25 references).[41]

(d) references in the immediate context to Jewish νόμος, as established on grounds a, b or c (thirteen references).[42]

Thus, the evidence we most often have for a connection between νόμος and Jews is not any specific reference to Scripture or to the Sinaitic code, but a reference simply to Judaism—directly, or negatively (by reference to Gentiles), or indirectly (by reference to circumcision). This is not entirely fortuitous. Even though Paul seems usually to take it for granted that his (often Gentile) audience will know what νόμος he refers to, in every letter his first reference to νόμος is accompanied by a marker that this νόμος is specifically Jewish. In 1 Cor 9:8-9 Paul speaks first of νόμος unqualified, but immediately adds that he is speaking of ὁ Μωϋσέως νόμος. In Phil 3:5 Paul introduces νόμος in a catalog of points which mark his Jewish identity. In Gal 2:15-16 ἔργα νόμου are presented as things which Ἰουδαῖοι φύσει "know" (εἰδέναι).[43] In Rom 2:12 the division of people into those who act ἀνόμως and ἐν νόμῳ immediately follows the division of people into Ἰουδαῖοι and Ἕλληνες in 2:9-10; then in 2:14 νόμος is expressly said to be something which ἔθνη do not have.

It may be objected that in these places Paul has not in fact gone out of his way to specify the connection between νόμος and Judaism; rather, in each case his argument has independently required him to speak of Jews. I do not think

---

[39] Rom 2:12a, b, 13a, b, 14a, b, c, 17, 18, 20, 23a, b; 9:31a, b; 1 Cor 9:20a, b, c, d; Gal 2:16a, b, c; Phil 3:5.

[40] Gal 5:3; 6:13. There are also references to circumcision in the immediate context of Rom 2:25-27, but there it is the uncircumcised who do νόμος. This therefore does not afford a direct (but rather a paradoxical) link to Jewish νόμος.

[41] Rom 2:15, 3:21a, 31a, b; 4:13, 14, 15a, 16; 6:14, 15; 7:1a, b, 4, 5, 6, 12, 14, 16; 8:3, 4; 10:4; 1 Cor 15:56; Gal 3:12, 24; 4:4.

[42] Rom 2:15, 25a, b, 26, 27a, b; 3:28; Gal 2:19a, b, 21; 3:2, 5; 4:21a.

[43] This passage also follows Paul's recital of the dispute in Antioch over Jewish food laws (2:11-14), which ends with a speech by Paul using the terms Ἰουδαῖος, Ἰουδαϊκῶς and ἰουδαΐζειν (2:14). (In Chapter 5 I will argue that Paul has borrowed the phrase ἐξ ἔργων νόμου from language used by others in Galatia; if so, the phrase required no explanation in a letter to Galatia.)

this objection has force; it is a fair comment on Phil 3:5, but it does not account for the other passages under discussion. First, in Gal 2:14-15 and Rom 2:9-10 the references to Jews are not inescapable; for example, Paul might have used νόμος to indicate what 'Ιουδαῖ- indicates.⁴⁴ Second, I noted in Chapter 3 the many places where νόμος appears without any express reference to Jews or to anything else which clearly fixes the term's reference;⁴⁵ it is a striking coincidence, if it is only a coincidence, that Paul does not allow this to happen in any of his initial references to νόμος. Third, 1 Cor 9:8-9 is decisive. Here Paul refers to Moses only to clarify his reference to νόμος, and he does this for his Gentile readers' benefit, lest they misunderstand that reference.

1 Corinthians thus shows that Paul deliberately identified νόμος in his initial reference to it, if it was not already naturally identified in the context, as in Phil 3:5. In 1 Corinthians Paul uses Μωϋσέως to make this identification, perhaps because that comes naturally to his mind when he is quoting from the Pentateuch;⁴⁶ elsewhere the identification is established by connection with 'Ιουδαῖοι.

Against this pronounced tendency to connect νόμος with 'Ιουδαῖος another attribute of Jewish νόμος must be noted. Paul's question in 1 Cor 9:8 (Μὴ κατὰ ἄνθρωπον ταῦτα λαλῶ ἢ καὶ ὁ νόμος ταῦτα οὐ λέγει;) evidently presumes that what νόμος says is not κατὰ ἄνθρωπον.⁴⁷ Other ancient Greek literature shows two different connections between νόμος and God. On the one hand, a divine law governs all humans;⁴⁸ on the other hand, one source

---

⁴⁴ E.g., in Gal 2:14: εἰ σὺ ἐν νόμῳ ὑπάρχων ἀνόμως καὶ οὐχὶ ὑπὸ νόμον ζῇς κ.τ.λ. In this case, however, Paul could have been prompted by his recollection of what he actually said in Antioch.

⁴⁵ This is most common in Galatians and Romans, but the clearest example is 1 Cor 15:56.

⁴⁶ Cf. Rom 10:5.

⁴⁷ Presumably this is not an attribute of νόμος as such, but rather of the specific νόμος to which Paul refers.

⁴⁸ For example, Sophocles (Antigone 454-55), ἄγραπτα κἀσφαλῆ θεῶν νόμιμα, "the unwritten immutable laws of the gods"; Plato, Republic, 9.590D-91A; Musonius Rufus (Lutz, Roman Socrates, 104.35), ὁ νόμος ὁ τοῦ Διός . . . ἀγαθὸν εἶναι κελεύει τὸν ἄνθρωπον, "the law of Zeus [which] commands a human to be good"; Plutarch, (Uneducated Ruler, 780E), δίκη μὲν οὖν νόμου τέλος ἐστί, νόμος δ' ἄρχοντες ἔργον, ἄρχων δ' εἰκων θεοῦ τοῦ πάντα κοσμοῦντος, "justice is the end of the law, but the law is the work of the ruler, and the ruler is the image of God who orders all things"; Epictetus (Discourses, 1.29.4; cf. 1.13.5, 2.16.28, 3.24.42), τὸν νόμον ὁ θεὸς τέθεικεν, "the law which God established," and (ibid., 1.29.19; cf. 3.17.6) νόμος . . . τῆς φύσεως καὶ τοῦ θεοῦ, "the law of nature and God"; Marcus Aurelius (Meditations, 7.9): κόσμος τε γὰρ εἷς ἐξ ἁπάντων, καὶ θεὸς εἷς διὰ πάντων, καὶ οὐσία μία, καὶ νόμος εἷς, λόγος κοινὸς πάντων τῶν νοερῶν ζῴων, καὶ ἀλήθεια μία, "For

testifies that although actual law, νόμος πόλεως, is of human origin, there is nevertheless a convention that such law comes from the gods.[49] We need to examine the connection between God and νόμος carefully; Paul's precise words are important.

Often Paul separates νόμος from God; according to Gal 2:19, for instance, living "for God" requires death "to νόμος," and in Phil 3:9 δικαιοσύνη ἐκ θεοῦ is opposed to διακαιοσύνη ἐκ νόμου. Other passages, especially in Galatians, hint at a more complete separation of νόμος from God. According to Gal 3:19, νόμος came δι' ἀγγέλων ἐν χειρὶ μεσίτου. Verse 20 then speaks of God, but in a way that has baffled interpreters:[50]

ὁ δὲ μεσίτης ἑνὸς οὐκ ἔστιν,

ὁ δὲ θεὸς εἷς ἐστιν.

Without exploring all of the difficulties presented by this verse, we can see that it presents the major and minor premise of a syllogism which yields the unstated conclusion:

[ὁ μεσίτης θεοῦ οὐκ ἔστιν]

"The mediator is not of God": since ὁ νόμος was given ἐν χειρὶ μεσίτου, God is evidently being separated from this giving—and yet not entirely. For the mediator stands between two parties, identifying with neither one (ὁ δὲ μεσίτης ἑνὸς οὐκ ἔστιν), and apparently one of these two is God.[51] We are left, then, to think of ὁ νόμος as a kind of compromise such as mediators typically produce, which by their nature fully satisfy neither party. The μεσίτης, and the νόμος which he brings, are neither of humans nor of God.

Then in Gal 4:1-11, νόμος is by implication compared to ἀσθενῆ καὶ πτωχὰ στοιχεῖα (4:9) and to οἱ φύσει μὴ ὄντες θεοί (4:8). Even more circumspect is Gal 1:14-16. Here Paul implicitly contrasts αἱ πατρικαὶ παραδόσεις (1:14) with ἀποκάλυψις τοῦ υἱοῦ [τοῦ θεοῦ] (1:16). Although neither νόμος

---

there is one universe out of all things, and one God through all things, and one substance and one law, the common reason of all intelligent beings, and one truth."

[49] Diodorus Siculus, *Library of History*, 1.94.2; cf. Plato (*Laws* 4, 705E-6A, 709B-C), who affirms that God lies behind all νόμοι, but at the same time leaves the framing of νόμοι in human hands.

[50] Burton (*Galatians*, 191) quotes a count of "about three hundred [different] interpretations."

[51] The alternative, that the parties are humans and angels, only excludes God if the angels are not themselves acting for God. Although apocalyptic literature knows fallen angels, I do not know of any writing in which angels, without further specification, could be presumed to be fallen; nor do I see any hint of fallen angels in this verse. This theory also fails to yield a persuasive interpretation of the reference to God in 3:20.

nor θεός is named,[52] the reference to θεός in 1:15 (ὁ ἀφορίσας με ἐκ κοιλίας μητρός μου) is unmistakable, and that to νόμος in 1:14 is almost as clear. Did not Paul's ancestors deliver νόμος to him?[53] It is sometimes supposed that Paul means *oral* traditions, as distinct from νόμος,[54] but this surely misses the point. Nowhere does Paul distinguish the two. Burton relies on non-Pauline passages which draw the distinction precisely to uphold νόμος as opposed to traditions which distort it[55]—not Paul's position. In Galatians in particular a distinction between νόμος and associated παραδόσεις is implausible. What could that have meant to Paul's Gentile audience?[56] How is it pertinent to Paul's argument? And if this distinction is pertinent, why does it appear nowhere else in the letter?[57]

But in these passages from Galatians Paul is careful not to declare the separation of νόμος from God at which he hints. Where he does refer explicitly to God, as in Gal 2:19 or Phil 3:9, he still says nothing inconsistent with the presumption of 1 Cor 9:8; he never asserts that the words of νόμος are κατὰ ἄνθρωπον. When Paul speaks of what νόμος says, he cites it as authoritative;[58]

---

[52] Nestle-Aland[26] includes ὁ θεός (bracketed) in 1:15, but these words are omitted in diverse authorities including P[46], B, F, G, lat and syp. As Burton says (*Galatians*, 51-52), "Transcriptional probability strongly favors the text without ὁ θεός as original, since there is an obvious motive for the (correct) interpretative gloss, but none for its omission." See also Metzger, *Textual Commentary*, 590 (minority report of Metzger and Wikgren).

[53] The use of παράδοσις for written tradition is attested at 2 Thess 2:15; Josephus, *C.Ap.*, 1.4 §20, 1.10 §53.

[54] So Burton, *Galatians*, 48; Bruce, *Galatians*, 91; Schlier, *Galaterbrief*, 51-52.

[55] Matt 15:2; Mark 7:3, 5; Josephus, *Ant.* 13.10.6 §297. See Burton, *Galatians*, 48.

This opposition between νόμος and παραδόσεις is in fact the principal basis for distinguishing the two. If, instead, one regards the traditions (Pharisaic, or whatever) as faithfully interpreting νόμος, there is no separate entity at all. Thus it cannot be assumed that Paul would ever have drawn a distinction between νόμος and παραδόσεις—much less that he does so here.

[56] Mussner, *Galaterbrief*, 80.

[57] Still less plausible is the thesis that "πατρικός denotes the religious inheritance of the father's house . . . with specific reference to the immediate father . . . [and not to] the laws, institutions or customs of the fathers or people" (Schrenk, "πατρικός," 1022, following Zahn [*Galaterbrief*, 61]). The argument presses much too far some possible distinctions in the observed use of πατρικός, πατρῷος and πάτριος (as to which, note that Aristotle (*Politics*, 3.9.3 (1285a19, 24)) uses the first and third synonymously, while LSJ, s.v. πατρῷος II, distinguishes the second and third in Attic prose exactly opposite to the way Gutbrod and Zahn distinguish them). At most, πατρικός *might* be used to distinguish what one received from one's immediate family from more general traditions, but there is nothing to suggest such a distinction here. See esp. Schlier, (*Galaterbrief*, 141); see also Betz (*Galatians*, 68 n. 118), Bruce (*Galatians*, 91), Burton (*Galatians*, 48), Mussner (*Galaterbrief*, 80).

[58] Rom 3:19a, 21b; 1 Cor 9:8-9; 14:21, [34]; Gal 4:21b.

even in Galatians, where he comes closest to rejecting νόμος, he still cites νόμος as the source for the authoritative story of the two sons of Abraham.[59] Moreover, in Romans 2 νόμος (Jewish νόμος, as we have seen) and θεός are expressly connected:

... οἱ ποιηταὶ νόμου δικαιωθήσονται [παρὰ τῷ θεῷ] (2:13)

... διὰ τῆς παραβάσεως τοῦ νόμου τὸν θεὸν ἀτιμάζεις (2:23)

Here also, τὸ ἔργον τοῦ νόμου written in the hearts of Gentiles (2:15) is associated—obscurely, it is true—with God's judgment (2:16). Later in Romans we also hear of [ὁ] νόμος [τοῦ] θεοῦ (7:25; 8:7).[60]

Paul's portrait of Jewish νόμος is also complicated by the difficulty, noted in Chapter 2, that in Rom 2 Paul speaks of Gentiles doing τὰ τοῦ νόμου (2:14), and of the uncircumcised "keeping" (φυλάσσειν) τὰ δικαιώματα τοῦ νόμου (2:26) and "accomplishing" (τελεῖν) τὸν νόμον (2:27). How can this be? Is Paul speaking hypothetically, about a case that does not exist?[61] Or does he delete from νόμος those things, such as circumcision and food laws, which Gentiles in fact do not observe? And if Paul does thus eliminate from νόμος the things peculiar to Jews, does he do so inadvertently,[62] or because he holds that the content of νόμος actually changes?[63] If Paul speaks hypothetically or inadvertently we can draw no conclusions about his concept of νόμος; but if he does mean that νόμος changes, then it appears that νόμος to some extent transcends specific provisions. Something of this kind might also be implied in Rom 13:8 (ὁ γὰρ ἀγαπῶν τὸν ἕτερον νόμον πεπλήρωκεν) and Gal 5:14 (ὁ γὰρ πᾶς νόμος ἐν ἑνὶ λόγῳ πεπλήρωται, ἐν τῷ· ἀγαπήσεις τὸν πλησίον σου ὡς σεαυτόν). Gal 3:21b-c, where Paul raises the possibility that a different νόμος might have been given, is also relevant here.

Finally, I have suggested that παραδόσεις as used in Gal 1:14 includes νόμος; there now remains the question of whether νόμος itself includes specifically oral traditions of the kind recorded in the Mishnah. We have it

---

[59] Gal 4:21-31. Paul also speaks in Gal 5:14 of fulfilling νόμος.

[60] The articles are omitted in 7:25 and present in 8:7.

[61] van Dülmen, Theologie, 77.

[62] Räisänen, Paul, 28.

[63] Käsemann (Romans, 73) and Wilckens (Römer, 1.155-56) believe that in 2:26-27 Paul is speaking eschatologically; Cranfield (Romans, 1.173) believes that Paul means that, with Christ's coming, "a grateful and humble faith in God and the life turned in the direction of obedience which is its fruit" fulfills ὁ νόμος.

from Josephus that the Pharisees treated διαδοχὴ πατέρων as νόμιμα, but this does not tell us what Paul's usage was.[64] But even if we had no direct evidence on the relation of oral traditions to written νόμος, I think we could still take it for granted that anyone concerned with applying any νόμος as rules for conduct would find it necessary to interpret that νόμος in order to apply it to particular situations, and that in so doing the interpreter would inevitably draw on traditional interpretations— especially if the interpreter claimed adherence to a school (such as the Pharisees) in such matters. Would the term νόμος include those traditions? In the first place, traditional interpretations could be considered inherent in the νόμος, rather than distinct from it; in the second place, if the traditions were regarded as separate from the written νόμος, they could nevertheless be incorporated under the term νόμος, as the common Greek equation of ἔθος and νόμος ἄγραφος shows.[65] Thus it would not be surprising if νόμος for Paul did include specific oral traditions, which would still fit within the idea of νόμος as verbal (component 1). These traditions could be included either implicitly as inherent in written νόμος or explicitly as a separate category of νόμος. But neither Josephus nor Paul resolves this matter for us.[66]

Our picture of Jewish νόμος in Paul's letters is therefore as follows:

(1) Like every νόμος, it is characterized by the seven components of meaning identified in Chapter 2 of this dissertation.

(2) It includes the specific elements, or kinds of elements, identified in this chapter at nn. 37-38.

(3) But some of these elements may not be essential parts of νόμος.

(4) Especially, it is identified by connection with Jews.

(5) It is also associated with God; but Paul has some ambivalence about this association.

(6) It may include oral traditions.

---

[64] Ant. 13.10.6 §297. Although Josephus himself uses νόμιμα here rather than νόμος or νόμοι, his terminology is not necessarily identical to Paul's. For one thing, Josephus very commonly uses the plural νόμοι to refer to Jewish matters, while Paul never does.

[65] That is, ἔθος can be νόμος, even though it is expressly said to be unwritten. See Aristotle, Politics, 3.11.6 (1287b.5-7); Dio Chrysostom, Orations, 76.1, 3; Dionysius of Halicarnassus, Roman Antiquities, 2.74.1).

Note, however, that the expression νόμος ἄγραφος in itself implies that νόμος is ordinarily written.

[66] In Gal 1:14 Paul refers explicitly to his ancestral traditions (αἱ πατρικαί μου παραδόσεις), but not to νόμος; this passage therefore does not clarify the relationship between the referents of the two terms.

With these elements I think we have already an outline of an account of Jewish νόμος. But I still have not confronted the questions with which I began: has Jewish νόμος one or, as Bauer and others suggest, several referents? And in either case, how should this referent, or these referents, be described? These questions raise some theoretical issues related to the general question of how terms are connected to the objects they signify. How, in general, does one go about describing a term's object? My analysis of Jewish νόμος is based on an analysis of this general problem, which I set out in an appendix to this chapter. Like the appendix to Chapter 1, this appendix is somewhat technical, and the balance of this chapter may be read without it. I include the appendix to show the relation between my work and contemporary linguistics and philosophy of language; the decisive question, however, is whether I make sense of what Paul wrote.

Analysis of Jewish νόμος in Paul's Letters

To describe Jewish νόμος by identifying distinct objects such as the Sinaitic Code (or the Pentateuch, or Scripture in general) raises three kinds of problems. First, such an approach suggests that these distinct objects correspond to distinct senses of νόμος and gives no account of the relations among these senses; but Paul (e.g., at Gal 4:21) evidently considered these senses either part of one νόμος, or at least closely related.

Second, the identification of Jewish νόμος with distinct objects fails to indicate the respects in which this νόμος resembles or differs from other νόμοι, whether literal (ὁ νόμος τῶν Ῥωμαίων) or metaphorical (ὁ νόμος τῆς ἁμαρτίας).

Third, such an identification of Jewish νόμος is fundamentally inadequate because (1) it evades the need to specify so far as possible the concepts on which any connection between a term and its objects depends, and (2) it fails to indicate, so far as may be done, the life setting from which—rather than from any physical objects—the term fundamentally derives its significance. Both of these points are elaborated in the appendix to this chapter.

To begin with, then, in order to specify the connection between the term νόμος and an entity in the real world to which that term corresponds, we require concepts. For any particular νόμος, Jewish or otherwise, my starting point is the seven components of the meaning of νόμος described in Chapter 2 and shown both there and in this chapter to apply whatever the specific referent of νόμος may be. These are:

1a. νόμος is *verbal*.

1b. νόμος is *perceived*.

2. νόμος is a *standard for judgment.*

3. νόμος is a *guide for conduct.*

4. νόμος *controls.*

5. νόμος is tied to *particular people.*

6. νόμος has a *source.*

7. People put *themselves under* νόμος.

These components relate to the meaning of νόμος generally, without specifying any particular referent. But our texts authorize us to make component 5 more specific; for as we have seen (Table 4, at the beginning of this chapter), the expressions which testify to component 5[67] always refer to either clear or probable Jewish νόμος. Therefore we may say:

5'. *Jewish* νόμος *is tied to the Jewish people.*

This gives us the following tentative identification of Jewish νόμος:

Those words[68] *given to*[69] *and possessed by the Jewish people,*[70] *which guide*[71] *and control*[72] *those who accept*[73] *them and according to which those who accept them are judged.*[74]

In this definition the reference to Jews does much more than tie the general definition of νόμος to particular writings; it ties νόμος to the lives of the Jewish people. It places the focus not on the particular writings which Bauer and others identify, but on how these writings function in Jewish life. In Charles Fillmore's terminology,[75] this definition recognizes that νόμος

---

[67] Principally οἱ ἐκ νόμου, οἱ ἐν νόμῳ and οἱ ὑπὸ νόμον. See the appendix to Chapter 2.

[68] Component 1; oral forms might satisfy this component, but I think Rom 2:15 (γραπτόν ἐν καρδίαις αὐτῶν) shows that νόμος is ordinarily associated with writing. Component 6 also is important here.

[69] Component 6. Note, however, that the source of Jewish νόμος could be (at least in part) the Jewish people themselves. Cf. Gal 1:14-16; 3:19; see above, at nn. 49-57.

[70] Component 5'. I use "possessed by" to specify a link between the words and the Jewish people. Theologically one might prefer to say that the words are God's; but I think this belongs to the realm of *assertion.* That is why, as I have noted (at nn. 49-60), Paul can be ambivalent about the relation between νόμος and God; he could not be ambivalent if Jewish νόμος were divine by definition.

[71] Component 3.

[72] Component 4

[73] Component 7.

[74] Component 2.

[75] See the appendix to this chapter, at nn. 19-21.

depends on a "scene," a place in life invoked by the term, and it identifies that scene as Jewish life and tradition.[76]

Support From Greek and Hellenistic Sources

I have already noted that the idea of νόμος as connected to particular peoples was standard in Paul's time.[77] The emphasis I now place on this point for understanding Jewish νόμος in Paul's letters invites further exploration of Greek and Hellenistic treatments of νόμος. Such treatments testify to the intimate connection of νόμος to the lives of the people possessing the νόμος. Aristotle considered νόμος to be effective only when people had become accustomed to it over time:

ὁ γὰρ νόμος ἰσχὺν οὐδεμίαν ἔχει πρὸς τὸ πείθεσθαι πλὴν παρὰ τό ἔθος, τοῦτο δ᾽ οὐ γίνεται εἰ μὴ διὰ χρόνου πλῆθος,

law has no power to persuade except by custom, and this happens only over a long time.[78]

Plato wrote that νόμοι depend on ἄγραφα νόμιμα . . . οὓς πατρίους νόμους ἐπονομάζουσιν, "unwritten laws . . . which are called ancestral laws":[79]

δεσμοὶ γὰρ οὗτοι πάσης εἰσὶ πολιτείας, μεταξὺ πάντων ὄντες τῶν ἐν γράμμασι τεθέντων τε καὶ κειμένων καὶ τῶν ἔτι τεθησομένων, ἀτεχνῶς οἷον πάτρια καὶ παντάπασιν ἀρχαῖα νόμιμα, ἃ καλῶς μεν τεθέντα καὶ ἐθισθέντα πάσῃ σωτηρίᾳ περικαλύψαντα ἔχει τοὺς τότε γραφέντας νόμους . . .

For these are bonds of the whole polity, situated between all that has been put and remains in writing and what is still to be established, just like ancestral patterns so ancient they seem always to have been known, which, being well established and the people being accustomed to them, wrap round in security the laws already written . . .[80]

He goes on to say that νόμοι, ἔθη, and ἐπιτηδεύματα all hold together the state, and none is stable (μόνιμος) without the others.[81]

---

[76] The importance of tradition follows from the statement that νόμος is possessed by Jews; this possession is by traditio, the handing on of νόμος. (This aspect of the definition excludes the commands of a Jewish ruler from νόμος, unless they should become part of Jewish tradition.)

[77] See earlier in this chapter, at n. 14.

[78] Politics, 2.5.14 (1269a.20-23).

[79] Laws VII, 793A.

[80] Ibid., 793B-C.

[81] Ibid., 793D. Similarly, Dio Chrysostom (Orations 32.50) associated δικαιοσύνη, ἀρετή, πατρῷοι γέροι, χρηστός βασιλεύς and νόμοι as those things for which a good person would suffer and die. Cf. Cicero (De Re Publica I.ii), for whom virtues come from

Supporting evidence also appears in the general association of νόμος with ἔθος, "custom." Dionysius of Halicarnassus wrote that Rome's Twelve Tables incorporated ἅπαντας τοὺς πατρίους ἐθισμούς τε καὶ νόμους ἅμα, "all the ancestral customs and laws together,"[82] and that when Tarquinus Superbus conquered Rome he overthrew its ἔθη τε καὶ νόμους καὶ πάντα τὸν ἐπιχώριον κόσμον, "customs and laws and whole native order."[83] We see a similar conception in Philo, who treats νόμιμα and νόμοι as parallel or identical to ἔθη,[84] and so also in Josephus. Especially interesting is a passage in which Josephus treats νόμοι and ἔθη τὰ πάτρια as equivalent:

τούτους ἐκέλευον ἀφικομένους εἰς τὸ πλῆθος τῶν Γαλιλαίων πυθέσθαι παρ᾽ αὐτῶν τὴν αἰτίαν δι᾽ ἣν ἐμὲ φιλοῦσιν· εἰ δὲ φαῖεν ὅτι πόλεως εἴην τῆς Ἱεροσολύμων, καὶ αὐτοὺς ἐξ ἐκείνων λέγειν ὑπάρχειν τοὺς τέσσαρας, εἰ δὲ διὰ τὴν ἐμπειρίαν τῶν νόμων, μηδ᾽ αὐτοὺς ἀγνοεῖν ἔθη τὰ πάτρια φάσκειν . . .

These were ordered to go to the crowd of Galileans and ask the reason they were attached to me. If they said, because I was from Jerusalem, they would say that the four of them were also from there; if because of [my] acquaintance with the laws, they would declare that neither were they ignorant of the ancestral customs . . .[85]

Similarly in Against Apion, Josephus says of those who left Egypt in the Exodus:

εἴτε γὰρ Αἰγύπτοι τὸ γένος ἦσαν, οὐκ ἂν ἐκ τῶν πατρίων ἐθῶν οὕτω ῥᾳδίως μετεβάλοντο, εἴτ᾽ ἀλλαχόθεν ἦσαν, πάντως τινὲς ὑπῆρχον αὐτοῖς νόμοι διὰ μακρᾶς συνηθείας πεφυλαγμένοι.

For if they were Egyptians, they would not readily have changed their ancestral customs; if they came from elsewhere, surely they had some laws, preserved by long practice.[86]

Here both τῶν πατρίων ἐθῶν and συνηθείας testify to the association of νόμος with custom.[87]

---

training, confirmed by custom and enforced by laws (disciplinis informata alia moribus confirmarunt, sanxerunt autem alia legibus).

[82] Roman Antiquities 2.27.3.

[83] Ibid., 4.41.2.

[84] Of cities in general: De Iosepho 6 §29 (νόμιμα), 34 §202 (νόμοι); of Jews in particular: ibid., 9 §42 (νόμιμα).

[85] Life 39 §198.

[86] Ag.Ap. 1.35 §317.

[87] Ephraim Urbach takes νόμος in a similar sense when he argues that it is in fact an appropriate rendering of תּוֹרָה:

The association of ἔθος with what could also be called νόμος is also found in Acts, and specifically in speeches attributed to Jews; thus in 6:14 we have τὰ ἔθη ἃ παρέδωκεν ἡμῖν Μωϋσῆς, "the customs which Moses delivered to us"; in 15:1, τῷ ἔθει τῷ Μωϋσέως, "according to the custom of Moses"; and in 21:21, ἀποστασίαν ὑπὸ Μωϋσέως ... λέγων ... τοῖς ἔθεσιν περιπατεῖν, "you teach apostasy from Moses ... saying not ... to follow the customs." Finally, the argument of Joseph Modrzjewski on the meaning of πολιτικοὶ νόμοι in Ptolemaic Egypt is suggestive here. The best known use of this phrase is in a judgment dated 227 or 226 B.C.E., in the following passage from a judicial decree:

> ἐπειδὴ καὶ τὸ διάγραμμα, ὃ καὶ παρέδετο ἐν τοῖς δικαιώμασιν
> ἡ Ἡράκλεια, συντάσσει καὶ δικάζειν [.........-]κῶς, ὅσα μὲν ἐν τοῖς
> βασιλέως Πτολεμαίου διαγράμμασιν εἰδῇ γεγραμμένα ἢ ἐμφανίζηι
> τις ἡμῖν, κατὰ τὰ διαγράμματα, ὅσα τε μὴ ἔστιν ἐν τοῖς διαγράμμασιν
> ἀλλ' ἐν τοῖς πολιτικοῖς νόμοις, κατὰ τοὺς νόμους, τὰ δ' ἄλλα γνώμηι
> τῆι δικαιοτάτηι [.......

... whereas the regulations which Herakleia [one of the litigants] put in among the submissions directs [us] to give judgment ... whatever someone knows or shows us in the regulations of King Ptolemy, according to the regulations; whatever is not in the regulations but is in the πολιτικοὶ νόμοι, according to the νόμοι; other matters, by the most equitable view.[88]

Modrzjewski proposes that here πολιτικοὶ νόμοι must mean the customs (ἔθη) of the Greek-speaking populace; for no formal Greek νόμος could have

---

... the term "Torah" was not a word but an "institution", embodying the covenant between the people and its God, and reflecting a complex of precepts and statutes, customs and traditions linked to the history of the people and the acts of its rulers, kings and prophets. If this was the connotation of "Torah", it could not be translated διδαχή or διδασκαλία, but only νόμος, in the sense in which it was interpreted also by Pindar, Νόμος ὁ πάντων ὁ βασιλεύς, and as Plato understood it, namely as "The constitution and living regime of a people, which is not comprised of a number of agreements and treaties, but is an institution of customs and traditions that are linked to one another by innumerable threads that tie them to the past of the people."

Urbach, Sages, 289-90, translating Schroeder, "νόμος," 203-4.

88 The decree exists in two copies, P.Petrie III.21 and P.Gurob 2, which in this passage largely fill each other's gaps. It is reprinted in many collections, including CPJ 19 and Hunt and Edgar, Select Papyri, No. 256. I follow these editors in the reading συντάσσει, where the original editor (P.Gurob 2.41) had συνσ[τ]ησαι; the difference is not important for my purposes.

been in effect in Egypt.[89] This decree is well removed in both time and place from Paul,[90] but it shows a pattern consistent with other Hellenistic sources.

Application to Particular Issues

My provisional definition of Jewish νόμος provides a ground from which to approach various questions about that νόμος in Paul's letters.

May νόμος include oral tradition? The definition leaves that question open, and appropriately so; we do not have sufficient data from Paul to know how he would answer this question.

Does νόμος incorporate separate objects? According to the definition I propose it does, but without marking them as separate senses of νόμος. The Sinaitic and other codes, the Pentateuch, Jewish Scripture—all are νόμος insofar as they meet the terms of the definition, which does not restrict νόμος to these objects either separately or together.

May the content of νόμος shift? Here it seems to me we have a question which presses at the boundaries of the scene on which νόμος depends. Because my definition is not framed in terms of a specific content, it would appear that its content may shift, provided it complies with the terms which the definition does contain. But if I am correct in identifying the νόμος possessed by the Jews with the *traditions* of the Jews, then the idea of shifting content is anomalous; it does not fit the life setting on which the term is ordinarily based.[91] How does one change one's traditions?[92] Paul allows for the possibility of rejecting the traditions; this is component 7. But rejection and

---

[89] Modrzjewski, "La règle." Cf. also Préaux, *Monde Hellénistique*, 2.592-93.

[90] According to Modrzjewski ("La règle," 131 n.24), the phrase πολιτικοὶ νόμοι is not attested in Egypt after the Ptolemaic era.

[91] Another way of putting this is that the meaning of a term ordinarily presumes a certain "scene," and that when we step outside that scene difficulties arise; thus, for example, "[t]he prototype 'scenario' for *widow* does not cover the case of a woman who murdered her husband . . . If we do not know whether to use the word *widow* in these cases, it is not because we are unsure of the meaning of the word, but because the prototype scene that provided our knowledge of the word *widow* simply does not cover all these cases." (Fillmore, "Topics," 84, 87). See further the appendix to this chapter, at nn. 19-21.

[92] Traditions do change, over time; but an innovation is by definition not a tradition until it has become so by being handed down over time. From a historical perspective one may be able to identify layers of traditions and date them to periods, but Paul gives no sign of this sort of historical consciousness. When he speaks of Jewish νόμος coming into existence (component 6: Rom 4:15; 5:13, 20; Gal 3:19, 21) he speaks as though it was then what it is now.

We may compare the rabbinic conceit (*m.Abot* 1.1) that the entire Torah, oral as well as written, was delivered to Moses on Mt. Sinai; thus Torah does not change.

alteration are quite different. In Gal 3:21, where Paul raises the possibility that νόμος might have been other than it is, he refers the possibility back to the time when νόμος was given; he does not speak of a change by those who received νόμος.[93]

What then of Romans 2? What can be the content of the νόμος spoken of there, which Gentiles do? It may be that the problems with this chapter arise precisely because νόμος is used outside of its ordinary setting—deliberately so.[94] For Romans 2 I can make this clearer by introducing a more concise version of my definition:

Νόμος is what Jews do.

To be a Jew is to do νόμος, and to do νόμος is to be a Jew.[95]

I propose this, not as a substitute for the full definition, but as an approximate version that will serve ordinarily, much as we might say that "to run" means "to move quickly," even though in fact there are other ways of moving quickly, and running can be slow.[96] We might say, adapting Fillmore's presentation,[97] that "run" as described by this approximate definition calls on a scene in which there are two ways to get from Point A to Point B, to walk and to run, and one of these is slow while the other is fast; probably most of our usage of "walk" and "run" derives from this simplified scene, and only calls on other scenes, with more complicated distinctions, on the less frequent occasions (typically having to do with children) when "hop," "skip," and "gallop" are at issue.[98]

---

[93] Paul speaks of a (hypothetical) νόμος with different effect rather than with different contents; the contents of this νόμος might hypothetically be the same as those of the actual νόμος. But this is hypothesis built on hypothesis; the question receives no attention from Paul.

[94] One can, in Fillmore's example (see n. 91) use "widow" for a woman who has murdered her husband; the effect is to emphasize a discrepancy between expectations and reality. In this case the discrepancy is between a concept of how wives should relate to husbands and how this husband and wife actually related to each other.

[95] This, naturally, is an idealized definition. No Jews will have done the entire νόμος—some of which could not be performed in Paul's time (e.g., Exod 21:12-13, which provides for capital punishment and places of refuge, presumes a Jewish political authority doubtful in Roman Palestine and certainly absent in the Diaspora)—and many will have done very little of it.

[96] I take the example from Nida, *Componential Analysis*, 21.

[97] See n. 91.

[98] Here I am discussing only one of the many meanings of "run." An extended discussion of this word appears in Nida, *Componential Analysis*, 138-50; it appears that some of the other meanings of "run" draw especially on the association of "run" with speed. In Nida's terminology (see the appendix to Chapter 1, at n. 32), *speed* is probably a supplementary component of the meaning of "run."

Now, this concise definition makes clearer what the more extended one also implies: that Jewish νόμος has to do with the Jewish community; the Jewish community is part of the scene which νόμος invokes. Therefore a reference to non-Jews doing νόμος is anomalous, for it removes νόμος from the Jewish community. In Rom 2:14[99] Paul minimizes the anomaly, for he writes of Gentiles who do τὰ τοῦ νόμου, not νόμος itself; in making this distinction Paul provides evidence that the scene for νόμος is indeed the Jewish community. But in 2:26-27[100] this distinction is no longer made; the anomaly is not avoided. To the contrary, the anomaly is exaggerated, for here Paul writes not of ἔθνη but of ἡ ἀκροβυστία. In another context we could regard these two terms as synonymous,[101] but the choice of ἀκροβυστία to speak of Gentiles who do νόμος creates an oxymoron that emphasizes the anomaly. The anomaly would be present even without ἀκροβυστία. Even if we think of a Gentile who has himself circumcised—and this in itself is anomalous, for no Jew has to do this; practically speaking it is as if the Jew were born circumcised—still for such a Gentile to do νόμος, as a Gentile and outside the Jewish community, is anomalous. The oxymoronic use of ἀκροβυστία tells us that this anomaly is deliberate, and that Paul wants to make sure that it is not missed.

Verse 26 points directly at the anomaly. ἐὰν οὖν ἡ ἀκροβυστία τὰ δικαιώματα τοῦ νόμου φυλάσσῃ, οὐχ ἡ ἀκροβυστία αὐτοῦ εἰς περιτομὴν λογισθήσεται; We might paraphrase: "If one who is not a Jew does what Jews do, is he not a Jew?" Here Paul invokes the reciprocal definitions that I have proposed for "Jew" and νόμος, but divorced from the setting, or scene, on which these definitions actually depend. To paraphrase Fillmore:[102] if we do not know whether to use the word νόμος when a Gentile does what Jews call νόμος, it is not because we are unsure of the meaning of the word, but because the prototype scene that provided the setting for our knowledge of the word νόμος simply does not cover this case.

In Rom 2:26-27 Paul deliberately steps outside the scene invoked by νόμος. His purpose, as it appears in 2:28-29, is evidently to challenge his hearers' understanding that Judaism is a matter of birth (cf. ἡ ἐκ φύσεως ἀκροβυσ-

---

[99] "Ὅταν γὰρ ἔθνη τὰ μὴ νόμον ἔχοντα φύσει τὰ τοῦ νόμου ποιῶσιν, οὗτοι νόμον μὴ ἔχοντες ἑαυτοῖς εἰσιν νόμος.

[100] Ἐὰν οὖν ἡ ἀκροβυστία τὰ δικαιώματα τοῦ νόμου φυλάσσῃ, οὐχ ἡ ἀκροβυστία αὐτοῦ εἰς περιτομὴν λογισθήσεται; καὶ κρίνει ἡ ἐκ φύσεως ἀκροβυστία τὸν νόμον τελοῦσα σὲ τόν διὰ γράμματος καὶ περιτομῆς παραβάτην νόμου.

[101] Cf. Rom 3:30, 4:9, where ἀκροβυστία is evidently used to mean Gentiles.

[102] See above, at n. 91.

τία, Rom 2:27, and φύσει 'Ιουδαῖοι, Gal 2:15).[103] Rather, Judaism is understood in terms of the proposition I introduce above (at n. 95): νόμος is what Jews do; or, inverted: Jews are those who do νόμος. But there is no revision here of the content of νόμος. To the contrary, Paul simply accepts and presses the connection between νόμος and Jew; his argument depends on this.[104]

Are some parts of νόμος more important than others? This issue is presented by Rom 13:8 and Gal 5:14, which speak of "fulfilling" (πληροῦν) νόμος through the love commandment. These passages do not imply a change in the content of νόμος at any particular time, nor do they suggest that νόμος contains only the love commandment—to the contrary, only if νόμος contains more than one commandment will there be any occasion to speak of either "summing up" or "fully performing" νόμος in that commandment.[105] These verses do pose certain questions about discrimination within νόμος: what is the relation of the love commandment to the rest of νόμος? does Paul claim for it priority over the other commandments, or simply that, in fact, to perform the love commandment one must also perform the others (and vice versa)? and so forth. But these questions turn on the interpretation of πληρόω rather than on the interpretation of νόμος. There is nothing in this use of νόμος to challenge my proposed definition.

What is the relation of νόμος to God? My definition is silent on this; the defining marks of νόμος lie elsewhere. This is demonstrated by Paul's ambivalence on the relation between νόμος and God.[106] If νόμος is divine, that char-

---

[103] Paul is also conscious of the difficulty in speaking of the uncircumcised doing the νόμος which requires circumcision, and he deals with this also in 2:28-29 by making circumcision as well as Judaism a matter of heart and spirit, not appearance and letter.

[104] The argument of Rom 2 also depends on another connection, a connection between Judaism and God. This is alluded to at certain points in the chapter (e.g., 2:17: ... σὺ 'Ιουδαῖος ἐπονομάζῃ καὶ ἐπαναπαύῃ νόμῳ καὶ καυχᾶσαι ἐν θεῷ), and it underlies the argument about "real" Judaism and νόμος-observance: why would real Judaism be important, except for the implied connection to God? Nevertheless the connection to God is not part of the *meaning* of νόμος. Paul probably makes use of the connection here because he supposes that it will be taken for granted by a Jewish audience (even so, he remarks in 2:12 that there is destruction ἀνόμως just as there is judgment διὰ νόμου); but his own ambivalence elsewhere about the relation between νόμος and God (see above, at nn. 49-60) shows that Paul does not consider that relation to hold as a matter of definition.

[105] Πληρόω allows both of these interpretations. Gal 5:14, where νόμος is the subject and the verb is passive, is often translated "the whole of the law is summarized in . . ." (JB, NJB; cf. NEB, BAGD s.v. 3); but "fully obeyed" is also a possible rendering (Burton, Galatians, 294-96; Bruce, Galatians, 241; cf. Betz, Galatians [distinguishing "fulfilling" from "doing"]). Rom 13:8, where πληρόω is active and the one who loves is the subject, is generally translated in the sense of "obey."

[106] See above, at nn. 49-60.

acter is—linguistically—secondary: not part of the term's meaning, but a consequence of its use to refer to Jewish νόμος, which has to do with (although it is not identical to) these particular words/scripture/tradition. This is not a matter of divine νόμος in general or in the abstract (pace Burton), but of this particular νόμος, which is divine.

Results

To my proposed definition of the *meaning* of νόμος, developed in Chapter 2 and further supported by the analysis in the first part of this chapter, I have now added a closely related definition of Paul's principal reference for νόμος: Jewish νόμος. In substance, I have said, Jewish νόμος is the νόμος of Jews.

This recalls the hypothesis which I introduced at the close of Chapter 3: that Paul's understanding of Jewish νόμος is shaped in part by his understanding of νόμος in general. The argument of this chapter has tended to confirm this hypothesis, but the question which follows from the hypothesis remains unexamined: Does Paul draw on this general understanding of νόμος in his critique of Jewish νόμος? Moreover, the entire argument of this dissertation has proceeded thus far on the basis of general patterns in the use of νόμος; although specific uses have been considered, I have not yet subjected any passage to sustained analysis.

In the balance of this dissertation I want to undertake such an analysis of two passages in which νόμος is prominent. My hypothesis about Paul's general understanding of νόμος will be tested against these passages. Further, I will examine how Paul's general understanding of νόμος contributes to his critique of νόμος. For this purpose two passages critical of νόμος will be useful, and in order to give my analysis as broad a base as possible, I will take one passage from Galatians and one from Romans: Gal 2:15-21 and Rom 7:14 - 8:7.

These two passages are Paul's first and last extended discussions of νόμος.[107] Gal 2:16 introduces νόμος in that letter, while the fourteen occurrences of νόμος in Rom 7:14 - 8:7 (nearly one per verse) are followed only by the scattered references in 9:31, 10:4-5 and 13:8, 10. But these passages have

---

[107] With most scholars, I take Galatians to precede Romans; e.g., Betz, *Galatians*, 11; Bruce, *Galatians*, 55; Burton, *Galatians*, xlvi; Jewett, *Chronology*, end-paper; Kümmel, *Introduction*, 311; Lüdemann, *Paul*, 86-87. (Although there is a general consensus on this conclusion, the arguments advanced vary considerably: Burton and Kümmel rely on comparisons of thought and language, Bruce on a chronology inferred from Acts, Betz on Rom 15:25 and Acts 20:2-3, Lüdemann on the inference that sometime after the writing of 1 Cor 16:1 and Gal 2:10 but before the writing of Rom 15:26 Galatia withdrew from the Jerusalem collection. Of these arguments, I find the last most persuasive.)

also intrinsic interest for my subject. Gal 2:16 introduces the enigmatic phrase ἔργα νόμου, which runs through both Galatians and Romans; in the same verse is also, apparently in opposition to ἔργα νόμου, πίστις Χριστοῦ as well; 2:19 presents the further enigma of διὰ νόμου νόμῳ ἀπέθανον. As a whole, this passage interweaves Paul's understanding and experience of Christ with his understanding, and perhaps his experience, of νόμος.

Rom 7:14 - 8:7 contains the bulk of Paul's uses of νόμος with a noun in the genitive, and for that reason alone it is central to my study of the meaning of νόμος. Moreover, the first-person passages in Romans 7—vv. 9-13 as well as 14-25—are a famous problem in interpretation, as are the dual νόμοι, of sin and of God, found in 7:23, 25 and 8:2, 7.

I will take up Gal 2:15-21 first, as the earlier passage; this will occupy Chapter 5. Romans 7:18 - 8:7 will occupy Chapter 6.

Appendix To Chapter 4

THE RELATION BETWEEN TERMS AND OBJECTS

Preliminary Note: Meaning and Reference. Throughout this dissertation I have distinguished between a term's *meaning*, the general sense or senses which it suggests apart from context, and its *reference*, the particular entity to which it refers in a particular context. But with νόμος, and especially with Jewish νόμος, this distinction is not so precise as it is with a term like "bicycle." On the one hand the distinction is useful in allowing us to see that νόμος *referring* to Jewish νόμος evidently bears important elements of *meaning* that are also present when other νόμοι are referred to; Jewish νόμος is to this extent comparable to all other νόμος. But on the other hand, when we turn to analyze the referent of Jewish νόμος, our problem is very much like that of analyzing meaning. It is doubtful that we can say that there is a unique object, *these words in this book* (like *that bicycle there in the corner*), to which νόμος refers; although this might work for some passages it will not work for others.[1] Here, our problems in analyzing *reference* are just the same as they would be if the Greek term νόμος always meant Jewish νόμος, so that it was *meaning* we were analyzing. What was said in the appendix to Chapter 1 about distinguishing multiple meanings from a single broad meaning there-

---

[1] We shall also find that a description like *these words in this book* would not in any event be a satisfactory description of the referent. See below, at n. 16.

fore applies here to the question of whether Jewish νόμος has multiple referents, or only one.[2]

Models for Reference: Ogden and Richards; C. S. Peirce. How do words relate to entities? I take my starting point from the triangle of meaning used first in 1923 by C. K. Ogden and I. A. Richards, a classic model still often reproduced:[3]

THOUGHT OR REFERENCE

SYMBOL   REFERENT

I need to pause briefly here to note that Ogden and Richards use "reference" and "referent" in a sense different from that which I give these terms; they are speaking generally of a term's relation to the kind of objects for which the term stands, which is more or less what Lyons means by "denotation."[4] Although Ogden and Richards's use of "reference" is a common one, I will (except in quotations) use "denotation" instead.

The principal point made by this diagram is that there is only an indirect relation between symbols, such as words, and the things for which symbols stand; this indirect relation is by way of the top of the triangle, and not straight across the bottom. How is it that the word "bicycle" is connected with certain objects in the physical world? The connection is that these objects fit certain thoughts, or concepts—for example, having two wheels—which are associated with "bicycle." In explaining Ogden and Richards's model, Ullmann quotes the scholastic maxim "vox significat mediantibus conceptibus (the word signifies through the medium of concepts) . . ."[5] Something like this model seems to lie behind our practice of defining words: a dictionary's

---

[2] In the terms Lyons uses in his treatise (*Semantics* 1.177-215), we pass from questions of "reference" to questions of "sense" and "denotation."

[3] Ogden and Richards, *Meaning*, 14; see Ullmann, *Semantics*, 55-57; Lyons, *Semantics*, 1.96-99; Silva, *Biblical Words*, 103. I have omitted some elements of the Ogden-Richards diagram.

[4] Lyons (*Semantics*, 1.206-15). Lyons himself (ibid., 1.96) uses the term "signification" to describe the Ogden-Richards triangle. The distinction between "signification" and "denotation" is not important for my discussion.

[5] Ullmann, *Semantics*, 56.

definition of "bicycle" supplies the concepts which mediate between that term and the objects to which we apply the term.[6]

Two important aspects of such definitions are that the definitions themselves are composed of signs, and that they do not incorporate everything that might be said about the objects which they describe. Both of these point are emphasized in the account of C. S. Peirce, which is analogous to the Ogden-Richards triangle.[7] According to Peirce,

> A sign, or *representamen*, is something which stands for something in some respect or capacity. It addresses somebody, that is, creates in the mind of that person an equivalent sign, or perhaps a more developed sign. That sign which it creates I call the *interpretant* of the first sign. The sign stands for something, its *object*. It stands for that object, not in all respects, but in reference to a sort of idea, which I have sometimes called the *ground* of the representamen.[8]

Peirce's *representamen* thus corresponds roughly to Ogden and Richards's *symbol*, his *interpretant* to their *thought or reference*, and his *object* to their *referent*. But for Peirce, "sign" includes not only individual words but propositions and arguments, which are themselves composed of signs. Thus Peirce emphasizes the similarity between a sign and the thought in a hearer's or user's mind;[9] this thought (Peirce's "interpretant") also takes the form of a sign, and, therefore, it too has to be interpreted. As Peirce says, the interpretant has an interpretant, which again has an interpretant: an infinite regress.[10] This seems odd, but it corresponds to the multiple possibilities of language: we can explain the meaning of a term, and then explain the explanation, and so forth. A definition is composed of terms which must themselves be defined. This will be significant when we move from the relation between the Ogden-Richards and Peirce models of meaning and definitions to the relation

---

[6] In this discussion I will limit myself to terms which denote non-linguistic objects, following Lyons (*Semantics*, 1.114), Silva (*Biblical Words*, 102), and Ullmann (*Semantics*, 56); thus I avoid the question of what object might be denoted by (say) "justice."

[7] Ogden and Richards devote an appendix to Peirce's views (*Meaning*, 431-44), but most of Peirce's writings on this subject were unpublished until volume 2 of his posthumously collected papers appeared in 1932.

[8] Peirce, *Papers*, 2 ¶228 (emphasis in the original).

[9] I take Peirce's description "a sign . . . addresses somebody" to be applicable to both hearers and users.

[10] Peirce refers expressly to this infinite regress at *Collected Papers*, 2 ¶¶92, 274, 303. In Peirce's view the signs actually expand, so to speak, geometrically; for the interpretant has *two* objects: the original object of the original sign, but also the original sign itself, "or rather the relation thereof to its Object." The relation between the interpretant and each of these objects yields another interpretant, which also has two objects, and so forth. Ibid., 2 ¶274.

between these models and *the actual thought processes which are involved in the use of words.*

The second point to which Peirce draws our attention is that a sign stands for an object "not in all respects, but in reference to a sort of idea . . ." This "sort of idea" may prove difficult to define; in a narrow sense, it emerges when we note that although bicycles are generally made of metal and have rubber tires, these features are not part of the definition of "bicycle": the term could be applied to a wooden bicycle. Thus "bicycle" does not identify every feature generally associated with bicycles. But what is the "sort of idea" which tells us that the materials used in construction are not part of the meaning of "bicycle"? It might be simply that our definition omits reference to materials; but then Peirce's *ground* would be simply another name for his *interpretant*, while Peirce himself distinguishes between the two. In fact the passage which I have quoted implies that, just as *interpretant* (a sign) mediates between *representamen* (also a sign) and *object*, so *ground* (an idea) mediates between *interpretant* and *object*. This too will be important in considering how these models of meaning relate to actual thought, the question to which I now turn.

The Models Applied: Thought and Use.[11] I have outlined the Ogden-Richards and Peirce models because, as I have indicated, they underlie the way we generally attempt to define words, including the way we define νόμος.[12] When we pass, however, to the actual ways in which we use language, we will see that some refinements of these models are necessary.

If the definition of a term identifies the concepts which mediate between the term and its referent, does this mean that when one *says* or *hears* "bicycle" one *thinks* "two wheels, handlebars [etc.]"? The thought might actually be somewhat different: perhaps what will flash though one's mind will be an image of one's own bicycle. But in any case, I do not understand these models to present a depiction of one's actual thought processes. The way in which Peirce's model leads to an infinite regress makes this clear; this may represent the logical structure of language, but not the thought processes involved in the use of language.[13]

One might not have any particular thought connected with "bicycle" when one hears the word in conversation. If I hear, "Jane's bicycle is gone, so she must have left for home," perhaps I will be thinking about Jane, and home, and what I will do now, and any number of things other than bicycles.

---

[11] In this section I draw heavily on the approach of Ludwig Wittgenstein in *Philosophical Investigation*, esp. I ¶¶1-202.

[12] BAGD's definitions (Chapter 4, at n. 30) illustrate this.

[13] Peirce was a philosopher, not a linguist, and he regarded his "doctrine of signs" as another name for "logic." *Collected Papers*, 2 ¶227.

Nevertheless I have heard the word, and if someone asks me how Jane went home, probably I can say, "by bicycle," and if I am asked what I mean by "bicycle" I will be able to give some answer. *At that point* the image of my bicycle, or of Jane's, might indeed flash though my mind; probably I will *say* something about two wheels and handlebars, but I may also, or principally, appeal rather to my questioner's experience: "You know, those things you see people ride down the street, they have two wheels, and pedals . . ."

My concept of "bicycle," then, may rest latent most of the time when I hear or say the word; nevertheless I can express this concept. When I do express it, I may do so in terms like those used by the dictionary—with "bicycle" this will probably be fairly easy, although everyone knows the experience of being unable to define a word that one is familiar with. But this conceptual analysis of "bicycle" will probably need to be reinforced by reference to what my auditor has seen, and it is in fact based on my own experience of the objects we call bicycles. Someone who had never seen a bicycle would not easily understand a definition without an illustration; even the definition and illustration together would not entirely succeed if one did not understand what bicycles were used for, and how, and by whom. In a society in which bicycles were used in a stationary position to pump water, or valued as symbols of status, works of art or religious artifacts, our dictionary definition—even though it fit the physical object—would miss the point.[14]

In Wittgenstein's words, "to imagine a language means to imagine a form of life."[15] Or as Lyons says:

> Nor indeed is the denotation of most lexemes determined solely, or even principally, by the physical properties of their denotata. Much more important seems to be the role or function of the objects, properties, activities, processes and events in the life and culture of the society using the language.[16]

In this way we can give a full meaning to Peirce's view that signs stand for objects only in respect to "a sort of idea":[17] this idea, Peirce's "ground," is actually the place of the object in the lives of those who speak of it.[18] We

---

14 Even of physical objects, different aspects might become important—for instance, the material of which they are made.

15 Wittgenstein, *Philosophical Investigations*, I ¶19.

16 Lyons, *Semantics*, 1:210.

17 See above, at n. 8.

18 Alternatively, we could think of this Sitz im Leben of the object as described by Peirce's expanding network of "interpretants." I am less interested in Peirce's precise terminology, however, than in the point that the "thought or reference" (to return to Ogden and Richards's terminology) which connects word to object cannot be fully summarized by discrete concepts. Peirce makes this point in various ways, Wittgenstein in others.

cannot take a term's object as an isolated object, even when the object is
something so prosaic as a bicycle; what "bicycle" means to those who use the
term depends on a pattern of life that our conceptual definition of the term
presumes rather than states. The concepts are useful if we understand the pattern and misleading if we do not. Charles Fillmore makes an analogous point
with his contention that "meanings" are relativized to "scenes."[19] Fillmore
illustrates his use of "scene" with the term "widow":

> A widow is a woman whose husband has died. The prototype "scenario" for
> widow does not cover the case of a woman who murdered her husband, or of a
> woman who had three husbands and now has only two left, or of a woman whose
> divorce became final on the day of her husband's death. If we do not know
> whether to use the word *widow* in these cases, it is not because we are unsure of
> the meaning of the word, but because the prototype scene that provided our
> knowledge of the word *widow* simply does not cover all these cases.[20]

Fillmore summarizes his thesis thus:

> The point I am making is that for a great many words and phrases in our
> language, we can only understand them if we first know something else, and this
> something else may not be analyzable. If you know what birds look like, then I
> can identify a certain part of a prototypic bird and tell you that part of it is called
> its "beak." To understand what is meant by such verbs as *wink, crawl, sneeze,*
> *yawn,* etc., you have to know about bodies—especially human bodies—and what
> kinds of things their owners can do with them, and what kinds of internal things
> can happen to them. . . . to understand what is meant by *déjà vu* you have to have
> had certain mental experiences.[21]

Especially will this be true of νόμος. If νόμος should refer simply to the
five books of the Pentateuch, still one could hardly be said to understand this
term unless one knew not merely what physical objects these books are, but
that these books' significance lies in the words they contain, and moreover in
understanding these words in a certain way—not as interesting stories or
historical artifacts, but as words associated with God on the one hand and the
Jewish people on the other. Understanding this, in turn, requires understanding the lives of Jews, and also the lives of those non-Jews for whom, as Paul's
letters testify, νόμος also became important. All this, and not simply the books
of the Pentateuch, constitutes the referent for νόμος as Pentateuch.

---

[19] Fillmore, "Topics," 84.

[20] Ibid., 87.

[21] Ibid., 84. Fillmore applies this analysis according to "scenes" to concepts as well as
to words standing for non-linguistic objects (ibid., 134).

In this we have a clue to the difficulty lexicographers and exegetes have in establishing a discrete sense for Jewish νόμος: Mosaic code, Pentateuch, or Scripture. Each of these terms successfully describes a physical object, namely, certain groups of words; but the very attempt to describe a physical object misses the point, which is, what is Jewish νόμος in the life of Jews? In answering this question, the physical limits to certain groups of words may be of only minor importance.[22]

We can also see with νόμος how an understanding of what Scriptures meant for Jews does not supplant the need for an attempt to identify particular concepts associated with νόμος. For Paul, Scripture was not only νόμος; it was also γραφή (e.g., 1 Cor 15:3, 4; Gal 3:8, 22) and perhaps γράμμα (Rom 2:27, 29; 7:6; 2 Cor 3:6-7); but if each of these words has the same object, it does not follow that the terms are identical. Each, rather, may represent the object understood in a different way, according to the different meanings of νόμος, γραφή and γράμμα; I tried to show in Chapter 2 of this dissertation (at nn. 94-102; Table 3) how these different understandings can be indicated by distinguishing among the particular concepts associated with the particular terms.[23]

---

[22] A different kind of problem emerges with definitions like that which Burton (*Galatians*, 457) gives for what he considers the most common sense (64 occurrences) of νόμος in Paul:

> Divine law viewed as a purely legalistic system made up of statutes on the basis of obedience or disobedience to which it justifies or condemns men as matter of debt without grace; the law detached in thought and distinguished from all other elements or aspects of divine revelation . . .

Burton's description incorporates a great deal which is not part of the contemplated scene, but rather a judgment on that scene; it belongs in the realm of *assertion* rather than *meaning* or *reference*.

[23] This also shows how mediating concepts are important to the meaning of a term even when that term appears to be used as the name for a unique object. If νόμος refers to Pentateuch (and I have argued that this is an oversimplification), still it refers to it *as understood in a particular way*. Just as with generic terms like "bicycle," the reference is not direct but only by way of the concepts which specify *how* the object is understood.

Chapter 5

Νόμος IN GALATIANS 2:15-21

In the last seven verses of the second chapter of Galatians νόμος appears six times:

οὐ δικαιωθῆναι ἐξ ἔργων νόμου (three times)
διὰ νόμου . . . ἀπέθανον
νόμῳ ἀπέθανον
διὰ νόμου [οὐ] δικαιοσύνη

As before, I wish to explore both the meaning and the referent for νόμος in these expressions; but now I shall do so against an examination of the passage as a whole, in its context in Galatians.

The chief interest of this examination will lie in what it shows about the meaning of νόμος. As to reference, the examination will confirm that νόμος in Gal 2:15-21 refers to Jewish νόμος. But more significantly, Gal 2:15-21 shows which elements of the general meaning of νόμος are important to Paul's understanding of Jewish νόμος in particular. We shall see that the critical point is not the relation between Jewish νόμος and God—a relationship, as we saw in the last chapter, about which Paul is ambivalent—but the relationship between Jewish νόμος and the Jewish people. Given the sharp division between human and divine authority which Paul posits in his letter to the Galatians, the status of νόμος is questionable at best; for it follows from components 5 and 7 of the meaning of νόμος[1] that νόμος is intrinsically linked to human matters.

---

[1] νόμος relates to particular people; people submit to νόμος.

The Setting of Gal 2:15-21

Although Paul, following his usual practice, introduces νόμος in 2:16 without any express statement of what this term refers to, the preceding portion of the letter deals with several subjects that illuminate Paul's use of νόμος; moreover, the verses immediately before 2:15 appear to provide the setting for what Paul says in 2:15-21. Each of these topics invites some preliminary comment.

Intimations of νόμος in Gal 1:10 to 2:14

To begin with, Paul has mentioned two topics usually associated with the observance of Jewish νόμος. First, circumcision: ἀλλ' οὐδὲ Τίτος ὁ σὺν ἐμοί, ῞Ελλην ὤν, ἠναγκάσθη περιτμηθῆναι (2:3); second, table-fellowship of Jews with Gentiles: πρὸ τοῦ γὰρ ἐλθεῖν τινας ἀπὸ Ἰακώβου μετὰ τῶν ἐθνῶν συνήσθιεν [Κηφᾶς]· ὅτε δὲ ἦλθον, ὑπέστελλεν καὶ ἀφώριζεν ἑαυτὸν φοβούμενος τοὺς ἐκ περιτομῆς (2:12).[2] We cannot, however, tie these specific points directly to the ἔργα νόμου of 2:16. Paul does not make this direct connection, and moreover, he immediately puts each of these specific points of Jewish practice in broader context. Following his reference to circumcision in 2:3 he speaks in 2:4 of the "false brothers"—evidently those who wanted to circumcise Titus—as wanting to "enslave us." This must mean more than circumcision, for otherwise the "us" does not fit; presumably Paul and Barnabas were already circumcised.[3] No other specifics are supplied in this paragraph, however. In 2:7-9 Paul again uses the terms περιτομή and ἀκροβυστία, but evidently in the broad senses of Jews on the one hand and Gentiles on the other (in 2:8 περιτομή and τὰ ἔθνη are opposed).

Similarly, although the charge Paul makes against Peter in 2:14 may be prompted by conduct relating to Jewish food laws, the charge itself is framed

---

[2] Jewish law will not have forbidden Jews to eat with Gentiles (Segal, "Romans 7," 366), but it will have forbidden them to eat foods which Gentiles could (and presumably did) eat. Paul's charge in 2:14 that Peter forced Gentiles to Judaize implies that at least some Gentiles were submitting to Jewish food rules in order to maintain table-fellowship with Peter and other Jewish-Christians.

[3] If one accepts the textual variant omitting οἷς οὐδὲ at the beginning of 2:5 (found principally in Latin: D* b Ir[lat] Tert MVict Ambst Hier[ms]), then Paul is apparently saying that "we" were not enslaved *even though* Titus submitted to circumcision. On this view even less importance attaches to an individual command than if οἷς οὐδὲ is original—as it almost surely is; see, e.g., Metzger, *Textual Commentary*, 591-92; Betz, *Galatians*, 91; Burton, *Galatians*, 85-86; Schlier, *Galater*, 72-73; Mussner, *Galater*, 110; Lagrange, *Galates*, 33.

generally: εἰ σὺ Ἰουδαῖος ὑπάρχων ἐθνικῶς ζῇς,[4] πῶς τὰ ἔθνη ἀναγκάζεις ἰουδαΐζειν; Thus the issue is not simply compliance with specified commands, but life ἐθνικῶς or Ἰουδαϊκῶς.

Moreover, in neither of these passages is Paul's concern limited to obedience to *rules* of any scope; although Paul speaks of enslavement (καταδουλόω, 2:4, cf. ἀναγκάζω, 2:14), in neither case does he speak of enslavement by rules; it is rather people ("the false brothers" in 2:4, Peter in 2:14) who are said to be requiring things of Gentile Christians. If Paul's relation to νόμος is an issue in these passages (and Paul does not use that term in them), it is an issue bound up with Paul's relation to people associated with νόμος.

The issue of life ἐθνικῶς or Ἰουδαϊκῶς is also treated, in another context, in chapter 1:

Ἠκούσατε γὰρ τὴν ἐμὴν **ἀναστροφήν** ποτε ἐν τῷ Ἰουδαϊσμῷ, ὅτι καθ᾽ ὑπερβολὴν ἐδίωκον τὴν ἐκκλησίαν τοῦ θεοῦ καὶ ἐπόρθουν αὐτήν, καὶ προέκοπτον ἐν τῷ Ἰουδαϊσμῷ ὑπὲρ πολλοὺς συνηλικιώτας ἐν τῷ γένει μου, περισσοτέρως ζηλωτὴς ὑπάρχων τῶν πατρικῶν μου παραδόσεων. (Gal 1:13-14)[5]

Immediately after this Paul describes how, in contrast, he was called by ἀποκάλυψις τοῦ υἱοῦ θεοῦ to preach among the Gentiles (Gal 1:15-16). We have therefore in Gal 1:10-16 a series of contrasts, beginning with the basic one of ἄνθρωπος and θεός announced in 1:16[6] and developed in 1:10-12:[7]

ἄνθρωπος	θεός
ἐν τῷ Ἰουδαϊσμῷ	ἐν τοῖς ἔθνεσιν
αἱ πατρικαί μου παραδόσεις	ἡ ἀποκάλυψις τοῦ υἱοῦ θεοῦ

These three contrasts parallel one another. The opposition of αἱ πατρικαί μου παραδόσεις and ἡ ἀποκάλυψις τοῦ υἱοῦ θεοῦ invokes that of ἄνθρωπος and θεός, and suggests that παραδόσεις are human—as indeed the term's literal meaning, emphasized by its description as ancestral, also suggests. But the content of παραδόσεις in 1:14 plainly includes Ἰουδαϊσμός,[8] so that

---

4 I omit καὶ οὐχὶ Ἰουδαϊκῶς before ζῇς; it is missing from P46, and those manuscripts which have it differ in their placement of it, as well as in the form of οὐκ. But the sense is not altered.

5 I have discussed this passage, in connection with Paul's view of the relationship between νόμος and God, in Chapter 4 (at nn. 52-57).

6 Παῦλος ἀπόστολος οὐκ ἐπ᾽ ἀνθρώπων οὐδὲ δι᾽ ἀνθρώπου ἀλλὰ διὰ Ἰησοῦ Χριστοῦ καὶ θεοῦ πατρὸς . . .

7 Ἄρτι γὰρ ἀνθρώπους πείθω ἢ τὸν θεόν; . . . οὐδὲ γὰρ ἐγὼ παρὰ ἀνθρώπου παρέλαβον [τὸ εὐαγγέλιον] οὔτε ἐδιδάχθην ἀλλὰ δι᾽ ἀποκαλύψεως Ἰησοῦ Χριστοῦ.

8 I have discussed the evident relation of παραδόσεις to νόμος in Chapter 4 (at nn. 64-66). Presumably there are also other, Gentile παραδόσεις, but none are at issue here.

'Ιουδαϊσμός is *now set against* ἡ ἀποκάλυψις τοῦ υἱοῦ θεοῦ and, by further implication, treated as human rather than divine.[9]

Thus, in 1:1 through 2:14 Paul has already called attention to particular points of Jewish conduct in which Gentiles should not be required to engage; he has set these issues in the context of Jewish conduct in general; and he has implied that such issues are related to human tradition and not to divine revelation.

The Connection Between Gal 2:11-14 and 15-21

In 2:14 Paul addresses Peter; in 3:1 he addresses the Galatians; is 2:15-21 part of the speech to Peter or not? Most commentators think it is, chiefly because no unmistakable break occurs until 3:1;[10] but recently Betz has argued that 2:15-21 is, according to ancient rhetorical practice, a *propositio* which both summarizes the entire *narratio* found in 1:12-2:14, and introduces the *probatio* to follow (3:1-4:31).[11] Betz's analysis does not actually settle the question of where the speech to Peter ends, for Paul could have used his speech to Peter as a summary statement. But Betz hits the central point, which is that Paul's words must be analyzed according to their function in this letter, and not according to their possible function at an earlier time.[12] Even if Paul recalled every word of his speech in Antioch, he would not have repeated those words here (either verbatim or paraphrased) except to make a point to the Galatians;[13] and if the meaning of these words depended at any important point on their being understood as part of the Antiochene *rather than* the Galatian situation, would Paul not have made that understanding clear?

In fact there is a break at 2:15, marked by the stylistic device of asyndeton, the absence of a connective particle.[14] Paul might have chosen to

---

These parallels should not be pushed too far, by linking Gentiles to God; there might be some sense in which Paul would allow this, in view of the Gospel's greater success among Gentiles (see Rom 9:30-32; but also 11:25-32), but he does not treat this subject here.

[9] J. L. Martyn ("Apocalyptic Antinomies") has shown the importance in Galatians of paired opposites, and especially of the shifts in such pairs which has resulted from the coming of Christ. The Jew/Gentile opposition is one which has disappeared (ibid., 414-15; see Gal 3:27-28); the ἀποκάλυψις of 1:16 is what has caused the shift (ibid., 417).

[10] E.g., Barrett, *Freedom*, 18; Lightfoot, *Galatians*, 113-14; Schlier, *Galater*, 87; Burton, *Galatians*, 117-18; Mussner, *Galater*, 167 n.2; Bruce, *Galatians*, 136.

[11] Betz, *Galatians*, 113-14.

[12] The usefulness of Betz's technical term *propositio* is less clear (see Smit, "Deliberative Speech," 33).

[13] Schlier, *Galater*, 88; Betz, *Galatians*, 113-14.

[14] See Schwyzer, *Grammatik*, 2.632-33, 701; Smyth, *Grammar*, 484-85; Robertson, *Grammar*, 443-44; Denniston, *Particles*, xliii-xlvi.

indicate the end of his speech to Peter by asyndeton rather than by such other devices as an abrupt change in topic or viewpoint (cf. 'Ω ἀνόητοι Γαλάται [3:1]) because he wished to move smoothly from the speech to Peter (2:14) into an exposition of that speech for the Galatians.[15] Moreover, 2:14 is an appropriate conclusion to Paul's account of what happened at Antioch. Schlier's claim that "v. 14 allein hätte ja keinen Sinn"[16] overlooks the relation between that verse and what precedes it. Verse 14 demonstrates precisely what Paul claimed at the outset in 2:11: "Οτε δὲ ἦλθεν Κηφᾶς εἰς Ἀντιόχειαν, κατὰ πρόσωπον αὐτῷ ἀντέστην, ὅτι κατεγνωσμένος ἦν. Two points are made in Gal 2:11. The first is that Paul opposed Peter, a point which is important for Paul's thesis that his authority comes from God

---

[15] This asyndeton does not settle the matter, for asyndeton is a rhetorical device that can be employed simply to "lend . . . solemnity and weight to the words . . ."(BDF §462(2), adding that it "is not a *conscious* rhetorical device" (emphasis added); I do not know how this judgment could be made). In Galatians, asyndeton appears between independent clauses or sentences some 45 times. Often the reason is clearly identifiable: there is asyndeton (a) at the introduction of a new topic (1:6; 3:1, 15a; 4:12, 21; 5:7; 6:1, 11, 17, 18; 5:1 may also belong here, but the UBS³ text—in distinction to Nestle-Aland²⁶—begins a new paragraph at 5:2 instead of 5:1), or (b) at the beginning of a quotation formula (1:9b; 2:14b; 3:2b, 15b; and perhaps the proverbs in 2:6c and 5:9), or (c) with the break in an argument that typically follows a question (1:10c; 2:14b; 3:2a, 3a, 4a, 4b, 15b, 21b; 4:10, 17; 5:8). This last is not automatic; when the argument flows smoothly from question to following statement there is no asyndeton (see Gal 4:15n; Rom 2:27; 4:1, 9; 1 Cor 6:8).

Otherwise emphasis appears to be the usual reason for asyndeton in Galatians, but this emphasis usually accompanies at least a minor break in the discourse; see, for example, 1:9 (ὡς προειρήκαμεν καὶ ἄρτι πάλιν λέγω) and 5:2 (Ἴδε ἐγὼ Παῦλος λέγω ὑμῖν); less dramatic are 2:21; 3:28a; 4:12b, 19; 5:10, 12). Probably this explains the use of asyndeton when Christ stands at the beginning of a sentence (2:19b; 3:13). Finally, Paul introduces parallel phrases of equivalent meaning with asyndeton (3:28b, c); this (in addition to emphasis) might account for 2:19b; so Bultmann, "Galater 2:15-18," 397.

It will be noted that not every paragraph begins with asyndeton; compare 3:15 (asyndeton) with 3:10 and 19 (no asyndeton). Robertson remarks (*Grammar*, 444; emphasis added): "In Paul's Epistles one would expect little asyndeton *between the paragraphs especially in the argumentative portions.* In general this is true, and yet occasionally even in Ro. asyndeton is met as in 9:1, 13:1." These are major breaks that provide no parallel for the asyndeton in Gal 2:15. It could be that the asyndeton of 2:15 is simply emphatic; but the reason for this emphasis is not clear. If 2:15 continues the address to Peter, and especially if it amplifies Paul's charge against Peter, γάρ or another connective would be expected. (2:15 follows a question, a common place for asyndeton; but as I have just noted, it is not the question itself but the break that often follows a question which brings asyndeton; I do not see such a break here.)

No firm conclusion can be drawn from the absence of any such connective, but it does cast doubt on the theory that 2:14-15 is a continuous address to Peter.

[16] Schlier, *Galater*, 87.

and not from any human (1:10-12, 16a-17, 18-19; 2:6). Gal 2:14 recounts this opposition, and thereafter this theme largely fades from view.

The second point is the reason for Paul's opposition to Peter: ὅτι [Κηφᾶς] κατεγνωσμένος ἦν. This periphrastic pluperfect form implies that Peter was condemned before Paul opposed him; 2:14 shows that it was Peter's own shifting conduct that condemned him—a theme to which, as we shall see, Paul returns in 2:17 and 18.

We are therefore alerted by 2:14, read as the confirmation of 2:11, that the charge of inconsistent conduct is a major one. How it is important, and how it relates to the Galatians, is taken up in 2:15-21.[17]

The Argument in Gal 2:15-21

I now turn to an analysis of Paul's argument in Gal 2:15-21. I will proceed verse by verse, beginning the discussion of each verse with the text of the verse in Greek and ending with a paraphrase in English that will summarize my conclusions.[18] A more literal translation of 2:15-21 appears, at the end of my exegetical discussion.

Verse 15

In v. 15 Paul defines and describes the subject of the long and complex sentence running to the end of v. 16:

Ἡμεῖς φύσει Ἰουδαῖοι καὶ οὐκ ἐξ ἐθνῶν ἁμαρτωλοί[19]

---

[17] A major difficulty with taking 2:14-21 to be continuous discourse is the great distance travelled from Antioch to the end of v. 21; thus Lightfoot (*Galatians*, 113-14) concludes:

> St. Paul's narrative in fact loses itself in the reflexions suggested by it. Text and comment are so blended together that they cannot be separated without violence.

See also Bruce (*Galatians*, 136), Burton (*Galatians*, 117). But if Paul's speech at Antioch ends with 2:14 there is a clear division between 2:11-14 and 2:15-21; 2:11-14 is a distinct anecdote, emphasizing the inconsistent conduct which condemned Peter, and we would expect 2:15-21 to expound the implications of this anecdote for the situation at Galatia.

[18] Except at the end of v. 15, which is not a separate sentence; my paraphrase of v. 15 appears at the end of v. 16.

[19] It is sometimes argued that 2:15 is a separate sentence; e.g., Bultmann ("Galater 2,15-18," 394). On this view a copula must be supplied to the verse, in one of these ways: (1) "We *are* Jews by nature and not Gentile sinners"; (2) "We Jews by nature *are* also not Gentile sinners"; or (3) "We, Jews by nature and not Gentiles, *are* sinners." None of these is plausible. (1) fails to define the subject and thus is possible only if this verse is part of Paul's speech at Antioch, so that the context defines the subject. (2) is pointless. (3) is

Like the rest of the sentence to come, this seems to be more elaborate than is strictly necessary. Ἡμεῖς φύσει Ἰουδαῖοι defines the subject as people of Jewish birth, but it does not fully define it, for in v. 16 we learn that "we" also "believe in Christ Jesus"—that is, are Christians of Jewish birth.[20] Does "we" then mean all Jewish Christians, or only some group of them? Paul, Peter, Barnabas and confreres are the obvious examples of Jewish Christians at this point; Paul, however, does not limit himself to these examples, but speaks of Jewish Christians as a group.[21]

Paul adds, however: καὶ οὐκ ἐξ ἐθνῶν ἁμαρτωλοί. What does this mean, and why does Paul say it? The meaning is clear except for ἁμαρτωλοί, and this is usually understood to be equivalent to ἔθνη: that is, Gentiles are *ipso facto* sinners.[22] But the evidence does not show that ἁμαρτωλός is a technical term for Gentiles, but only that it is a pejorative, often applied to Gentiles yet not necessarily to Gentiles as such;[23] it is also applied to Jews.[24] The best case for a technical sense in fact rests on this verse, for it is hard to see why Paul of all people would apply such a pejorative to Gentiles.[25] But this difficulty cannot be solved by appealing to technical usage; even if the term is technical it is still pejorative, and Paul goes out of his way to use it here, having already defined his subject as (a) Jews and (b) not Gentiles, a description which is

---

dubious for its separation of "Gentiles" and "sinners," a point discussed further in the text below. Finally, if Paul's meaning were one that required a copula for clear expression, it is hard to see why he would not have included the copula.

[20] Here φύσει Ἰουδαῖοι might suggest that these are Jews who are now outside Judaism; but it is not clear whether the word φύσει can bear this weight. Alternatively, Paul's use of φύσει might be taken simply as a Jewish boast in the privilege of Jewish birth (cf. Rom 2:9-10; 3:1-2; 9:4-5; Phil 3:4-6).

[21] It is interesting that Paul can say simply φύσει Ἰουδαῖοι for Christians, not specifying their belief in Christ for another twenty-one words, just as though all Jews believed in Christ. Does this reflect the situation in Galatia?

[22] Lightfoot, *Galatians*, 115; TDNT, s.v., 1 (1964) 326; cf. Schlier, *Galater*, 89; Betz, *Galatians*, 115 n.25.

In contrast, H. Neitzel ("Galater 2,11-21," 18-27) contends in a lengthy article that "sinners" applies to "Jews" and *not* Gentiles: "We, Jews by nature and not Gentiles, [are] sinners." Neitzel's argument neglects the possibility that Paul might have spoken ironically; he also relies on the Antiochene setting to the exclusion of the Galatian.

[23] Ps 9:17 ((LXX); Tob 13:8; 1 Macc 1:10, 34; Isa 14:5.

[24] 1 Macc 2:44, according to which ἁμαρτωλοί fled to the Gentiles. 1 Macc 2:48 and 62 are ambiguous, as are most of the numerous occurrences in Psalms. The term is also very common in Sirach, without an indication that Gentiles are meant. In Mark 14:41, Matt 26:45, the apparent reference for ἁμαρτωλῶν is Judas and the crowd sent by the chief priests and elders. ἁμαρτωλοί is also applied to Jews in Gal 2:17; see below.

[25] This is equally a problem whether we think of the Galatians or, if this is a speech in Antioch, of the mixed congregation there.

redundant even before we come to ἁμαρτωλοί. Rather than a technical term for Gentiles, ἁμαρτωλός is more likely a stock epithet which can be applied to Gentiles or to Jews; it is opposed to 'Ιουδαῖος in the sense that overall the conduct of Jews and Gentiles differs on various points, as Paul has remarked in 1:13-14; 2:7-9, 12-14—a rough differentiation which holds even if in practice many Jews neglect many Jewish practices. 'Αμαρτωλός is then applied to the Gentile side of this division on the presupposition that (on the whole) Jewish conduct is right and Gentile conduct wrong.

But why should Paul adopt this usage and the presupposition on which it depends? Two things may be said. The first is that the usage and presupposition must have been known in Galatia, or v. 15 will not have been understood; indeed, if circumcision was attractive to the Galatians it appears that they accepted—at least in part—the view that Jewish conduct is right. The second point is that Paul's choice of ἁμαρτωλός in v. 15 cannot be understood except in light of its use in v. 17, for which v. 15 prepares the way; but we cannot leap to that later verse before assessing the impact of the earlier. Taken as a whole, v. 15 emphasizes Jewish pre-eminence: φύσει specifies that born Jews are meant; since οὐκ ἐξ ἐθνῶν following φύσει 'Ιουδαῖοι is literally redundant,[26] its presence is emphatic; ἁμαρτωλοί gratuitously lays against Gentiles a charge which actually lies against many Jews as well.[27]

Verse 16

We now proceed to the substance of Gal 2:15-16. The chief issue for this dissertation is the meaning of the thrice-repeated phrase ἐξ ἔργων νόμου, but this must be examined in its context. Verse 16, whose subject is specified in v. 15, consists of the following succession of clauses and phrases:

1	εἰδότες[28] ὅτι οὐ δικαιοῦται ἄνθρωπος
2	ἐξ ἔργων νόμου
3	ἐὰν μὴ διὰ πίστεως 'Ιησοῦ Χριστοῦ,
4	καὶ ἡμεῖς εἰς Χριστὸν 'Ιησοῦν ἐπιστεύσαμεν,
3'	ἵνα δικαιωθῶμεν ἐκ πίστεως Χριστοῦ
2'a	καὶ οὐκ ἐξ ἔργων νόμου,
2'b	ὅτι ἐξ ἔργων νόμου
1'	οὐ δικαιωθήσεται πᾶσα σάρξ.

---

[26] Unless a contrast is meant between born Jews and converts. But then ἁμαρτωλοί is out of place.

[27] For my paraphrase of v. 15, see the end of my discussion of v. 16.

[28] I omit the δέ which many manuscripts have at this point; see below, at nn. 37, 39.

I present the sentence in this way to show its roughly chiastic structure; the central element (both grammatically and structurally) is καὶ ἡμεῖς εἰς Χριστὸν Ἰησοῦν ἐπιστεύσαμεν, flanked by the roughly equivalent expressions 3 and 3', 2 and 2', 1 and 1'.²⁹ Structure and simple repetition emphasize two thrice-repeated themes: the negative οὐ δικαιοῦσθαι ἐξ ἔργων νόμου and the positive πιστ–Ἰησοῦ[ν].³⁰ The first of these themes begins and ends the verse, while the second forms its center.³¹ The key elements of the two themes are joined both in 1-3 (ὅτι οὐ δικαιοῦται ἄνθρωπος ἐξ ἔργων νόμου ἐὰν μὴ διὰ πίστεως Ἰησοῦ Χριστοῦ) and in 3'-1' (ἵνα δικαιωθῶμεν ἐκ πίστεως Χριστοῦ καὶ οὐκ ἐξ ἔργων νόμου, ὅτι ἐξ ἔργων νόμου οὐ δικαιωθήσεται πᾶσα σάρξ), but the first of these statements has a critical ambiguity: ἐὰν μὴ might mean either "unless" (i.e., "unless [also] through faith")³² or "but" (i.e., "but [rather] through faith").³³ Taken alone, the clause in 1-3 could mean that both πίστεως Χριστοῦ and ἔργων νόμου are required for salvation; not until 3'-1' is the opposition between πίστις and ἔργα stated clearly.

The final effect of v. 16 is thus to set ἔργα νόμου and πίστις Χριστοῦ against each other, but in a certain respect: in their relation to δικαιοῦν. Nothing is said against ἔργα νόμου except that one is not justified ἐξ ἔργων νόμου; at the same time, nothing at all is said in favor of ἔργα νόμου.

All this is apparent apart from the particular meanings of δικαιοῦν, ἐξ ἔργων νόμου, διὰ/ἐκ πίστεως Χριστοῦ, and εἰς Χριστὸν πιστεύειν. There is good reason to approach these terms warily, especially ἔργα νόμου and πίστις Χριστοῦ, on which interpreters have vigorously disagreed. To close in upon these difficulties full attention must be given to the surrounding terrain, not only the relation in which these terms are placed by v. 16 but their relation to the balance of the letter.

---

²⁹ This is not entirely symmetrical; 2' is doubled and δικαιόω is found in 3' but not in 3 (where, however, it is understood). The symmetry might have been preserved by omitting 2'a, which is redundant, and repeating the δικαιοῦται in 3, which would have clarified that phrase's meaning (see below, at n. 33); but the asymmetry may be intended to call attention to the additional, unbalanced elements in 2' and 3'.

³⁰ The latter expression, in contrast to the former, shows variations between noun and verb; between different prepositions; in the identification of Christ; and probably (see below, at nn. 62-70) in the relation between πίστις and Christ.

³¹ Schlier remarks (Galater, 88): "Durch die überladene Satzkonstruktion erhält die Aussage, ἡμεῖς φύσει Ἰουδαῖοι εἰς Χριστὸν Ἰησοῦν ἐπιστεύσαμεν, sofort das ihr zukommende Gewicht." This does not do justice to Paul's sentence; it is not simply overloaded but artfully balanced, and its elements cannot be stripped away as if that would leave the essential kernel.

³² Smyth, Grammar, ¶ 2346(a); BDF, § 376.

³³ Moulton and Howard, Grammar, 468; Burton, Galatians, 121. This is the usual rendering (AV, RSV, NEB, JB, NAB), but it depends on the second half of 2:16.

First, the preliminary proposition οὐ δικαιοῦται ἄνθρωπος ἐξ ἔργων νόμου ἐὰν μὴ διὰ πίστεως Ἰησοῦ Χριστοῦ is one which those born Jews identified in v. 15—presumably Jewish Christians—are said to "know" (εἰδότες ὅτι). How "know"? Occasionally in Paul οἶδα refers to something experienced,[34] but much more often to a general proposition of some kind,[35] even to propositions about future events which cannot be based on experience.[36] εἰδότες therefore does not of itself imply any reference to some experience which has taught Jews the inadequacy of ἔργα νόμου. Paul does not even assert that this knowledge is peculiar to Jews; yet he only claims it for Jews, and his extraordinary emphasis on Jewish precedence in v. 15 prepares us for some claim resting on that precedence. It is true that Paul's most exaggerated claim, that Jews are not sinners, is undercut (as we shall see) in vv. 17-18. But we are still at the beginning of v. 16, the clause immediately following οὐκ . . . ἁμαρτωλοί, where Jewish precedence is not yet questioned.

The relation between the description of Jews in v. 15 and the following εἰδότες is complicated by the doubtful δέ after εἰδότες, on which the manuscripts are divided.[37] If δέ is present it might be taken to imply contrast between Ἰουδαῖοι and εἰδότες. But this would be an unusual use of δέ.[38] I think it more likely that the presence or absence of δέ depends chiefly on whether or not v. 15 is construed as a separate sentence: if v. 15 is independent, a particle is needed in v. 16 to avoid an implausible asyndeton, but if v. 15 is a phrase in apposition to ἡμεῖς, then no particle is required. The scribal confusion over δέ thus reflects the uncertain syntax of vv. 15-16.[39] But if I am

---

[34] Gal 4:13; 1 Cor 1:16; in both of these passages, something recalled.

[35] E.g., Rom 3:19: οἴδαμεν δὲ ὅτι ὅσα ὁ νόμος λέγει τοῖς ἐν τῷ νόμῳ λάλει.

[36] E.g., 1 Cor 6:2: οὐκ οἴδατε ὅτι οἱ ἅγιοι τὸν κόσμον κρινοῦσιν; (cf. 1 Cor 6:3, 9). In 1 Cor 14:16, τί λέγεις οὐκ οἶδεν, the sense is "understand."

[37] With δέ : ℵ, B, C, D*, F, G, H, 81, 104, 1175, 2464 pc lat. Without: P[46], A, D[2], Ψ, Majority Text, sy[h]. Nestle-Aland[26] includes δέ, but in brackets. The extrinsic evidence is inconclusive, with weighty manuscripts on both sides: according to Metzger (Text, 37-60, 213-16), most of the witnesses for δέ are Western (C, D*, f, G, perhaps B), but the Alexandrian witnesses are divided (ℵ, H with δέ, P[46], A without); or, according to Aland's different terminology (Text, 106-16), there are Category I witnesses both with δέ (ℵ, B) and without it (P[46], A).

[38] I find no other place in Paul's seven undisputed letters where δέ contrasts a participial phrase with a noun to which the phrase is in apposition (see Aland, Konkordanz, s.v. δέ). The closest parallel is 2 Cor 6:10, where (twice) two participles are contrasted with each other; but the opposition is expressed by the participles themselves (λυπούμενοι, χαίροντες· πτωχοὶ πολλούς, πλουτίζοντες); in a third contrasting pair the particle is καί rather than δέ.

[39] The presence of so much authority both for and against the presence of a connective particle is unusual. The most nearly comparable case in Galatians is 1:10c, where D', Majority Text and sy[c] have γάρ. In Romans, see 3:2 (γάρ), 5:9 (οὖν), 14:5 (γάρ) and 16:1

right that Paul's speech in Antioch ends with v. 14, the syntactic problem is solved; v. 15 is pointless as an independent sentence, ("We Jews are not Gentile sinners"), and so δέ is superfluous.

It is thus suggested that Jewish Christians in particular[40] know ὅτι οὐ δικαιοῦται ἄνθρωπος ἐξ ἔργων νόμου. Does it follow that their knowledge extends also to the following ἐαν μή clause? Syntactically, this too is dependent on ὅτι. We may grant the immediate implausibility of supposing Jews to have special knowledge about πίστις Χριστοῦ; but perhaps this implausibility is the product of succeeding centuries and not of the first century. Both Gal 3 and Rom 4 present Abraham as a model of πίστις; Ἰουδαῖοι φύσει might therefore be expected to know something about faith. Moreover, Rom 3:21-22 says that Scripture (ὁ νόμος καί αἱ προφῆται) bears witness to δικαοσύνη . . . θεοῦ διὰ πίστεως Ἰησοῦ Χριστοῦ. This implies that Scripture (correctly understood) speaks specifically of πίστις Χριστοῦ.[41]

It can at least be said that all the knowledge attributed to Ἰουδαῖοι φύσει by the first clause of v. 16 is attributed to them not as the consequence but as the occasion of their belief (εἰδότες ὅτι οὐ δικαιοῦται . . .), for prior knowledge is presupposed in the statements of the purpose of their belief (ἵνα δικαιωθῶμεν . . .)[42] and of the basis of their belief (ὅτι . . . οὐ δικαιωθήσεται . . .). This triple statement (εἰδότες . . ., ἵνα . . ., ὅτι . . .) may partly serve the purpose of allowing Paul to repeat his key phrases in slightly different language, but it also implies that knowledge logically (and perhaps temporally) precedes belief.[43]

Let us now turn to the key terms and phrases of this verse: δικαιοῦσθαι, ἐξ ἔργων νόμου, διὰ/ἐκ πίστεως Χριστοῦ, and πιστεύειν εἰς Χριστὸν. I have remarked that this passage introduces νόμος in this letter, and without any explicit statement of what is meant; and this is equally true of the rest of these

---

(δέ). (In each of these cases Nestle-Aland[26] includes the particle, but in Gal 2:16; Rom 3:2; 14:5 the particle is bracketed; the editors' confusion mirrors the scribes'.)

[40] φύσει Ἰουδαῖοι. The limitation to Christians is implied by the main clause (4) of 2:16.

[41] The exact meaning of the ἐαν μή clause depends partly on the meaning of πίστις Ἰησοῦ Χριστοῦ, to which I turn below; here I am still trying to mark out the boundaries of this problem, before trying to apprehend the words themselves.

[42] ἵνα could imply only result and not purpose, and ὅτι could then explain the result. But purpose is so clearly implied by the εἰδότες clause that mere result must be ruled out.

[43] It does not necessarily follow that this knowledge is sufficient for faith, nor even that it is essential for it.

terms. Moreover: here these terms first emerge as significant ones in the Pauline corpus.[44]

For my purposes, not much need be said about δικαιοῦσθαι; there is no dispute that its basic sense is "the state of being right with God."[45] The middle and passive voices used here are noteworthy; Paul uses the active voice with this word only at Gal 3:8; Rom 3:26, 30; 4:5; 8:30 (twice), 33, and in all of these places the subject is God,[46] so that the passive here is probably divine. In view of my interest in νόμος, it is noteworthy that δικαιοῦσθαι can be used forensically, but this must not be overemphasized; the term has no necessary connection with νόμος, as both the Septuagint and Josephus show.[47] Paul himself does not draw any link between the terms but rather, in 2:21, denies that νόμος is connected to δικαιοσύνη.[48] If he has such a link in mind, he uses it only ironically, as in 2:21: εἰ γὰρ διὰ νόμου δικαιοσύνη, ἄρα Χριστὸς δωρεὰν ἀπέθανεν.

Now ἐξ ἔργων νόμου. I begin with Marcus Barth's observation:

---

[44] δίκαιος, -οσύνη, -όω, -ως and -ωσις appear 89 times in the seven undisputed letters, but 13 of those appearances are in Galatians and 58 in Romans. πιστεύω and πίστις appear 133 times, 26 times in Galatians and 61 in Romans (πιστός, used differently, is found eight times in 1 and 2 Corinthians and 1 Thessalonians, only once in Galatians). The association of these three terms with each other and with νόμος is unique to Galatians and Romans.

[45] Bruce, Galatians, 138. See, in addition to the other commentaries on Galatians, Bultmann, Theology, 1.270-87; TDNT, 2 (1964) 202-10.

[46] Implicitly in Rom 4:5, explicitly in the other passages.

[47] δικαιοῦν appears in legal codes only at Exod 23:7 and Deut 25:1, not very much when measured against the total bulk of codes in the LXX. In both of these passages the word means "to justify," as also—and in a forensic setting—in 3 Kgdms 8:32 and Isa 1:17; but this is a general sense which also appears in non-legal settings: e.g., Isa 42:61; Sir 13:22; 26:29. In the more technical sense of "to judge," often with other legal terminology, see 1 Kgdms 12:7; 2 Kgdms 15:4. Sometimes the term is associated with other legal terminology, but the term itself means "to justify," so that a technical legal sense may or may not lie in the background: e.g., τὰ κρίματα κυρίου ἀληθινὰ δεδικαιωμένα (Ps 18:9; cf. Ps 50:4).

In Josephus a technical sense "to condemn" is found at Ant. 17.9.1 §206, and "to judge" (here, θανάτῳ) at Ant. 18.6.5 §178. The more general sense "to be right" appears at Ant. 17.10.1 §251; 19.6.3 §305. In two passages the sense generally is "to justify," but the subject of the verb is νόμος or νόμοι (Ant. 4.8.33 §278; 9.9.1 §187); here a forensic sense of δικαιοῦν has perhaps suggested the term to Josephus, but its actual sense is more general.

[48] If 2:21 is Paul's answer to those who claim that δικαιοσύνη does come διὰ νόμου, then these others might be making use of a semantic link between νόμος and δικαιοσύνη.

The nature of "works of law" (which cannot be defined with the aid of LXX, Qumran, Apocalypticists, Tannaites) must be elucidated by the only group of documents in which they are mentioned,[49] the Pauline epistles . . .[50]

In Paul the precise phrase ἐξ ἔργων νόμου is found seven times (Gal 2:16[3]; 3:2, 5, 10; Rom 3:20), and four times in connection with οὐ δικαιοῦσθαι or -θῆναι (Gal 2:16; Rom 3:20); in five of these passages ἔργα νόμου are also contrasted with πίστις Χριστοῦ (Gal 3:16) or ἀκοῆς πίστεως (Gal 3:2, 5). These passages are predominantly in Galatians; eight other passages in Romans display some half-dozen variations on the theme. In one passage ἔργα νόμου are opposed to δικαιοῦσθαι, but without ἐξ and with χωρίς in place of

---

[49] There is a Hebrew parallel מעשי תורה, apparently found in 4QFlor. 1.6-7, but this does not elucidate Paul. This passage reads, according to Allegro ("Fragments," 352) and DJD 5.53:

ויואמר לבנות לוא מקדש אדם להיות מקטירים בוא לוא לפנית
מעשי תורה

Here the reading מעשי תודה, "thanksgiving" or "thank offerings," has been proposed in place of מעשי תורה (see Strugnell, "Notes," 221). But even if we set this possibility aside, the passage is of little help in interpreting Paul. First, the meaning of מעשי תורה is obscure; evidently it is parallel to מקטירים, "burning [offerings]," but is this term to be taken literally (so that מעשי תורה is a synonym for sacrifices) or figuratively (so that מעשי תורה has some more general meaning, to which sacrifices are likened)? The latter view underlies Vermes's rendering (Dead Sea Scrolls, 293), ". . . that then they may send up, like the smoke of incense, the works of the law," but this is speculative. A related question is the interpretation of מקדש אדם, which might mean "temple made by humans," or "temple of humans"; on this, see Dupont-Sommer, Essene Writings, 312 n. 5.

Second, this single occurrence of a Hebrew phrase in a particular context cannot establish an idiomatic sense even in Hebrew and even at Qumran; the phrase may be simply an ad hoc formulation whose sense (whatever it is) depends on the context. A connection with Paul's Greek phrase is entirely speculative. For the same reasons, the apparent existence of another, still unpublished reference to מעשי תורה (see Dunn, Romans, 1.154), although of great interest, is not likely to contribute significantly to our understanding of Paul.

Twice the Community Rule (1 QS 5.21; 6.18) speaks of judging a community member לפי שכלו ומעשיו בתורה, "according to his understanding and deeds with regard to the Torah." Here the repetition of the phrase suggests that it may be an idiom. But it is not the same as Paul's Greek idiom.

[50] Barth, Ephesians 1.246. I cut off this sentence just as Barth is about to give his definition ("these works stem from a random selection of individual commandments and prohibitions from the bulk of Israel's legal tradition" [emphasis added]), with which, as will be seen, I disagree.

Barth's parenthetical phrase, "which cannot be defined with the aid of . . .," is correct as stated; the other literature he lists may be the source of hypotheses about Paul's meaning, but our knowledge of that meaning finally depends on Paul's texts.

οὐ (3:28). In another passage ἔργα (without νόμου) are opposed to δικαιοσύνη, again without ἐξ and with χωρίς for οὐ (4:6). In one passage ἐξ ἔργων appears without νόμου and is opposed to δικαιοῦσθαι (4:12); in three others ἐξ ἔργων appears without νόμου and is denigrated, although without express reference to δικαιοῦσθαι (9:12, 32; 11:6); in one of these ἔργα are opposed to πίστις (9:32). In 3:27 the phrase is inverted—νόμος ἔργων—but the contrast to πίστις (νόμος πίστεως) is present. Once ἔργον νόμου appears, without particular similarities to the usage of ἔργα νόμου (2:15). Finally, just as ἔργα can be used in expressions similar to those in which ἔργα νόμου appears, so also νόμος can be opposed to both δικαιοσύνη (Rom 3:21; 4:13; Gal 2:21; 3:11, 21) and πίστις (Rom 3:21-22; 4:14; 10:5-6; Gal 3:23; Phil 3:9).

It cannot be presumed from this that any of these similar expressions are equivalent to one another, especially when this would lead to such conflicting conclusions as that ἔργα νόμου means νόμος (on the strength of Gal 2:21, 3:21),[51] but that, on the other hand, it means ἔργα (on the strength of Rom 4:2, 6; 9:12, 32; 11:6).[52] It would be particularly dangerous to construe Paul's initial usage of this phrase in Gal 2:16 by his later usage in Romans. What is most striking about the usage in Romans, viewed against that in Galatians, is how the fixed syntactical pattern ἐξ ἔργων νόμου of the earlier letter is adapted and varied—now at one point, now at another—in the later. Why is the pattern so rigid in Galatians—not only with δικαιοῦσθαι (2:16), but without it? This is what one would expect if this fixed pattern in Galatians comes not from Paul but from Galatia; and if from Galatia, then almost certainly from those "troublers" of the Galatians (1:7) who wish them to be circumcised (6:13)—or, as J. Louis Martyn calls them in an effort to step back from Pauline polemic, "the Teachers."[53]

If the phrase ἐξ ἔργων νόμου is the Teachers', used by them to preach circumcision (6:13), days and seasons (4:10)—no doubt among other things—then the phrase is intended to have a positive meaning. In their mouths it cannot mean, as Barth says it means for Paul, "a random selection of individual commandments,"[54] nor will it mean this in the ears of the Galatians who are attracted to the Teachers' views. Rather, if Barth is right at all, Paul would be saying "ἔργα νόμου amount to a random selection of commandments

[51] E.g., Betz, Galatians, 126; Westerholm, Israel's Law, 117-18; van Dülmen, Theologie, 23.

[52] E.g., Moo, "Law," 94-96; cf. Lambrecht, "Gestezesverständnis," 126-27. Lohmeyer ("Gesetzeswerk," 64) equates all three expressions: ἐξ ἔργων νόμου, ἐξ ἔργων and ἐκ νόμου.

[53] Martyn, "Law-Observant Mission."

[54] Barth, Ephesians, 1.246,

. . ." But for the *meaning* of the phrase (not forgetting the initial ἐξ) we must look further. To be specific, we must look further in Galatians, not in Romans. Three points will now provide guidance. The first is that 2:15-21 is Paul's application to the Galatians of the Antioch incident, and especially of Paul's judgment that in Antioch Peter was condemned by his own conduct (2:11, 14).[55] The second point is that we must read the term νόμος against the background of 1:1 - 2:14, where in three particular passages (1:13-14; 2:3-4, 12-13) Paul refers to aspects of Jewish νόμος but sets them in a broader context of Jewish life;[56] the most proximate expression of this point is in 2:14, where Paul criticizes Peter for forcing Gentiles to live Ἰουδαϊκῶς.

The third point is Paul's statement that Ἰουδαῖοι φύσει know that they are not justified ἐξ ἔργων νόμου. Inasmuch as Ἰουδαῖοι φύσει are precisely those who have lived Ἰουδαϊκῶς, the juxtaposition of all these expressions suggests that ἐξ ἔργων νόμου and Ἰουδαϊκῶς are equivalent. Both are adverbial expressions meaning "to do as Jews do"; for Paul, the emphasis is not on the performance of specified commands on (for example) circumcision or food, but on the general phenomenon of taking up a way of life belonging to the Jewish people and not to others. This is how Paul views the issue in Antioch, where Paul appeals to the very conduct of Ἰουδαῖοι φύσει to demonstrate that life Ἰουδαϊκῶς is not necessary.[57] If the phrase ἐξ ἔργων νόμου does come from the Teachers whom Paul opposes, this equivalence with Ἰουδαϊκῶς probably does not; it is much more likely that Ἰουδαϊκῶς, ἰουδαΐζειν and Ἰουδαϊσμός are Paul's terms for what he understands the Teachers to mean by ἐξ ἔργων νόμου.

This is precisely what is to be expected on the basis of my argument in Chapter 4 that Jewish νόμος was for Paul the particular νόμος that belonged to the Jewish people. The words νόμος and Ἰουδαϊκῶς, -ΐζειν, -ϊσμός and -ός are intimately connected for Paul, and it is consistent with this that in Gal 1:12 - 2:14 he should repeatedly try to shift the discussion from particular com-

---

55 See above, at nn. 16-17.

56 See above, "Intimations of νόμος in Gal 1:10 - 2:14."

57 For a similar conclusion, see Dunn, "New Perspective," 107-10; ibid., "Works of Law," 527. I think, however, that Dunn goes too far in dividing νόμος into one part (the cultic) which distinctively marks Jews, and another part which does not (ibid., 527-28); elsewhere (ibid., 526) Dunn himself remarks that νόμος as a whole "has this identity-affirming, boundary-marking function." This parallels my view that the term νόμος itself implies a link to a specific people; but in my view this link is not dependent on whether the νόμος or any part of it is perceived as "boundary-marking." Against Dunn, I do not think that Paul is especially concerned about νόμος "in its social function" (ibid., 531).

mandments to ᾽Ιουδαϊσμός. These are the terms that Paul sets for the discussion of νόμος in 2:15-21, and therefore in the balance of the letter.[58] The reconstruction of the original meaning of ἐξ ἔργων νόμου cannot be separated from the reconstruction of the Teachers' doctrine in general, a problem which goes well beyond the scope of this dissertation.[59] It is apparent, however, that the Galatians were being urged to obey certain commandments of Jewish νόμος, at least including circumcision (6:13), and probably others relating to the calendar (4:10);[60] the fulfillment of these commandments was described as ἔργα νόμου, and δικαιοσύνη was said to result from such fulfillment—as the Teachers put it, to result ἐξ ἔργων νόμου.

Thus οὐ δικαιοῦται ἄνθρωπος ἐξ ἔργων νόμου is an expression in partly borrowed language of what Paul might have said by οὐ δικαιοῦται ἄνθρωπος ᾽Ιουδαϊκῶς. Paul seems to presume that this principle will be granted by the congregations in Galatia; it resembles οὐκ ἔνι ᾽Ιουδαῖος οὐδὲ ῞Ελλην . . . πάντες γὰρ ὑμεῖς εἷς ἐστε ἐν Χριστῷ ᾽Ιησοῦ (3:28), which is often taken as a

---

[58] If I am right about the origin and use of the phrase ἐξ ἔργων νόμου in Galatians, then some of the difficulties in its subsequent interpretation are partly explained. Discussion has proved difficult on such matters as the grammatical link between ἔργα and νόμος—the question that inspired Ernst Lohmeyer's analysis of the phrase, even though in the end Lohmeyer ("Gesetzeswerk," 33-37, 73-74) had to leave the grammatical question unresolved. Perhaps this matter can be left with Robertson's observation (*Grammar*, 493): "The Specifying Case. It [the genitive] is this and no other. . . . It is the case of genus (γένος) or kind." To this Robertson adds (ibid., 493-94) that particular implications often emerge from different words and contexts; thus ἡ τοῦ πνεύματος βλασφημία (Matt 12:31) "is the 'Spirit-blasphemy.' From the context we know that it is blasphemy against the spirit, though the genitive does not mean 'against.'" ἔργα νόμου, similarly, are "law-works"; the rest is context.

Neither have convincing answers been provided to the related substantive questions: are ἔργα νόμου all of the works required by νόμος, or some of them? is the emphasis on ἔργα rather than on νόμου, so that the key is that these are *human* achievements? Some of the difficulty is a consequence of having the phrase preserved only in the writings of one to whom it did not come naturally, and who moreover had no need to clarify its meaning, for he knew it to be familiar to his audience.

[59] Lohmeyer's careful study of ἔργα νόμου ("Gesetzeswerk," esp. 38-58) might accordingly be turned to good account in a study of the Teachers' theology. This would require collation of Lohmeyer's work with other evidence from Galatians about the Teachers.

[60] Other commandments may also have been at issue, but I think it doubtful that food laws were; if they were, why doesn't Paul—with the Antioch incident for ammunition—refer to them directly? In any event, Gal 5:3 indicates that the Teachers were not advocating strict obedience to every commandment. It is left to Paul to observe that νόμος is a whole: you cannot be half-Jewish, either you are a Jew or you are not.

pre-Pauline baptismal formula that may have been common ground for all sides in Galatia.[61] This brings us to the third key phrase in 2:16, πίστις Χριστοῦ.[62] Here there are two basic theories: that the genitive is objective, so that the expression as a whole refers (like ἡμεῖς εἰς Χριστὸν Ἰησοῦν ἐπιστεύσαμεν) to what believers do; or that the genitive is subjective, the expression referring to what Christ did.[63] The general usage of πίστις with a noun in the genitive establishes that the subjective genitive is ordinary with πίστις; see, for example, Rom 3:3 (τὴν πίστιν τοῦ θεοῦ) and 4:16 (ἐκ πίστεως Ἀβραάμ).[64] That this understanding also fits Paul's use of πίστις Χριστοῦ has now been shown by Hays and Hooker;[65] in Hooker's words, "Believing faith depends on the faith/faithfulness of Christ: it is the response to Christ's faith, and claims it as one's own."[66] This interpretation is especially convincing for passages such as Rom 3:22, Gal 3:22 and Phil 3:9, for it recognizes meaning and not mere redundancy to the dual expressions "from faith"/"to faith" found in these verses. Gal 2:16 is less clear, since the expression (διὰ πίστεως / ἐπιστεύσαμεν) is not so clearly redundant; if Χριστοῦ is objective, Paul is saying, "We knew we had to believe, so we believed";[67] and indeed although Hays concludes that the subjective genitive is preferable everywhere except in Gal 2:16, there he finds the choice difficult.[68]

But we need not be so cautious; once it is established on the grammatical evidence that the standard meaning is subjective, an objective meaning can emerge only if (a) the phrase is shown to have the objective meaning either

---

[61] E.g., Betz, Galatians, 181-85. Whether the Teachers are part of this consensus is very difficult to say; but if they think δικαιοσύνη is the product of both πίστις and ἔργα νόμου, that might explain Paul's ambiguous statement of the relationship between these two in the first part of 2:16. The ambiguity allows the statement to appear acceptable to all.

[62] So 2:16c; in 2:16a the manuscripts vary between Ἰησοῦ Χριστοῦ and Χριστοῦ Ἰησοῦ, and in 2:20 the equivalent phrase is probably πίστις τοῦ υἱοῦ τοῦ θεοῦ κ.τ.λ. (although some important manuscripts read πίστις τοῦ θεοῦ). I do not see that there is any substantive difference among the three expressions; but the variations (including the variation between διὰ and ἐκ) do make it probable that the phrase, unlike ἐκ ἔργων νόμου, is Paul's own.

[63] A detailed discussion of the debate appears in Hays, Faith, 157-76; see also, more recently, Hooker, "ΠΙΣΤΙΣ."

[64] Howard, "On the 'Faith'"; Howard, "Faith"; Hays, Faith, 162-64. Hultgren ("Pistis Christou") has argued that the subjective genitive with πίστις requires the definite article; for a reply, see Williams, "Again Pistis," 431-36.

[65] Hays, Faith, 164-77; Hooker, "ΠΙΣΤΙΣ."

[66] Hooker, "ΠΙΣΤΙΣ," 340.

[67] But this is peculiar, although not redundant. Is it Paul's view that one believes because one knows one needs to?

[68] Hays, Faith, 175.

(i) in Paul's usual speech, or (ii) in the Galatians'; or (b) something in the immediate context requires the objective understanding. But if the phrase is subjective elsewhere in Galatians (2:20; 3:22) and Romans (3:22, 26) then grounds (a)(i) and (ii) are excluded; as we shall see, Gal 2:20 in particular shows that the subjective understanding is presumed in our text. We are left with ground (b), that 2:16 itself requires an objective understanding. This indeed is argued, on the ground that εἰς Χριστὸν 'Ιησοῦν ἐπιστεύσαμεν determines the meaning of πίστις Χριστοῦ.[69] But this is a non sequitur. If πίστις Χριστοῦ is subjective, then the argument runs something like: "Inasmuch as we are justified by Christ's faithful obedience to God, we trust in Christ [and do not rely on extraneous matters such as ἔργα νόμου]." The shift in the sense of the πιστ- root is not merely a rhetorical device, for there is a parallel between Christ's trust in God and ours in Christ.[70]

This gives a particular shape to the opposition between πίστις Χριστοῦ and ἔργα νόμου found in 2:16. If πίστις Χριστοῦ means "Christ's faithfulness," this faithfulness was pre-eminently exhibited in Christ's death on the cross, which Paul expressly mentions in 2:19 (Χριστῷ συνεσταύρωμαι), and links with πίστις Χριστοῦ in 2:20 (ἐν πίστει ζῶ τῇ τοῦ υἱοῦ τοῦ θεοῦ τοῦ ἀγαπήσαντός με καὶ παραδόντος ἑαυτὸν ὑπὲρ ἐμοῦ). But by this death, as Paul will say in Gal 3:13, Christ was accursed. Exactly at this point Christ did not live as a Jew—or, to put it in the language of 2:16, ἐξ ἔργων νόμου.

From this, however, it follows that ἔργα νόμου and πίστις Χριστοῦ oppose one another only in a certain respect, and that this opposition is not the same as that between ἔργα νόμου and πιστεύειν εἰς Χριστόν. ἔργα νόμου and πίστις Χριστοῦ are parallel grammatically and as competing principles of justification; these parallels dominate the rhetoric of 2:16 and tend to obscure the fact that ἔργα νόμου and πιστεύειν εἰς Χριστόν, which are parallel only as competing principles of action, do not compete in the same way. It may be

---

[69] E.g., Betz, Galatians, 117-18; Bruce, Galatians, 139.

[70] There has not been a recent full-scale defense of the objective interpretation of Χριστοῦ, but that interpretation has been so popular that more will surely be heard. Hooker ("ΠΙΣΤΙΣ," 321-24) has suggested that the objective interpretation reflects a fear lest the importance of believers' faith be undermined; she tries to quiet that fear.

One argument against the subjective interpretation is that Paul often uses people as the subject of πιστεύειν, but never Christ. Such a usage would certainly support the subjective interpretation, but its absence does not refute it; although (on the subjective interpretation) Paul could have replaced πίστις Χριστοῦ with a phrase resting on Χριστὸς ἐπιστεύσαμεν, any gain in clarity would have been paid for by a loss in compactness and felicity of expression. Moreover, some ground for attributing πίστις to Christ can be found in the references to his ὑπακοή (Rom 5:19; Phil 2:8); see Johnson, "Rom 3:21-26"; Hays, Faith, 166-67.

that one cannot trust in both ἔργα and Χριστός for justification; πιστεύειν εἰς Χριστόν and πιστεύειν εἰς ἔργα would then be an exact opposition. But Paul does not state the matter in this way in 2:16;[71] instead he seeks to establish a conflict between life ἐξ ἔργων νόμου and πιστεύειν εἰς Χριστόν, which are not inconsistent.[72]

The succeeding verses show, however, that inconsistency is central to Paul's argument. To establish an inconsistency Paul must take the argument in a different direction; but before we proceed, let us pause to recapitulate the argument to this point by paraphrasing Paul's train of thought in Gal 2:15-16:

> Galatians, there are some among you who are urging you to take up the life of the Jewish people—for this is what they mean by their phrase ἐξ ἔργων νόμου. Now in this matter you would do well to attend to the example of those who are born Jews, like me, and also Peter (one of the celebrated leaders of the church in Jerusalem—a pillar, as some call them). According to the exaggerated view which you are being encouraged to take of the Jewish way of life, we born Jews possess a remarkable advantage, being singled out from all of humanity, the only ones who are not sinners. Very well, then; let us grant for the moment that we as Jews have this advantage. You will agree to begin with that we Jews have recognized that our Jewish way of life is not adequate of itself to make us acceptable to God; we know—none better!—that we become acceptable only through Christ's faithful obedience to God. Therefore we have placed our trust in Christ, in order that we might be acceptable through Christ's faithful obedience, and not because we live as Jews; for no one is acceptable simply through living as a Jew.

---

[71] Probably the Teachers and the Galatians do not speak of πιστεύειν εἰς ἔργα.

[72] That is, not strictly inconsistent. One may say that, if one relies for justification on the faithfulness Christ exhibited while becoming a curse under νόμος, one ought not to think it important to live under νόμος oneself. But why should one not live that way—provided simply one understands that such a life is not necessary for justification?

One can fashion a strict opposition by interpreting the phrase ἐξ ἔργων νόμου to imply such a reliance on ἔργα νόμου that it is in fact inconsistent with πιστεύειν εἰς Χριστόν; see, e.g., Barrett (Romans, 70; emphasis in the original), taking ἔργα νόμου to mean "not good works simply, but works done in obedience to the law and regarded as, in themselves, a means of justification." But this is a dubious interpretation of the Greek phrase; moreover, it places too much weight on finding an inconsistency which Paul himself holds back from asserting, and which would not have been at all obvious either to the Teachers in Galatia or to those who were attracted to their teaching.

Verse 17

Rhetorically, verse 17 contrasts sharply with v. 16; in place of the enormous but balanced structure of the previous verse, now the argument proceeds dialectically: proposition, inference, denial.

εἰ δὲ ζητοῦντες δικαιωθῆναι ἐν Χριστῷ εὑρέθημεν καὶ αὐτοὶ ἁμαρτωλοί, ἆρα Χριστὸς ἁμαρτίας διάκονος; μὴ γένοιτο.

Here the subject, αὐτοὶ [ἡμεῖς], is evidently the φύσει Ἰουδαῖοι of vv. 15-16; ἁμαρτωλοί is also recalled from v. 15.

Our chief tasks here are specifying the relation between ἁμαρτωλοί and ἁμαρτία, and deciding whether μὴ γένοιτο denies the protasis or the apodosis of the preceding conditional sentence. My starting point is that the meaning of ἁμαρτωλοί here is determined by its meaning in 2:15; the term will not have abruptly altered its meaning without some clear indication of a shift, and there is none. A corollary is that the use in v. 15 establishes the sense in both vv. 15 and 17, for v. 15 is heard first.[73] Therefore, if in v. 15 ἁμαρτωλοί refers to what Gentiles rather than Jews do,[74] that is also what it refers to in v. 17.[75] The καὶ of καὶ αὐτοὶ also points in this direction: "we too," that is, we as well as the Gentiles. Finally, this follows from the argument of v. 16; for if "we" do not live ἐξ ἔργων νόμου, and if thus "we" live ἐθνικῶς rather than Ἰουδαϊκῶς, then "we" have crossed to the Gentile side of v. 15's classification. This provides an explanation for Paul's surprising use of the pejorative ἁμαρτωλοί for Gentiles in 2:15; there Paul's application of the term to Gentiles was part of a claim for the privilege and authority of born Jews, a privilege and authority which the Galatian teachers have claimed supports their view that we should live ἐξ ἔργων νόμου;[76] but now, this privilege and authority are turned against the Teachers' position: for φύσει Ἰουδαῖοι have themselves lived as Gentiles

---

[73] I do not mean that the use in v. 17 is irrelevant to establishing the meaning in v. 15; if that meaning is ambiguous v. 17 may provide some help in choosing among the possibilities left open by v. 15.

[74] See above, following n. 25.

[75] Against Betz, Galatians, 119-20; Schlier, Galater, 95. The Jew-Gentile distinction is so strong in v. 15, and the placement of ἁμαρτωλός on the Gentile side of that distinction is so clear, that the more general sense of ἁμαρτωλός has no occasion to emerge. Here too the general Jew-Gentile distinction of 2:12-14 (cf. also 2:3-10) helps to determine the meaning.

[76] We cannot be certain whether the Teachers would have put the matter this way; the identification between Ἰουδαῖοι φύσει and νόμος might be Paul's and not the Teachers'. But for Paul, understanding νόμος in the way I have described in Chapter 4, this connection is a matter of course.

rather than as Jews. Paul's use of ἁμαρτωλοί, not only here but in v. 15, now can be seen to be ironic.[77] One would expect the cognate ἁμαρτία to have an analogous meaning; but the change in word form allows Paul some flexibility. Moreover, μὴ γένοιτο suggests that the apodosis of v. 17 does not follow from the protasis, alerting the hearer to the possibility of a change in meaning from ἁμαρτωλοί (protasis) to ἁμαρτία (apodosis).[78] ἁμαρτία, unlike ἁμαρτωλοί, is therefore not bound by its context to Gentiles; it is rather "sin" in general, as elsewhere in Paul, which (in principle) either Gentiles or Jews may serve.[79]

But does μὴ γένοιτο deny the premise or the conclusion of v. 17? This depends on whether the sentence is a conditional question or a conditional assertion. These two types of conditional sentence may be illustrated from elsewhere in Paul: (1) a question, εἰ ἠπίστησάν τινες, μὴ ἡ ἀπιστία αὐτῶν τὴν πίστιν τοῦ θεοῦ καταργήσει; (Rom 3:3); (2) an assertion, εἰ δὲ ἀνάστασις νεκρῶν οὐκ ἔστιν, οὐδὲ Χριστὸς ἐγήγερται (1 Cor 15:13). In each case, as in Gal 2:17, the conclusion is rejected; but in the assertion the conclusion is put forth as a reductio ad absurdum of the premise, while in the question the premise is accepted, and only the inference from premise to conclusion is rejected. It is precisely the inference that a conditional question puts in issue:[80] if A is true, then is B true? Does A imply B? While a conditional question does not formally assert the truth of its premise, probably the premise is usually true, as it is in Rom 3:3; if the premise is false it usually will not matter what inferences could be drawn from it if it were true.

Now if Gal 2:17 is a question it requires an answer; and μὴ γένοιτο supplies one—as it also does to Rom 3:3 (see 3:4). If it is not a question μὴ γένοιτο seems superfluous; the refutation rests on the absurdity of the conclusion, and neither in 1 Cor 15:14 nor elsewhere when Paul argues by a conditional sentence incorporating a reductio ad absurdum does Paul expressly deny his premise.[81] One could explain μὴ γένοιτο by supposing that the conditional sentence is not a question put by Paul but rather the assertion of an

---

77 Fitzmyer, "Galatians," 784.

78 We shall see in a moment that this is not the only possible interpretation of μὴ γένοιτο. Nevertheless, the expression at least raises a question about the connection between the two clauses of v. 17.

79 Jewish sin is spoken of in, for example, Rom 3:9; 2:12.

80 Burton, Galatians, 128.

81 Rom 4:14; 1 Cor 15: 13, 15, 16, 17, 19, 29, 32; Gal 5:11. Neither does Paul put the condition of such sentences in the unreal form, which would signal the falseness of the premise; on the other hand, the use of the real form does not imply the truth of the premise. See Winger, "Unreal Conditions," 111.

objector (probably Peter), and μὴ γένοιτο is Paul's reply;[82] but this is implausible, not only because we cannot read the Antioch setting into 2:17 but because Paul gives his Galatian audience (which is his primary audience whatever the original source of 2:17) no hint of any such shift in person.[83]

Μὴ γένοιτο thus implies that 2:17 is a question,[84] and that the issue is whether or not the inference it suggests is valid; the premise, καὶ ἡμεῖς εὑρέθημεν ἁμαρτωλοί, is evidently accepted.[85] This is exactly what we would expect from our analysis of vv. 15-16: that 'Ιουδαῖοι φύσει, having decided not to live ἐξ ἔργων νόμου, that is, 'Ιουδαϊκῶς, have become ἁμαρτωλοί like the Gentiles.[86]

The rejected inference of 2:17 is evidently based on the resemblance between ἁμαρτωλοί in the premise and ἁμαρτία in the conclusion; but the resemblance is misleading. ἁμαρτία here, as elsewhere in Paul, has nothing to do with whether one is Jewish. Rather, it is a power;[87] sometimes it is virtually a person,[88] an entity which one might indeed serve.[89] The precise way in which Christ might be said to be ἁμαρτίας διάκονος is not developed; in terms of Paul's analysis elsewhere of ἁμαρτία, Bultmann is probably right when he says that the issue should be whether Christ frees one from sin, not whether

---

[82] Moule, *Idiom Book*, 196. The only non-Pauline use of μὴ γένοιτο in the New Testament, Luke 20:16, is in dialogue as a reply.

[83] It is often remarked that Paul only uses μὴ γένοιτο following questions; see, e.g., BDF, §§ 384, 440(2); Burton, *Galatians*, 126-27; Mussner, *Galater*, 176. On this, Bultmann ("Galater 2,15-18," 395 n.2) observes that there is no logical distinction between the rejection of an absurd question and the rejection of an absurd statement. But however that may be, there is a *rhetorical* distinction. Rhetorically, μὴ γένοιτο is a reply, and ordinarily to a question.

[84] The particle αρα introducing the main clause might have clarified the syntax; but, oddly enough, this particle has two alternative accents, ἆρα introducing a question and ἄρα introducing an inference (which, however, can also be a question, as in 2 Cor 1:17). As is often the case, the context illuminates the particle, rather than the particle the context.

[85] Although the premise is unchallenged it is not precisely affirmed; the sentence remains conditional. There are numerous examples, however, of conditional sentences in which the protasis evidently describes the real situation. See, for example, Gal 1:9, εἴ τις εὐαγγελίζεται παρ' ὃ παρελάβετε, and 2:14, εἰ σὺ 'Ιουδαῖος ὑπάρχων ἐθνικῶς ζῇς. In another place I have listed 39 evidently fulfilled conditions in Paul's seven undisputed letters (Winger, "If Anyone Preach," 46-47, 99); there are probably others whose truth was known to Paul and his audience, which we, not knowing the full context, cannot identify.

[86] Paul says "found" (εὑρέθημεν) rather than "became"; but I see no place in Paul where Paul uses εὑρίσκω with any suggestion that what is "found" is not true.

[87] See, for example, Gal 3:22 (συνέκλεισεν ἡ γραφὴ τὰ πάντα ὑπὸ ἁμαρτίαν) and Rom 6:12 (μὴ οὖν βασιλευέτω ἡ ἁμαρτία ἐν τῷ θνητῷ ὑμῶν σώματι).

[88] Rom 7:7 (χωρὶς γὰρ νόμου ἁμαρτία νεκρά).

[89] Paul does speak of serving ἁμαρτία, although his term for this is δοῦλος or δουλ[εύ/ό]ω (Rom 6:16, 17, 20) rather than διάκονος or διακονέω.

he brings one under sin.[90] But Paul is not developing such an argument here, only anticipating a conclusion which he supposes his audience might erroneously draw (or perhaps has already drawn).[91] Materially, it does not matter whether the term is actually on the lips of Paul's audience in Galatia or Paul merely puts it there; Paul himself denies it, and it would be pointless to over-analyze the reasons why someone else would affirm it.

Paul's argument in this verse has run:

So you see that, if you as Gentiles are "sinners," no less are we Jews, not only I but Peter. But what does this mean? That Christ produces sin? That is absurd!

But now Paul must explain why this is absurd.[92]

Verse 18

Verse 18 continues the argument of v. 17 with another conditional sentence:

εἰ γὰρ ἃ κατέλυσα ταῦτα πάλιν οἰκοδομῶ, παραβάτην ἐμαυτὸν συνιστάνω.

What is Paul talking about? I begin with the premise that he is supplying an explanation of μὴ γένοιτο; it surely requires one, and the γάρ at the beginning of this verse is a common prelude to an explanation.[93] The condition (εἰ γὰρ ἃ κατέλυσα ταῦτα πάλιν οἰκοδομῶ) should therefore be related to the situation under discussion: what Ἰουδαῖοι φύσει have done. Now the first person singular, new to this verse, focuses attention specifically on Paul,[94] but as he is himself a Jew by nature this does not change the terms of the discussion.[95] What have born Jews such as Paul broken down; what might

---

[90] Bultmann, "Galater 2,15-18," 395-96.

[91] Betz (*Galatians*, 120) suggests that the phrase Χριστὸς ἁμαρτίας διάκονος is in use at Galatia.

[92] Not everyone agrees that Paul gives such an explanation; see Lambrecht, "Line of Thought," proposing that 2:18 begins a new train of thought. It is a weakness in Lambrecht's thesis that he has Paul drop the argument of v. 17 without any explanation.

[93] Lambrecht, ("Line of Thought," 491) points out that γάρ may be "anknüpfend and fortführend." But this is not what the reader will be expecting here, and not, accordingly, what Paul is most likely to have provided. (On γάρ, see n. 114 below.)

[94] Against BDF (§281): "G2:18 (put as a real case [εἰ, not ἐάν], which, however, by no means applies to Paul . . ." This is confused; the condition does not imply that the subject *will* do this, only that he *could*; and this certainly applies to Paul.

[95] The first person singular is not emphatic here; perhaps it is meant to ease the transition to v. 19, where it is highly emphatic. Or Paul may drop the plural because many Jewish Christians (as Paul has recounted) have resumed life Ἰουδαϊκῶς; their rebuilding is actual. A stylistic reason for the singular is also possible; see below, at n. 98.

they build up again? An answer lies in two places: in vv. 15-16, where a general proposition is asserted, and in vv. 12-14, where a particular situation is described involving the proposition of v. 16. I have already equated the terminology of these verses, identifying ἐξ ἔργων νόμου of v. 16 with Ἰουδαϊκῶς of v. 14; both expressions describe what Jewish Christians ceased to do and then, according to vv. 13-14, took up again. In particular terms, this is the keeping of the Jewish food rules, but Paul eschews the particular. Verse 14 provides the most complete parallel, for in that verse Peter is accused of resuming what he had abandoned: building up what he had broken down.

But why is this rebuilding wrong? The form of v. 18 suggests that Paul draws on a general proposition,[96] the truth of which does not depend on the particular things one destroys and then rebuilds. Certainly it is stated as a general proposition. A similar Talmudic saying is noteworthy, and shows how such sayings may take a proverbial form:

אמרו לו כבר בנית ואי אתה יכול לסתור כבר גדרת ואי אתה
יכלו לפרוץ.

They said to him: You have already built and you cannot overthrow, you have made a fence and you cannot break it down.[97]

The use of the plural ἅ and the singular κατέλυσα and οἰκοδομῶ also tend to make the expression general.[98]

Understood as a general proposition, v. 18 implies that one should never reverse one's position. But we need to look more carefully at the effect of such a reversal, for it could be taken in at least two ways. As an inconsistency, a reversal of position might simply render one untrustworthy, so that neither of

---

[96] Notwithstanding the use of εἰ and the indicative mood, rather than ἐάν and the subjunctive. The division of conditions into simple and general according to the mood of the protasis (e.g., Smyth, Grammar, §§ 2298, 2335; Zerwick, Grammar, § 301; Burton, Moods, § 239) is dubious; contrast Robertson, Grammar, 1004-7; Schwyzer, Grammatik, 2.684; BDF, § 370. Paul often states a general condition in the indicative mood; see, e.g., εἰ βρῶμα σκανδαλίζει τόν ἀδελφόν μου, οὐ μὴ φάγω εἰς τὸν αἰῶνα (1 Cor 8:13). See further Winger, "If Anyone Preach," 14-20, 62-67.

[97] B. Ber. 63a, cited in Str-B, 3.537. The context is: when Hananiah the nephew of R. Joshua ben Hananiah began to intercalate years and fix new moons outside Palestine, two scholars were sent to him, whom he praised; but when they declared clean what he had declared unclean, he said they were worthless. They rebuked him in the language quoted.

The tradition is credited by R. Safra to R. Abbahu. According to Strack (Introduction, 113, 125), Hananiah was a second-generation Tanna (about 90-130 C.E.), and Abbahu a third-generation Amora; Strack does not list Safra.

[98] For the use of singular subjects in proverbial sayings, see Proverbs and Sirach, passim. Objects, however, may be plural (e.g., Sir 3:17, 23), and the sayings are thereby presumably more general.

one's positions has any authority. Alternatively, however, there may be grounds for giving priority to the first position, so that the reversal is held to be ineffective. This is what is implied in the Talmudic statement just quoted,[99] and also in a legal principle set out in *b. Sanh.* 44b: "Once a witness has testified, he cannot testify again."[100]

This argument is particularly forceful when applied to the renunciation of νόμος. One may, as did Paul himself, observe νόμος on some occasions and not on others; this suggests that one no longer treats it as νόμος, even when observing it; if the observance of certain practices is optional, the practices in question are no longer controlling (component 4) or a standard for judgment (component 5).

In 2:18, however, Paul does not refer to νόμος, but seems to base his argument on the more general presumption against recantation. That likewise seems to have been the principle relied on in Paul's question to Peter in Gal 2:14: πῶς τὰ ἔθνη ἀναγκάζεις ἰουδαΐζειν; Paul typically uses πῶς in a question in the sense of "how can," or "how will," with the implication that what is under discussion cannot or will not happen.[101] In Gal 2:14 I take Paul to be saying that Peter has no authority to require the Gentiles to Judaize; his own conduct amounts to a renunciation of Jewish life and deprives him of the authority to impose it on others. In 2:18 the point is generalized: the Jewish

---

[99] Above, at n. 95.

[100] The saying is an anonymous comment on a saying attributed to the sages. The context involves a change in testimony after sentence has been pronounced; it comes too late. (A change before sentence presumably disqualifies the witness's testimony; cf. *m. Sanh.* 5.3, which provides that the inconsistent testimony of two different witnesses renders both invalid.) In American jurisprudence the rule on recanted testimony is less sweeping, but in general recanted testimony remains valid; see for example the Illinois Supreme Court's formulation: "Recanting testimony is regarded as very unreliable, and a court will usually deny a new trial based on that ground where it is not satisfied that such testimony is true." *People v. Marquis,* 344 Ill. 261, 265, 176 N.E.2d 314, 315 (1931). On this ground a recent Illinois court, in a highly publicized case, declined to overturn a rape conviction despite the testimony of the supposed victim, six years after the trial, that she had fabricated the entire incident in order to explain her suspected pregnancy. *People v. Dotson,* 516 N.E.2d 718, 163 Ill.App. 419, 114 Ill.Dec. 563 (App.Ct.Ill., 1987).

This technical legal rule against recantation is not at stake in the case Paul presents, even if the rule goes back to Paul's time, and even if Paul knows the rule; but the principle behind the rule may be invoked—just as in *b. Ber.* 63a.

[101] E.g., οἵτινες ἀπεθάνομεν τῇ ἁμαρτίᾳ, πῶς ἔτι ζήσομεν ἐν αὐτῇ; (Rom 6:2). Cf. Rom 3:6; 8:32; 10:14a, b, c, 15; 1 Cor 14:7, 9, 16; 15:12; 2 Cor 3:8; Gal 4:9. Paul also uses πῶς neutrally, but less often, and then usually not in a question: Rom 4:10; 1 Cor 3:10; 7:32, 33, 34; 15:35; 1 Thess 1:9; 4:1; of which Rom 4:10 and 1 Cor 15:35 are questions.

Christians have, by their conduct, testified against ἔργα νόμου, and they cannot retract this testimony.[102] This suggests an answer to the puzzle left by 2:16: granting that justification is not ἐξ ἔργων νόμου but ἐκ πίστεως Χριστοῦ, why should we regard ἔργα νόμου and πίστις Χριστοῦ as opposed rather than complementary? The answer given in 2:18 does not lie in any inherent inconsistency of ἔργα and πίστις, but simply in the conduct of Paul, Peter, and Ἰουδαῖοι φύσει generally. They have in fact lived ἐθνικῶς while they sought δικαιοσύνη ἐκ πίστεως, and if Paul fails to show that it was necessary for them to do so, then this is not the point.[103] The point is that they—specifically including Peter and, as Paul now says, Paul himself—did live ἐθνικῶς, and this life, which cannot be revoked, condemns them if they require of Gentiles a life ἐξ ἔργων νόμου. Thus παραβάτην ἐμαυτὸν συνιστάνω in 2:18 is parallel to ὅτι κατεγνωσμένος ἦν in 2:11,[104] and 2:14 shows that it was Peter's former conduct which condemned his later conduct. In the language of 2:18, Paul's own καταλύειν would denounce him as a παραβάτης if he should build up ἔργα νόμου again.[105]

---

102 Note that the same principle could be turned against Paul's renunciation of Jewish life: one could say that he has no authority to do this. But for Paul, this is authorized by the revelation of Christ; it has nothing to do with his own authority. The principle against changing one's position is thus a limited one, invoked by Paul in a particular context. (In this it resembles all legal principles, which must always be weighed against one another in case of conflict.)

103 We can infer an explanation for Paul's life ἐθνικῶς—or ὡς ἄνομος—from 1 Cor 9:19-23, 10:23-33.

104 "Condemn" is the typical meaning of καταγιγνώσκω in Jewish literature; see, e.g., Deut 25:1: ἐὰν δὲ γένηται ἀντιλογία ἀνὰ μέσον ἀνθρώπων καὶ προσέλθωσιν εἰς κρίσιν καὶ κρίνωσιν καὶ δικαιώσωσιν τὸν δίκαιον καὶ καταγνῶσιν τοὺς ἀσεβοῦς ..., "if there is a dispute between people and they come to judgment, and [the judges] justify the righteous and condemn the wicked ..." Note, however, that the judicial setting of Deut 25:1 is not typical; see Josephus, J.W. 2.6.5 §135: ἤδη γὰρ κατεγνῶσθαί φασιν τὸν ἀπιστούμενον δίχα θεοῦ, "for they say that one who cannot be trusted without God [i.e., without taking an oath] is already condemned." If καταγιγνώσκω has a technical legal sense, its usual use does not depend on this sense.

105 Here it should be noted that both συνιστάνω and παραβάτης—and even καταλύω—are sometimes said to be legal terms; but if they are, the legal sense is not important in 2:18. καταλύω is relatively common (seventeen times in the New Testament), and its occasional use with τὸν νόμον as object does not (contra Betz, Galatians, 121 n.70) establish that any legal meaning adheres to καταλύω itself. If Paul really means Gal 2:18 to refer specifically to Jewish νόμος, his use of the general ἅ is surprising; moreover, in that case one would also expect another legal term in the second clause to balance καταλύω, but Betz concedes that οἰκοδομέω is not legal.

Συνιστάνω does have a technical legal sense, "to appoint [a representative]" seen in numerous of the Oxyrhynchus papyri: with an object, P.Oxy. I.94, 97; II.261, 320; absolute

To this point, Paul's response to the question of 2:17, whether Christ is ἁμαρτίας διάκονος, is to shift the terms of the discussion. He says, in substance, "Living ἐθνικῶς is not wrong (ἁμαρτία); to the contrary, returning to the life Ἰουδαϊκῶς which I have already left would be wrong (make me a παραβάτης)." Implicit in this is the proposition that ἁμαρτία is not to be defined (like ἁμαρτωλός) in relation to Jewish νόμος, but in relation to the conduct of those Jews (pre-eminently Paul) in whom Christ has been revealed.[106] How can such a major shift of authorities, from νόμος to particular Jews, take place silently?

If, as I have argued in both this and the preceding chapter, νόμος for Paul is defined in terms of Jews and Jews are defined in terms of νόμος, the shift from the authority of νόμος to the authority of Jews is less radical than appears at first. The usual understanding of νόμος depends on a scene in which νόμος and Jews are in agreement, and in that scene an appeal to the authority of either one is equally an appeal to the authority of the other. But

_____

(simply ὁ συνεσταμένος; it is this use which shows that the technical sense adheres to the term itself): II.243.1, 269.22, 329, 330, 331, 339, 349 (all first century C.E.) But this sense has no application in Gal 2:18; and while συνιστάνω is also found sometimes in connection with instituting or trying legal actions, this usage—as with καταλύω—is too sporadic and dependent on context to be technical. Thus Josephus twice uses the verb with δική as an object (J.W. 2.6.1 §80; Ant. 12.3.2 §126); but even in these two passages συνιστάνω and δική are not related in the same way; elsewhere Josephus uses δική 154 other times without συνιστάνω. The verb occurs 48 times in the LXX and fourteen other times in the New Testament (twelve in Paul, once in Colossians) without any suggestion of a legal sense.

With παραβάτης the issue is not so much technical usage as a fundamental semantic link with νόμος. This, in fact, can be demonstrated; a παραβάτης must be the transgressor of something, and this something is often νόμος (see Sir 19:24; 1 Esdr 8:24, 84; 3 Macc 7:12; Josephus, C.Ap. 2.176; Herm. Sim. 8.3.5; Euripedes, Ion, 231; Plato, Crito, 53E). The chief text is Rom 4:15: οὗ δὲ οὐκ ἔστιν νόμος οὐδὲ παράβασις. Moreover, παράβασις is distinguished from ἁμαρτία in precisely this respect: ἄχρι γὰρ νόμου ἁμαρτία ἦν ἐν κοσμῷ, ἁμαρτία δὲ οὐκ ἐλλογεῖται μὴ ὄντος νόμου (Rom 5:13). As a lexical mater, then, παράβασις implies νόμος, but ἁμαρτία does not.

But this is Rom 4-5; these ideas do not emerge in Galatians. Against Betz (Galatians, 121 n.71) and Bultmann ("Gal 2,15-18," 397), παραβάτης in 2:18 is unlikely to mean a violator of Jewish νόμος; the fact that Paul has just used ἁμαρτωλός in this sense makes it highly unlikely that he will use this second term in the same way. It is much more likely that Paul changes terms so that he can have one—παραβάτης—which is clearly negative (so Lightfoot, Galatians, 117).

Betz's contrary interpretation takes ἁμαρτωλός in 2:18 to mean, more generally, "living outside the realm of God's grace;" I think this unlikely for the reasons given above, in the text following n. 25. Moreover, Betz's interpretation depends on reading μὴ γένοιτο in v. 18 as a denial of the premise rather than the conclusion of the preceding conditional sentence; I have explained why I think this unlikely.

[106] In the language of Gal 1:16 (. . . ἀποκαλύψαι τὸν υἱὸν αὐτοῦ ἐν ἐμοί. . .).

behind Paul's discussion in Gal 2:18 lies something like the paradoxical formulations of Rom 2:25-29 which I discussed in Chapter 4; if Jewish νόμος refers to what Jews do, and what Jews do changes, what becomes of Jewish νόμος?[107] The situation no longer fits the scene on which our understanding of the term is based; νόμος is, so to speak, set over against itself. That Jewish life with which νόμος is associated, as exemplified in the lives of 'Ιουδαῖοι φύσει like Paul, Peter and Barnabas, is now opposed to those particular written expressions with which νόμος is also associated. Paul's claim that ἁμαρτία must be defined in terms of the former rather than the latter is not therefore an extraordinary one; only the situation is extraordinary.

The argument of 2:18 thus runs as follows:

> I insist: if you think that your relation with God depends on whether you have adopted a Jewish manner of life, consider those Jews by whose means Christ has been revealed to you. Jewish life is not what it was; it is something new, which you can see in our lives. How could I renounce this new life, by which I have borne witness to Christ among you? If I were to do so, that would truly make me a wrong-doer.

Verse 19

Verse 19 opens with an emphatic ἐγώ[108] which presses the argument on the authority of 'Ιουδαῖοι φύσει, and especially presses the appeal to Paul—but still to Paul as a Jew by birth:

ἐγὼ γὰρ διὰ νόμου νόμῳ ἀπέθανον, ἵνα θεῷ ζήσω.

The references to νόμος in the first clause of 2:19 make this argument more explicit; here νόμος is, paradoxically, an authority against νόμος. Paul states his position strongly, even extravagantly: διὰ νόμου νόμῳ ἀπέθανον. διὰ νόμου is difficult; is it *because* of νόμος, or even *by means* of νόμος, that Paul died to νόμος? Paul's words allow these suggestions, but he does not develop them, and his words can be taken in a weaker sense. Prepositions are notoriously difficult to translate, as the complexity of their lexical entries

---

[107] One could say that such people are no longer Jews; for Paul, however, they are: 'Ιουδαῖοι φύσει (2:15).

[108] ἐγώ is supernumerary to begin with, and it is further emphasized by its position at the beginning of the sentence. Compare the normal word order according to BDF (§472): verb, subject, object, supplementary participle, etc., but "any emphasis on an element in a sentence causes it to be moved forward . . ." Here every element of the main clause is pushed before the verb, and ἐγώ stands first of all.

suggests;[109] but although διὰ with the genitive can mean "by means of"[110] or "because of,"[111] Paul also uses it where neither instrument nor cause is likely, in what BAGD calls διὰ "of attendant circumstances."[112] Since the stronger senses are not explained or required by the context of 2:19,[113] the weak sense

---

[109] E.g., LSJ, s.v. διὰ A (with the genitive) (1 column, 14 senses); BAGD, s.v. διὰ A (with the genitive) (3 columns, 17 senses). The practical difficulties are much greater for those who have to rely on lexicons than for native speakers, however; English "by," for example, occupies 14 columns (93 senses) in the *Oxford English Dictionary*, but native speakers are not usually confused by the term in context.

[110] E.g., 1 Cor 14:9; Rom 5:10.

[111] The causal idea is usually conveyed by διὰ with the accusative, but it can be found with the genitive; e.g., Gal 5:13, and probably 3:18; Rom 5:11, 17a.

[112] BAGD s.v. διὰ, A.III.1.c; see, e.g., Rom 2:27 (. . . σὲ τὸν διὰ γράμματος καὶ περιτομῆς παραβάτην νόμου): but Paul does not seem to be saying that a Jew violates νόμος by means of or because of the letter and circumcision. BAGD also cites Rom 4:11; 8:25; 14:20; 2 Cor 2:4 (but not Gal 2:19).

[113] Attempts have been made to interpret διὰ νόμου in terms of what Paul says about νόμος later in Galatians, either the statement in 3:24 that νόμος was our παιδαγωγός (so Betz, *Galatians*, 122; Lightfoot, *Galatians*, 118), or the role of νόμος in Christ's death described in 3:13 (so Bläser, *Gesetz*, 225; Bruce, *Galatians*, 143; Bultmann, "Galater 2,15-18," 397; Fitzmyer, "Galatians," 785; Maurer, *Gestzeslehre*, 21; Moule, "Death," 372-73; van Dülmen, *Theologie*, 25-26; Schlier, *Galater*, 100). Neither of these roles fits 2:19 precisely, however; at best, the argument is that 2:19 draws out an implication of one or the other of these *later* passages which is *not* drawn out in the passage itself.

There are also some difficulties in drawing the necessary implications. According to 3:23-4:7, νόμος did not bring an end to its own role, which is what 2:19 implies. According to 3:13 νόμος cursed Christ but did not kill him, whereas 2:19 refers to death with Christ.

Burton, on the other hand (*Galatians*, 133; cf. Barrett, *Freedom*, 20; Mussner, *Galater*, 180; Ridderbos, *Galatians*, 104; Sanders, *Paul, the Law*, 83; Schlier, *Galater*, 99-100), interprets διὰ νόμου as a reference to Paul's own experience of life under νόμος as described in Rom 7. This is broadly consistent with my interpretation, but it is doubtful whether διὰ νόμου here could have suggested to the Galatians any of the particulars of Rom 7, and methodologically I think it is desirable to assume that Paul has designed his remarks to be understood by his audience. Räisänen (*Paul*, 58) suggests "the general and somewhat vague idea that [the law] point[ed] to Christ as the redeemer . . ."; this also cannot be shown from this letter.

Another possibility is to take the νόμος of διὰ νόμου to be something other than Jewish νόμος; thus Luther (*Works*, 26.155) supposes that Paul means "grace," and Neitzel ("Galater 2,11-21," 138) that he means "faith." These theses are especially intriguing in light of the use of παραβάτης in the previous verse; since παραβάτης implies a νόμος which has been transgressed (see above, n. 105), 2:18 suggests that a return to ἔργα νόμου would violate some higher νόμος. I think, however, that the absence of any clear reference to such a νόμος in the proximate context (Neitzel finds it necessary to look to Gal 6:2 and Rom 3:27; 8:2) makes this explanation of 2:19 unlikely.

is indicated; ἐγώ διὰ νόμου is then a way of saying, "I, having νόμος," which amounts to "I as a Jew." In short, Paul repeats the point made in 2:15.[114]

Following διὰ νόμου, the expression νόμῳ ἀπέθανον puts the contrast between Paul's Jewish past and his present relation to Judaism in the strongest possible way. The reference to death hyperbolically repeats the assertion of 2:18 that Paul cannot go back to what he has left behind; he has passed from that world to the next.[115] This passage from world to world is part and parcel of Paul's δικαιοσύνη, as the following clause (ἵνα θεῷ ζήσω) implies. There are three successive paradoxical contrasts in 2:19, thus:

$$\text{ἐγὼ γὰρ}$$

διὰ νόμου	νόμῳ ἀπέθανον
νόμῳ ἀπέθανον	ἵνα θεῷ ζήσω
ἵνα θεῷ ζήσω	Χριστῷ συνεσταύρωμαι.[116]

This jarring succession of thoughts returns in a different way to the issue left at the end of 2:16: why is it that πίστις Χριστοῦ and ἔργα νόμου conflict? Verses 17 and 18 develop one answer, which the beginning of v. 19 also develops, that in fact Paul and other Jewish Christians such as Peter have severed πίστις Χριστοῦ from ἔργα νόμου. Taken as a whole, v. 19 shows the sharp contrast between the two worlds presented by Paul's own experience, a contrast introduced in Gal 1:13-16: the old world of Ἰουδαϊσμός, the new world of ἀποκάλυψις τοῦ υἱοῦ θεοῦ. Here Paul says: νόμῳ ἀπέθανον ἵνα θεῷ ζήσω. Death to νόμος was necessary for life to God. Why? Paul himself merely asserts this and then changes the subject; there is perhaps the implicit premise that if one lives for X one cannot also live for Y (cf. Matt 6:24, Luke 16:13); we also know from Gal 1:13-16, among other places, that this was Paul's own

---

[114] This takes v. 19 to restate the thought of v. 18, not to explain it. One issue which has troubled commentators is the interpretation of γάρ here; if it gives, as BAGD (s.v. 1) say, "cause or reason," for what does it do? This is a blind alley; particles like prepositions are so protean that they are poor guides to the flow of the argument; BAGD (s.v. 4) also allows the vague sense "expressing continuation or connection." See Robertson (*Grammar*, 1191): "The precise relation between clauses or sentences is not set forth by γάρ. That must be gathered from the context if possible." This insight underlies the method of Denniston (*Particles*, 56-98). who outlines a variety of senses for γάρ based upon its actual usage; for instance, "Successive γάρ's [as in Gal 2:18, 19] have the same reference" (ibid., 64).

[115] Scroggs, *Christology*, 26.

[116] We may note here how close Paul is to the prosaic. Had he said διὰ νόμου θεῷ ζῶ few Jews would have taken exception; and in his own way, of course, Paul does say this (did the Teachers use such a phrase?). But the insertion of the intervening νόμῳ ἀπέθανον complicates Paul's statement considerably.

experience.[117] For Paul, Judaism was not neutral to the church; it was a measure of Paul's zeal for Judaism that he persecuted the church (Gal 1:13-14; Phil 3:6). Not until Paul had abandoned his zeal for the ancestral traditions (Gal 1:13-16) did he live to God.

Paul's own experience is tied also to the Galatians' experience, for it was Paul who brought the gospel to the Galatians—a circumstance to which he has alluded in 1:6-9, and which he will recall again in a moment (3:1). Paul expands his portrayal of his experience in the concluding phrases of 2:19 (ἵνα θεῷ ζήσω· Χριστῷ συνεσταύρωμαι); here his life/death language not only sharpens the contrast of old and new, it sets up the reference to crucifixion at the end of 2:19, which leads in turn to the account of πίστις Χριστοῦ in Paul's life in the following verse.

Thus in v. 19 Paul has argued in the following fashion:

I myself am a Jew, and I have put aside that Jewish life which you now wish to take up. I did this in order to take up the work to which God called me, the proclamation of the gospel among Gentiles such as you; and in putting Jewish life aside I in fact followed the pattern of our Lord.

Verse 20

Here a chain of remarks, each clarifying that which precedes it,[118] reaches its climax in an extended and virtually credal[119] formulation.

ζῶ δὲ οὐκέτι ἐγώ, ζῇ δὲ ἐν ἐμοὶ Χριστός· ὃ δὲ νῦν ζῶ ἐν σαρκί, ἐν πίστει ζῶ τῇ τοῦ υἱοῦ τοῦ θεοῦ τοῦ ἀγαπήσαντός με καὶ παραδόντος ἑαυτὸν ὑπὲρ ἐμοῦ.

In particular, ζῇ δὲ ἐν ἐμοὶ Χριστός is amplified by the balance of the verse, for Christ lives in Paul in the sense that πίστις Χριστοῦ enables Paul to

---

[117] Cf. Gaventa ("Autobiography," 318): "[Paul] sees in his experience a paradigm of the singularity of the gospel, and he uses his experience to call the Galatians into that singularity in their own faith-lives."

Another intriguing text with an autobiographical dimension is 1 Cor 1:18: Ὁ λόγος γὰρ ὁ τοῦ σταυροῦ τοῖς μὲν ἀπολλυμένοις μωρία ἐστίν, τοῖς δὲ σῳζομένοις ἡμῖν δύναμις θεοῦ ἐστιν. The word of the cross is either foolishness or power; one is either perishing or being saved—there is no middle ground. And how does Paul know about these sharply divided experiences? Presumably he—once among the perishing, now among those being saved—has experienced them.

[118] Thus, "crucified with Christ" is clarified by "I no longer live," "I no longer live" by "Christ lives in me," and this by "what I live . . ."

[119] Cf. 1 Cor 15:3 (ἀπέθανεν ὑπὲρ τῶν ἁμαρτιῶν ἡμῶν); see Mussner, Galater, 183.

endure the tribulations of life ἐν σαρκί.[120] Although Paul does not expressly refer to tribulations here, it is clear from the Corinthian correspondence (1 Cor 4:9-13; 2 Cor 1:4; 11:23-29; 12:7-10) that Paul considered bodily tribulations to be an important feature of his apostolic mission, and clearly Paul understands his life ἐν σαρκί to mean essentially his apostolic mission.[121] Probably these sufferings are alluded to here by Χριστῷ συνεσταύρωμαι in 2:19;[122] the analogy between Paul's and Jesus' sufferings, explicit in Phil 3:10,[123] is suggested not only by the term συνεσταύρωμαι but by the depiction of Christ in 2:20: τοῦ ἀγαπήσαντός με καὶ παραδόντος ἑαυτὸν ὑπὲρ ἐμοῦ. In this context πίστις . . . τοῦ υἱοῦ τοῦ θεοῦ is most naturally read as subjective. First, the subjective reading makes a logical connection with the preceding sentence; Paul explains that by "Christ lives in me" he means "the faith of Christ lives in me." Second, the descriptive phrases in apposition to "son of God" explain how this faith lives in Paul: Christ's faithfulness, which was exhibited in the death to which he went for the sake of those he loved, is seen also (as through a glass, darkly) in Paul's apostolate for the sake of the Galatians.

Verse 20 may thus be paraphrased:

Truly, I am no longer the individual I once was, to whom, as I have said, the traditions and practices of my people were so important. That person has passed away; in me, that human pattern of existence to which you now aspire has been replaced by existence in the pattern set by the Son of God, who out of His love for me gave Himself for me, as I have loved you and given myself for you.

Verses 19 and 20, with their language of life and death setting up Paul's reference to Christ's crucifixion and then to πίστις Χριστοῦ, have prepared also for Paul's allusion in 3:1 to the Galatians' experience of Paul's own preaching of Christ crucified. But before turning to this Paul turns back again to νόμος.

---

[120] ἐν πίστει may be instrumental, as ἐν often is; see BAGD, s.v. III; BDF §195.

[121] Cf. Phil 1:23-24: although it would be much better for Paul to be with Christ, τὸ δὲ ἐπιμένειν ἐν τῇ σαρκὶ ἀναγκαιότερον δι' ὑμᾶς.

[122] Many commentators take this for a reference to baptism (Schlier, Galater, 99-101; Mussner, Galater, 180-81; Bläser, Gesetz, 225); but see Barrett (Freedom, 20): ". . . it seems to me a striking fact that Paul does not mention baptism."

[123] . . . τοῦ γνῶναι . . . τὴν κοινωνίαν τῶν παθημάτων αὐτοῦ, συμμορφιζόμενος τῷ θανάτῳ αὐτοῦ . . . Cf., without reference to sufferings, 1 Cor 11:1: μιμηταί μου γίνεσθε καθὼς κἀγὼ Χριστοῦ.

Verse 21

A break in the discourse is signalled here by the absence of a connective particle:[124]

οὐκ ἀθετῶ τὴν χάριν τοῦ θεοῦ· εἰ γὰρ διὰ νόμου δικαιοσύνη, ἄρα Χριστὸς δωρεὰν ἀπέθανεν.

In this verse Paul sharpens the opposition between νόμος and Christ implied in 2:16, but there stated in terms of ἔργα νόμου and πίστις Χριστοῦ; here the opposition is directly between νόμος and Christ. To arrive at this opposition, which concludes our pericope and creates the transition to the extended discussion of Christ in Gal 3, Paul takes up a charge, real or imagined, that he nullifies ἡ χάρις τοῦ θεοῦ.[125] χάρις should be translated "gift," to avoid the usual modern implications of the term "grace." Paul uses χάρις in the general sense of "gift" when discussing the collection for Jerusalem,[126] and further, if Paul is here responding to others, the usage is probably not his own. The transition to the conditional sentence in 2:21b is best explained if "God's gift" is a term which the Teachers in Galatia use for νόμος.[127]

The terms ἀθετῶ, τὴν χάριν and δωρεάν are plays on a common theme, conveyed by translating v. 21:

> I do not make nothing what God gave for nothing; rather, if rectification is through νόμος, *then* Christ died for nothing.

That is, God's gift—as the participle παραδόντος in 2:20 has already suggested—is Christ crucified.[128] The plays on "nothing" serve to suggest the

---

124 On such asyndeton, see nn. 14-15 above.

125 Although this charge may be real, it proves so convenient to Paul's purposes that I suspect he has manufactured it; but (as will be seen) he has employed the Teachers' terminology to do so.

126 See especially 1 Cor 16:3; in 2 Cor 8:4, 6, 7, 19 the precise sense is less clear. For general usage, see LSJ, s.v. III. There are many examples in Sirach: 3:31, 7:33, 8:19; 17:22; 19:25.

127 But ἀθετῶ is probably Paul's word. Although this is often a legal term (see Gal 3:15, διαθήκην οὐδεὶς ἀθετεῖ) that is accordingly suitable for νόμος, νόμος is the referent rather than the meaning of χάρις. Thus the expression ἀθετῶ τὴν χάριν, by focussing on the referent of χάρις, undercuts the meaning: that νόμος is a gift. This language therefore serves Paul's purposes rather than the Teachers'.

Schlier (*Galater*, 104) thinks that χάρις may refer either to νόμος or specifically to circumcision. The latter seems improbable to me; certainly this was an issue in Galatia, but I see no reason to think that the Teachers so elevated this one point as to make it (to the exclusion of the rest of νόμος) ἡ χάρις τοῦ θεοῦ.

128 Or perhaps: what God gave is Christ, and the free gift is accomplished by the crucifixion.

high stakes: this is not, in Paul's view, a matter of a little of this and a little of that, but of this or that: all or nothing.

Implicit in this argument is the premise that Christ would not have died unless justification was otherwise impossible. One basis for this premise is the shocking nature of Christ's death on the cross, to which Paul refers in the next verse: Ὦ ἀνόητοι Γαλάται . . . οἷς κατ' ὀφθαλμοὺς Ἰησοῦς Χριστὸς προεγράφη ἐσταυρωμένος . . .[129] With this address Paul also appeals to the Galatians' own experience, in a way analagous to his appeal in 2:17-19 to his own experience and that of Ἰουδαῖοι φύσει in general: like the Jews, the Galatians have in fact received the spirit not ἐξ ἔργων νόμου (Gal 3:2, 5) but from Christ.[130]

We may thus paraphrase Paul's conclusion to our text:

You have been told that the practices of the Jewish people are a gift of God, and you have been warned not to treat that gift lightly. Galatians, you have been misled. It is very true that God's gift is of the utmost importance; but God's true gift is the gift of His Son, Jesus Christ. It is not I who trifle with God's gift; it is those who tell you that to satisfy God you must take up a Jewish life. For if this is so, then God's gift of Christ—Christ's horrible death upon the cross— was just an idle gesture.

Paul thus ends with the conclusion that δικαιοῦσθαι is not διὰ νόμου— almost the point at which he began: οὐ δικαιοῦται ἄνθρωπος ἐξ ἔργων νόμου (2:16). Just as the first formulation was based on the Teachers' vocabulary (ἐξ ἔργων νόμου), so also is the last; the Teachers' use of ἡ χάρις τοῦ θεοῦ has allowed Paul to move from ἔργα νόμου and πίστις Χριστοῦ to νόμος and Χριστός, and thus to state the opposition in the sharpest possible way: νόμος or Christ?

Verses 15-21 Translated

I have accompanied my exegesis of Gal 2:15-21 with highly paraphrastic renderings of each verse. A more literal translation, which better reflects the connection between Paul's Greek and my interpretation, will now be useful as a summary:

---

[129] Cf. 1 Cor 1:23: ἡμεῖς δὲ κηρύσσομεν Χριστὸν ἐσταυρωμένον, Ἰουδαίοις μὲν σκάνδαλον, ἔθνεσιν δὲ μωρίαν . . .

[130] On this point Paul employs a variety of terminology: speaking of the Galatians, Χριστὸς προεγράφη ἐσταυρωμένος (Gal 3:1) and ἐξ ἀκοῆς πίστεως (3:2, 5); of the Corinthians, κηρύσσομεν Χριστὸν ἐσταυρωμένον (1 Cor 1:23); of himself, ἀποκαλύψαι τὸν υἱὸν αὐτοῦ ἐν ἐμοί (Gal 1:16).

15 We who are Jews by birth, and not Gentile sinners, 16 know that a person is not rectified by life according to Jewish practice, but through the faith of Jesus Christ. Therefore we too [like the Gentiles] trusted in Christ Jesus, so that we might be rectified by the faith of Christ and not by our Jewish way of life; for no flesh is rectified by the Jewish way of life.

17 Now, if we too, as we seek rectification through Christ, are found to be sinners [like the Gentiles], does this mean that Christ produces sin? Certainly not! 18 Rather, if I were to build up again the [way of life] which I had destroyed, this [rebuilding] would make me a transgressor.

19 I, although myself a Jew, have died so far as Jewish practice is concerned, in order to live so far as God is concerned. I have been crucified with Christ; 20 I myself live only so far as Christ lives within me. My physical existence continues by means of the faith which the Son of God had, the Son of God who loved me and gave himself for me.

21 I do not make nothing what God gave for nothing; rather, if rectification comes through Jewish practice, *then* Christ died for nothing.

Results

My rendering of Gal 2:15-21 rests upon the following interpretations:

(1) Gal 2:15-21 appears in a context which has raised the broad issue of Jewish conduct, and implied that this is a matter of human tradition rather than divine revelation.

(2) The passage is not a part of Paul's speech to Peter at Antioch, but is Paul's discussion of the implications for the Galatians of all that he has recounted from 1:10 through 2:14.

(3) Paul begins in 2:15-16 by making a special claim for the authority of Ἰουδαῖοι φύσει, referring to Jewish Christians such as himself and Peter.

(4) Paul claims that this authority supports the entire introductory participial clause of 2:16, εἰδότες ὅτι οὐ δικαιοῦται ἄνθρωπος ἐξ ἔργων νόμου ἐὰν μὴ διὰ πίστεως Ἰησοῦ Χριστοῦ.

(5) The phrase ἐξ ἔργων νόμου:

(a) is not Paul's own, but is borrowed from the Teachers at Galatia;

(b) is interpreted by Paul to mean, broadly, Ἰουδαϊκῶς, "by doing as Jews do," and is not limited to specific issues, such as circumcision or purity, that may have been under discussion in Galatia.

(6) πίστις Χριστοῦ is subjective, referring to the πίστις which Christ had in God.

(7) 2:17 is a question, not a statement, of which the conclusion (not the premise) is denied.

(8) 2:18 refers to the conduct of Jewish Christians (including although not limited to Paul) in living ἐθνικῶς; the concluding clause (παραβάτην ἐμαυτὸν συνιστάνω) asserts that this conduct gives a witness against living Ἰουδαϊκῶς which remains valid even if Jewish Christians like Peter and Barnabas take up Jewish life again (ταῦτα πάλιν οἰκοδομῶ).

(9) Paul thus invokes, against the authority of Jewish **νόμος**, the authority of Jews. 2:19ab is another statement of this opposition: Paul, a Jew, has learned and demonstrated that Jewish life is not required.

(10) 2:20, like 2:16, appeals to the faith which Christ had in God, and displayed specifically in his giving of himself; Paul asserts that he lives by this same faith.

(11) In 2:21 Paul asserts that ἡ χάρις τοῦ θεοῦ is not the pattern of life contained in νόμος, as the Teachers claim, but rather Christ.

Within these conclusions are specific interpretations of several uses of νόμος (ἐξ ἔργων νόμου, διὰ νόμου νόμῳ ἀπέθανον, εἰ γὰρ διὰ νόμου δικαιοσύνη).[131] More generally, my exegesis confirms:

(1) that νόμος in this passage refers to Jewish νόμος.[132]

(2) that here Paul sees Jewish νόμος in essentially human terms, as the *way of life* of the Jewish people rather than the *command* of God.

---

[131] See points 5, 9, 11.

[132] Only in 2:19a, where νόμος could refer to a higher νόμος implied by the term παραβάτης in 2:18, was there any reason to doubt this. See above, nn. 105, 113.

Chapter 6

Νόμος IN ROMANS 7:14-25

Romans 7:1 - 8:11 offers a major test for any understanding of the term νόμος in Paul's letters. Here νόμος is found 28 times in 36 verses. Some take the discussion here—and especially that in 7:14-25—to be the core of Paul's analysis of why νόμος does not save, or justify;[1] but whether or not this is so, the varied uses of this term here provide an abundance of material for the analysis of its meaning and of its references, and of how its meaning and references function in Paul's argument. Here, precisely at what appears to be a climactic point in Paul's argument, appears the greatest concentration in his letters of references to νόμος (Jewish or otherwise):

εὑρίσκω ἄρα τὸν νόμον, τῷ θέλοντι ἐμοὶ ποιεῖν τὸ καλόν, ὅτι ἐμοὶ τὸ κακὸν παράκειται. συνήδομαι γὰρ τῷ νόμῳ τοῦ θεοῦ κατὰ τὸν ἔσω ἄνθρωπον, βλέπω δὲ ἕτερον νόμον ἐν τοῖς μέλεσίν μου ἀντιστρατευόμενον τῷ νόμῳ τοῦ νοός μου καὶ αἰχμαλωτίζοντά με ἐν τῷ νόμῳ τῆς ἁμαρτίας τῷ ὄντι ἐν τοῖς μέλεσίν μου. (Rom 7:21-23)[2]

---

[1] According to Bultmann ("Romans 7," 147), Romans 7 as a whole analyzes "the general situation of man under the law." In contrast, Sanders (*Paul, the Law*, 73-81) concludes that Rom 7:7-13 and 7:14-8:5 offer different, inconsistent accounts of the relation between law and sin, and that both of these accounts compete with still another account given at Gal 3:22-24 and Rom 5:20f.

[2] I have identified νόμος in 7:21 as a singular definite reference to a non-Jewish νόμος—namely, the νόμος specified by the following ὅτι-clause (Chapter 3, at nn. 74-75). In 7:22, 23a, b and c the phrase with νόμος specifies one νόμος out of a broader category of

Usually these five νόμος-expressions are taken to refer to only two distinct νόμοι, or even to the single Jewish νόμος. But I will argue in this chapter that this description of five battling νόμοι is to be taken seriously: it is precisely the multiplicity of these νόμοι, and their internecine warfare, which account for Paul's miserable (ταλαίπωρος [7:24]) condition. Paul's expressions are metaphorical, to be sure, and the metaphors are not fixed: after the lament of 7:24, Paul summarizes his state more concisely in 7:25b, this time with only two νόμοι: "Αρα οὖν αὐτὸς ἐγὼ τῷ μὲν νοΐ δουλεύω νόμῳ θεοῦ τῇ δὲ σαρκὶ νόμῳ ἁμαρτίας. Nevertheless, we shall see that the metaphors make a point about the nature of νόμος, and about the limitations of Jewish νόμος.

I shall also take issue with the prevailing interpretation of Romans 7 at a second point: I hold that when Paul uses the first person and the present tense, as he does (often emphatically) throughout 7:14-25, he is speaking about himself and about his condition at the time he writes. Various nuances of interpretation necessarily follow from this conclusion; some will prove to shed light on Paul's understanding of νόμος.[3]

Over all, the 28 occurrences of νόμος in Rom 7:1 - 8:11 include: fifteen with a clear or probable reference to Jewish νόμος;[4] ten with what I have called implicit general reference, expressions such as those in 7:22-23 with νόμος and another qualifying term (usually a noun in the genitive) implying the existence of some broader category of νόμος;[5] one reference to a νόμος whose content is evidently specified by the following clause;[6] and two references to a specific νόμος, ὁ νόμος τοῦ ἀνδρός, which may or may not be

---

νόμοι; I have said that νόμος itself thus makes an implicit general reference to this category of νόμοι (ibid., at nn. 17-23); what specific νόμοι are identified by these phrases (whether or not Jewish) I have not yet attempted to say. All of this I discuss further below, in the exegesis of 7:21-23.

[3] My basic arguments about the meaning and references of νόμος in Rom 7:14-25 do not depend on my understanding of ἐγώ. The meaning of ἐγώ is central, however, to the meaning of Rom 7 as a whole.

My departures from the usual view of Rom 7 partly reflect my starting point. The most influential writers on Rom 7, Bultmann, Bornkamm and Käsemann, come to this chapter with analyses of νόμος and sin, life and death, based on what Paul says about these subjects in other passages; much of their understanding of Rom 7 actually depend on this other material and not on the exegesis of Rom 7 itself (see, e.g., nn. 88, 90, 91 below). I, in contrast, have begun with Rom 7; I try to understand what this chapter is likely to have conveyed to Paul's audience, drawing on other parts of Romans only when their relation to this passage is clear.

[4] Clear: Rom 7:7b, c, 12, 14; 8:4; probable: 7:1a, b, 4, 5, 6, 7a, 8, 9, 16; 8:3.

[5] Rom 7:2b, 22, 23a, b, c, 25a, b; 8:2a, b, 7. These are ten out of Paul's fifteen implicit general references. 7:23a is ἕτερος νόμος, and the others are all genitival constructions.

[6] Rom 7:21: τὸν νόμον . . . ὅτι ἐμοὶ τὸ κακὸν παράκειται.

Jewish.[7] In all, five of the six kinds of reference I outline at the beginning of Chapter 4 are found in Rom 7:1 - 8:11.[8] The entire passage from 7:1 through 8:11 is, however, too long for detailed analysis here. A manageable passage is 7:14-25, culminating with the manifold uses of νόμος which I have just quoted. In these twelve verses νόμος appears nine times, twice with a clear or probable reference to Jewish νόμος,[9] six times with implicit general reference to unspecified νόμοι,[10] and once to a νόμος of specified content.[11] The precise beginning of this passage can be disputed; several text editions, translations and commentaries begin a new paragraph with v. 13 instead of v. 14,[12] but most recognize a paragraph break between vv. 13 and 14,[13] and many treat 7:14-25 as a distinct unit.[14] This division corresponds to the shift from the aorist tense which Paul uses in vv. 7-13 to the present tense employed in vv. 14-25; the point need not be pressed, however, for due attention must in any event be given to the context surrounding the passage under particular consideration. I shall want in particular to note the use of the phrases ὁ νόμος τοῦ πνεύματος τῆς ζωῆς, ὁ νόμος τῆς ἁμαρτίας καὶ τοῦ θανάτου and ὁ νόμος τοῦ θεοῦ in 8:2 and 7, resembling as they do expressions found in 7:22, 23 and 25. But it will be possible to analyze these kindred phrases without resolving every issue in 8:1-11.

The Setting of Rom 7:14-25

Our text comes roughly midway through Romans. Already Paul has had a great deal to say about νόμος;[15] from this prior discussion, three general points can be noted. The first relates to the general usage of νόμος to this point in Romans; the second, to the specific connections between νόμος and ἁμαρτία, which give the immediate occasion for the discussion in 7:7-25; the

---

[7] Rom 7:2a, 3. For the meaning of this phrase, see further n. 178.

[8] The only kind of reference not found in this passage is reference to a hypothetical different Jewish νόμος; this reference appears only in Gal 3:21 (εἰ γὰρ ἐδόθη νόμος ὁ δυνάμενος ζῳοποιῆσαι . . .)

[9] 7:14, 16.

[10] 7:22, 23a, b, c, 25a, b.

[11] 7:21.

[12] UBS[3]; AV, RSV, NAB; Cranfield, Romans, 1.340; Lagrange, Romains, 171; Wilckens, Römer, 2.83.

[13] Nestle-Aland[26]; NEB, JB, NJB, TEV; Barrett, Romans, 139; Dunn, Romans, 1.375; Sanday and Headlam, Romans, 177.

[14] Käsemann, Romans, 198-212; Kuss, Römer, 2.451-61; Murray, Romans, 256-73; Nygren, Romans, 284-303; Schlier, Römer, 228-35.

[15] νόμος appears 54 times from 1:1 through 7:13 (beginning in 2:12).

third, to the association in the immediately preceding passage, 7:7-13, of νόμος with ἐντολή.[16]

Νόμος in Rom 1:1 - 7:13: A Summary

In the great majority of the places where νόμος appears in Rom 1:1 - 7:13 it clearly or probably refers to Jewish νόμος;[17] but six passages depend on an indefinite, a general or a generic reference.[18] Rom 4:15b and 5:13b are especially important, for they establish not only that Paul knows of a generic sense of νόμος—which we could have assumed—but also that he uses this sense in argument: οὖ δὲ οὐκ ἔστιν νόμος οὐδὲ παράβασις (4:15b) and ἁμαρτία δὲ οὐκ ἐλλογεῖται μὴ ὄντος νόμου (5:13b).[19]

All of these references are active possibilities for νόμος in Romans. Paul's interest, however, is in Jewish νόμος, and not in νόμος as such. In Rom 7:7-13, which immediately precedes our text, the reference to Jewish νόμος is established by the quotation from the Septuagint in 7:7: τήν τε γὰρ ἐπιθυμίαν ἤδειν εἰ μὴ ὁ νόμος ἔλεγεν· οὐκ ἐπιθυμήσεις.[20] In view of Rom 1:1 - 7:13 as a whole, and of 7:7-13 in particular, there can hardly be any doubt that οἴδαμεν

---

[16] One much-disputed issue in the analysis of Romans is the occasion of the letter; see generally (besides the commentaries) Donfried, *Romans Debate*, and, more recently, Jewett, "Ambassadorial Letter"; Bruce, "Romans Debate"; Theobald, "Warum schrieb?"; Stuhlmacher, "Abfassungszweck"; Wedderburn, *Reasons for Romans*; and Marcus, "Circumcision." Many writers, including Donfried (*Romans Debate*, 120-49), Stuhlmacher ("Abfassungszweck") and Marcus ("Circumcision"), have argued cogently that in Rom 14:1-15:6 Paul addresses actual conflicts between Gentile and Jewish Christians in Rome relating to the observance by Gentiles of certain parts of Jewish νόμος; on this view, Paul in effect encourages the Gentiles ("the strong") to follow Jewish practices so as not to make their Jewish brothers and sisters ("the weak") stumble. If this is so, this reflects an attitude to νόμος different from that which appears in Galatians (where, however, the principal issue was evidently circumcision); this difference is reflected elsewhere in Romans in certain positive statements Paul makes about νόμος (3:31; 7:14) which have no parallel in Galatians.

But it is noteworthy that Paul carries on the discussion of 14:1 - 15:6 without using the term νόμος. If Paul does speak there of particular issues of νόμος-observance, he may wish to guard against against sweeping conclusions about νόμος-observance in general.

[17] Forty-six out of the 54; see Chapter 4, nn. 2, 3.

[18] Indefinite: 2:14d. Generic: 4:15b, 5:13b. General: 3:27a, b; 7:2b. The other two uses are in Rom 7:2a, 3; see above, at n. 7.

[19] See Chapter 3, at nn. 89-94.

[20] In treating Rom 7:7-13 in Chapter 3 (n. 96) I recognized the theoretical possibility of a general or generic reference in Rom 7:7a, 8 and 9. But nothing suggests that this possibility is actually taken up

γὰρ ὁ νόμος πνευματικός in 7:14 refers to Jewish νόμος.[21] But while this clear reference establishes the focus of 7:14-25, it does not explain the other uses of νόμος in this passage.

Νόμος and ἁμαρτία

On its face Rom 7:14-25 appears to be part of Paul's analysis of the relation between νόμος and ἁμαρτία, a further development of Paul's answer to the question posed in 7:7:

Τί οὖν ἐροῦμεν; ὁ νόμος ἁμαρτία; μὴ γένοιτο·

The vocabulary of 7:14-25 testifies to the continued prominence of this problem; νόμος is found eight times, ἁμαρτία five,[22] and each from the first verse to the last. The centrality of these terms to the text will emerge from the analysis below, but there is enough on the surface to justify a review of what Paul has already said about νόμος and ἁμαρτία.

We encountered both νόμος and ἁμαρτία in Gal 2:15-21; although the relationship between the two is not developed in that passage, it is implied in 2:17-18 that the *observance* of νόμος might in some circumstances be ἁμαρτία.[23] Later, in Gal 3:22-24, there appears to be an analogy between ἁμαρτία (v. 22[24]) and νόμος (vv. 23-24[25]). A connection between νόμος and ἁμαρτία is also declared in 1 Cor 15:56, where Paul remarks, with no explanation whatsoever, ἡ δὲ δύναμις τῆς ἁμαρτίας ὁ νόμος.

In Romans too we find νόμος connected to ἁμαρτία, and especially at two points just before our passage:

ἁμαρτία γὰρ ὑμῶν οὐ κυριεύσει· οὐ γάρ ἐστε ὑπὸ νόμον ἀλλὰ ὑπὸ χάριν. (6:14)

and:

ὅτε γὰρ ἦμεν ἐν τῇ σαρκί, τὰ παθήματα τῶν ἁμαρτιῶν τὰ διὰ τοῦ νόμου ἐνηργεῖτο ἐν τοῖς μέλεσιν ἡμῶν ... νυνὶ δὲ κατηργήθημεν ἀπὸ τοῦ νόμου ἀποθανόντες ἐν ᾧ κατειχόμεθα ... (7:5-6)

---

[21] See Chapter 3, following n. 73. The article excludes an indefinite reference; a generic reference is implausible on its face, for it would mean that νόμος *as such* is πνευματικός, which 7:23 and 25 rule out.

[22] Note also κακός (7:19, 21).

[23] See the exegesis of Gal 2:17-18 in Chapter 5.

[24] ἀλλὰ συνέκλεισεν ἡ γραφὴ τὰ πάντα ὑπὸ ἁμαρτίαν ...

[25] ὥστε ὁ νόμος παιδαγωγὸς ἡμῶν γέγονεν ...

In each of these places the rule of ἁμαρτία is connected with νόμος. More precisely: freedom from ἁμαρτία is connected with freedom from νόμος.[26] This naturally gives rise to the question of 7:7: ὁ νόμος ἁμαρτία; Having come so close in 7:6 to identifying νόμος and ἁμαρτία, Paul now denies (μὴ γένοιτο) that they are identical, and attempts to explain what the actual relation between them is.

We may be a little surprised to find this explanation here. νόμος first appeared in Rom 2:12, and the ἁμαρτ- word group appeared in the same verse;[27] through Rom 7:6 νόμος has appeared 47 times and words in the ἁμαρτ- group 38 times, and 22 times the two have appeared within two verses of each other (eight times in the same verse).[28] If the relationship between νόμος and ἁμαρτία has not yet been explained, or at any rate not satisfactorily explained, we have grounds for supposing that Paul has himself been working with two separate ideas—νόμος and ἁμαρτία—which he understands more clearly than he does their inter-relationship. In fact what Paul has said about νόμος and ἁμαρτία through 7:6 does not all point in the same direction.[29] Against the apparent association of νόμος and ἁμαρτία in Gal 2:17-18; 3:22-24; Rom 6:14 and 7:5-6, in Rom 2:12 Paul implies that the two are independent categories, for one can sin and be judged ἀνόμως as well as ἐν νόμῳ or διὰ νόμου.[30] Likewise Rom 5:13 tells us that sin exists without νόμος; yet this does not mean that νόμος and sin are unrelated, for the same verse tells us that, when νόμος does exist, it evidently provides a measure of sin.[31]

---

[26] The expression ἐλευθέρα ἐστιν ἀπὸ τοῦ νόμου is found at 7:3, and κατηργήθημεν ἀπὸ τοῦ νόμου at 7:6 (cf. 7:2). (Strictly speaking, καταργέω means something like "make ineffective" or "abolish" [BAGD, s.v.], or "leave idle" [LSJ, s.v.], so that when it is passive, as in 7:2, 6, one would expect its subject to be νόμος rather than believers. Burton [Galatians, 276], writing on κατηργήθητε ἀπὸ Χριστοῦ in Gal 5:4, terms this "a case of rhetorical inversion," and instances ἐθανατώθητε τῷ νόμῳ [rather than νόμος ἐθανατώθη ὑμῖν] in Rom 7:4 as another example. See also Gal 2:19: νόμῳ ἀπέθανον.)

[27] Ὅσοι γὰρ ἀνόμως ἥμαρτον, ἀνόμως καὶ ἀπολοῦνται, καὶ ὅσοι ἐν νόμῳ ἥμαρτον, διὰ νόμου κριθήσονται· In view of the general association between νόμος and judgment (aspect 2 of the meaning of νόμος), the idea of judgment without νόμος is particularly interesting. What will be the standard of judgment, if not νόμος? Paul does not explain; it might be a νόμος, but not the Jewish νόμος with which he is principally concerned.

[28] They appear together in Rom 2:12 (twice); 3:20; 5:13; 6:14, 15; 7:5.

[29] An entirely different usage (ἁμαρτάνειν εἰς person) appears in 1 Cor 8:12. This has no necessary relation to ἁμαρτ- in the different sense found in Romans.

[30] See n. 27.

[31] ἄχρι γὰρ νόμου ἁμαρτία ἦν ἐν κόσμῳ, ἁμαρτία δὲ οὐκ ἐλλογεῖται μὴ ὄντος νόμου, in which, as I argued in Chapter 3 (preceding n. 63, and at nn. 93-94), the first νόμος is Jewish but the second is generic. It therefore does not follow that every transgression of any particular νόμος (Jewish or otherwise) is sin, nor that all sin transgresses a particular νόμος.

In view of these varying perspectives on νόμος and ἁμαρτία, it will be prudent to take our cue from Rom 7:7-13, which immediately precedes our text. In 7:7 Paul puts the relation between νόμος and ἁμαρτία in terms of knowledge:

> ἀλλὰ τὴν ἁμαρτίαν οὐκ ἔγνων εἰ μὴ διὰ νόμου· τήν τε γὰρ ἐπιθυμίαν οὐκ ᾔδειν εἰ μὴ ὁ νόμος ἔλεγεν· οὐκ ἐπιθυμήσεις.

Here the general statement that νόμος brought knowledge of sin is followed by the specific one that it brought knowledge of desire,[32] implying that the knowledge of desire entails knowledge of sin. The following verses then evidently explicate the ἐπιθυμίαν . . . ᾔδειν of 7:7:

> ἀφορμὴν δὲ λαβοῦσα ἡ ἁμαρτία διὰ τῆς ἐντολῆς κατειργάσατο ἐν ἐμοὶ πᾶσαν ἐπιθυμίαν· χωρὶς γὰρ νόμου ἁμαρτία νεκρά. ἐγὼ δὲ ἔζων χωρὶς νόμου ποτέ, ἐλθούσης δὲ τῆς ἐντολῆς ἡ ἁμαρτία ἀνέζησεν . . .
> (Rom 7:8-9)

Thus sin lives (7:9) when it works "all desire" within one (7:8); sin does this διὰ τῆς ἐντολῆς (7:8) or διὰ νόμου (7:7); and the role of ἐντολή and νόμος is to bring knowledge of sin.

This theme of sin working through νόμος is repeated in 7:13, and then echoes through 7:14-25. The formulation of 7:13 is parallel to that of 7:8, but without reference to ἐπιθυμία:[33]

> . . . ἡ ἁμαρτία . . . διὰ τοῦ ἀγαθοῦ μοι κατεργαζομένη θάνατον . . .

Four parallels appear between 7:8 and 13: (1) ἡ ἁμαρτία is the subject; (2) κατεργάζομαι is the verb; (3) ἁμαρτία acts through (διὰ) ἐντολή or νόμος,[34] (4) in relation to (dative case) the speaker. Much the same pattern appears in 7:14-25, where κατεργάζομαι is used in vv. 15, 17, 18 and 20. It will be natural to connect its use in these verses with its use in vv. 8 and 13,[35] especially

---

[32] Or "covetousness," to which ἐπιθυμία refers in the context of the tenth commandment. Here, however, the omission of any object for ἐπιθυμία leaves open the possibility that Paul is thinking of "desire" more generally.

[33] It is unclear whether Paul's discussion of desire in 7:8 is an explication of the statement in 7:7 that τὴν ἁμαρτίαν οὐκ ἔγνων εἰ μὴ διὰ νόμου, or merely an illustration of it. In Rom 13:8 Paul treats as central the command to love one's neighbor, rather than the command not to desire.

[34] τοῦ ἀγαθοῦ in 7:13 might refer to either or both; see v. 12.

[35] Although κατεργάζομαι is not an uncommon term in Paul, it is not so common that its parallel uses in these six associated verses are likely to be unrelated. Of 19 appearances in Paul (out of 22 in the entire New Testament), and 11 in Romans, 6 are in Rom 7:7-20. (Contrast ποιέω: 22 uses in Romans [568 in the New Testament]; πράσσω is much rarer, except in Paul: 10 in Romans, 17 in Paul, 39 in the New Testament.)

when we observe that although Paul says in 7:15 that he "works," he corrects this in 7:17 and 20 to say that actually it is sin which "works" in him—just as sin "works" according to 7:8 and 13.[36] Thus the theme of 7:7-13, that sin "works" because νόμος gives one knowledge of sin, plays (as we shall see) a role in 7:14-25.

Νόμος and ἐντολή

In contrast to νόμος, ἐντολή is relatively unusual in Paul; he uses it only nine times, six of which are in Rom 7:7-13.[37] What is the relation of νόμος and ἐντολή, and why does Paul stress the latter here? That νόμος and ἐντολή here are connected seems plain, especially in 7:9-10, where the coming of ἐντολή means the end of the time χωρὶς νόμου. But various connections are possible. ἐντολή might be one command within νόμος,[38] or perhaps every command within νόμος,[39] or simply a synonym for νόμος.[40] None of these theories, however, entirely explains the use of ἐντολή; for according to them, νόμος includes ἐντολή, so that each of Paul's statements would evidently still be accurate if he had used νόμος instead of ἐντολή. If 7:7-13 is a defense of νόμος, why does Paul introduce another term?

Although it is possible that Paul simply wants to vary his terminology, that would not explain why he introduces this variation here and nowhere else in his discussions of νόμος. There are two other possible explanations. First, Paul may wish to *refer* only to that part of Jewish νόμος which is ἐντολή, excluding the rest of Jewish νόμος. Second, it might be that both terms refer to the same entity, but insofar as the terms have distinct *meanings* they call attention to different aspects of that entity.[41]

---

[36] Only the third element of the parallel, that this happens διὰ νόμου, is not expressly represented in 7:14-25—at least, in terms of the Jewish νόμος referred to in 7:8 and 13. But 7:21-23 shows, as we shall see, how other νόμοι make use of a weakness inherent in νόμος to prevent Jewish νόμος from accomplishing (κατεργάζομαι) good; sin thus does work evil διὰ νόμου in this other sense.

[37] The other uses are in Rom 13:9 and 1 Cor 7:19, 14:37. It also appears in Eph 2:15; 6:2; Col 4:10; 1 Tim 1:14.

[38] Perhaps οὐκ ἐπιθυμήσεις. So Cranfield (*Romans*, 1.352), on v. 10.
Another possibility, based on the supposition that 7:9-11 refers to Adam (see n. 50 below), is that ἐντολή refers to Gen 2:16-17 (LXX): ἐνετείλατο κύριος ὁ θεὸς τῷ Αδαμ λέγων . . . ἀπὸ δὲ τοῦ ξύλου τοῦ γινώσκειν καλὸν καὶ πονηρόν, οὐ φάγεσθε ἀπ᾽ αὐτου . . . But the allusion in Romans to Adam is so indirect, while the reference to νόμος and the Decalogue so clear, that this understanding of 7:9-11 is very doubtful.

[39] Cranfield (*Romans*, 1.353), on v. 12.

[40] Dunn, *Romans*, 1.380.

[41] Thus one might say "the leading port in the state" or "my home town," referring to the same city.

As to meaning, when I compared ἐντολή to νόμος in Chapter 2[42] it appeared that in the New Testament two of the components of meaning associated with νόμος are not found with ἐντολή: the association with judgment (component 2), and the association with a particular people (component 5). I have argued in Chapters 4 and 5 that the association of Jewish νόμος and Jewish people is usually central to Paul's references to Jewish νόμος. ἐντολή appears to be a term which avoids that association, and Paul may have chosen it for just that reason. In defending νόμος he does not wish to emphasize its Jewishness.[43]

It may also be that ἐντολή, by its transparent relationship to ἐντέλλω, calls attention to the one who commands: here, God (cf. τήρησις ἐντολῶν θεοῦ, 1 Cor 7:19).[44] This too would call attention away from the Jewish people.

As to reference, whether or not ἐντολή refers to the single command οὐκ ἐπιθυμήσεις to the exclusion of all others,[45] the term implies a focus on part of the range of Jewish νόμος: what is commanded. Paul clearly has this in mind; οὐκ ἐπιθυμήσεις is at least an illustration if not the full content.[46] Broader senses of νόμος, so significant in Rom 2 (see Chapter 4) and Galatians 2 (see Chapter 5), here recede into the background.

On both these grounds, then, the repeated use of ἐντολή in Rom 7:7-13 gives a focus to the discussion there of νόμος: in contrast to Gal 2:15-21, Paul in Rom 7:7-13 calls particular attention to specific commands found within νόμος, and away from the particular connection of νόμος with the Jewish people.

Romans 7:14-25

I will begin with an investigation of Paul's use of the first person throughout 7:14-25, and then proceed to a verse-by-verse analysis of the text. As with

---

[42] See following n. 99.

[43] This contrasts with Paul's argument in 7:1-3, which is based specifically on Jewish νόμος rather than Roman: the argument of vv. 2-3 does not work with Roman law, first because a Roman wife could divorce her husband, and second because the consequence of adultery (if discovered) was itself divorce. See Crook, *Law and Life*, 105-6. (It is possible that Paul, a provincial even if a citizen, was unaware of these details of Roman law. But if he was, and if he had Roman law in mind, then his γινώσκουσιν γὰρ νόμου λαλῶ [7:1] is odd.)

[44] Or possibly, according to Gal 3:19, the angels of God. (The distinction should not be overemphasized.)

[45] I think this improbable. Contrast Rom 13:8-9.

[46] In Rom 13:9 Paul lists four ἐντολαί, all from the Decalogue.

Gal 2:15-21 I will summarize my conclusions with a translation. Here, however, where the verse divisions are generally shorter and the argument usually clearer than in Galatians 2, I have chosen not to break my own discussion by inserting paraphrases at the end of each verse. The whole translation appears after my exegesis of 7:14-25.

Preliminary Observations: ἐγώ

A conspicuous feature of 7:7-25 is the introduction of verbs in the first person singular, used 26 times through 7:25,[47] eight times with the emphatic ἐγώ.[48] In vv. 7-13 the verbs associated with the first person are in the aorist or imperfect tense,[49] while in vv. 14-25 they are in the present tense.

The natural interpretation is that Paul is speaking of himself, past and present; but few follow this interpretation.[50] Rather, vv. 14-25—despite their

---

[47] And there ending sharply. Despite the continuities in subject and vocabulary (especially relating to νόμος) from 7:14-25 to 8:1-11, there is at most one first person in 8:1-11, the possible με of 8:2 (see n. 175).

[48] The first person singular also appears seventeen times in 7:7-25 in the oblique cases.

[49] Strictly speaking, ᾔδειν in v. 7 is pluperfect, but it functions as an imperfect. Both ἔγνων and ᾔδειν in v. 7 occur in the apodoses of conditional sentences which are evidently unreal; the secondary tense could be chosen for this reason (although ἄν is omitted). The unconditional aorists of vv. 8-13 make a clearer reference to the past.

[50] I will focus here on the present tense of vv. 14-25; vv. 7-13, with their past tense, seem to me too obscure to be helpful in construing the following passage. On the one hand, application of vv. 7-13 to Paul himself is made difficult by v. 9a: ἐγὼ δὲ ἔζων χωρὶς νόμου πότε, ἐλθούσης δὲ τῆς ἐντολῆς . . . When was there a time before the commandment came to Paul? A recent critical survey of various theories (e.g., that Paul speaks of the time before his Bar Mitzvah) is in Segal, "Romans 7," 362-64. Segal himself (ibid., 365) proposes that Paul speaks first of a time after his conversion when he did not observe Jewish νόμος, and then of a time when he "return[ed] to various customs afterwards as a courtesy to those whose sensibilities might be offended by his private beliefs [cf. 1 Cor 8:13, 9:20]. That moment was a crucial one in which sin again entered his actions."

This is a carefully thought-out proposal, further developed in Segal's Paul the Convert, 224-53. I am unpersuaded, however, because I think that if Paul's argument depended on so idiosyncratic an experience he would have provided some further explanation—especially in this letter to people unlikely to be familiar with the details of his life. As it stands, what is the likelihood that Paul's audience will see what Segal sees?

However, neither is any non-autobiographical reference convincing. Most critics think Paul has Adam in mind; in Käsemann's words (Romans, 196): "There is nothing in the passage which does not fit Adam, and everything fits Adam alone." (See also Dodd, Romans, 123; Schlier, Römer, 224; Wilckens, Römer, 2.81. Others are more restrained than Käsemann; Cranfield [Romans, 1.343-44] says Paul "draws upon the fundamental narrative of Genesis 2 and 3," and Dunn [Romans, 1.381] that "Paul is almost certainly speaking in typical terms, using the Adam narrative to characterize what is true of man ['adam] in general, everyman . . ." [emphasis in the original].)

present tense—are generally understood as describing the human situation before the coming of Christ.[51] On this view one cannot take both the first person and the present tense literally; if Paul is talking about himself he is not talking about his present self,[52] and if he is talking about the present he is not talking about himself.[53]

One is driven to this precarious position by the difficulty of accommodating the keynote proclamation of this passage, ἐγὼ δὲ σάρκινός εἰμι πεπραμένος ὑπὸ τὴν ἁμαρτίαν (7:14), with such other statements as νυνὶ δὲ [ὑμεῖς] ἐλευθερωθέντες ἀπὸ τῆς ἁμαρτίας δουλωθέντες δὲ τῷ θεῷ (6:22) and ὁ γὰρ νόμος τοῦ πνεύματος τῆς ζωῆς ἐν Χριστῷ Ἰησοῦ ἠλευθέρωσέν σε ἀπὸ τοῦ νόμου τῆς ἁμαρτίας καὶ τοῦ θανάτου (8:2).[54] These contradictory expressions thus invite us to take one group of expressions for rhetorical devices. But we have a choice. A rhetorical device serves a rhetorical purpose; what will have been Paul's purpose in representing himself to labor under present difficulties which he had in fact escaped? The first person and the present tense certainly make the picture more vivid; but to what end? I cannot think that such expressions are likely except under the apprehension that what they describe is at least a present, actual threat. But if the issue is freedom, then the perception that sin's power constantly threatens one, if one takes it with full seriousness, not radically different from the perception that it actually dominates one. In either case it would seem that the expression, "we have been freed from sin," is hyperbolic: itself a rhetorical device. This rhetorical device,

---

But one arrives at Adam as though this were the solution to a puzzle; every other possibility being eliminated, this remains. Yet if we can thus prove that Paul is thinking of Adam, we have not proved that he is thinking of him very much, or that he wants his readers to think of Adam at all. Paul says ἐγώ, not Ἀδάμ. Nothing here directly suggests Adam to the reader except the account two chapters earlier at 5:12-14; but not only does Paul make no allusion here to this account, he (if he is thinking of Adam) contradicts it. In 5:13 Paul says expressly that there was no νόμος at the time of Adam; in 7:7-13 the point is to describe the effect of νόμος. Adam is not the key to 7:7-13. Paul has hidden any use he has made of Adam's story; the key to Paul's meaning lies rather in the words he did use, ἐγώ among them.

[51] See especially Kümmel, Römer 7, 138; also, e.g., Bornkamm, "Sin," 100; Bultmann, "Romans 7," 147; Dodd, Romans, 125; Käsemann, Romans, 192; Kuss, Römer, 2.482; Sanday and Headlam, Romans, 186; Schlier, Römer, 221.

[52] Rather, he is talking of his past life under νόμος. So Dodd, Romans, 125; Wilckens, Römer, 278; and, by implication, Bornkamm, "Sin," 87.

[53] Rather, he is talking of the present condition of whose who are still under νόμος. So Käsemann, Romans, 192; Kümmel, Römer 7, 135; Kuss, Römer, 2.442; Lagrange, Romains, 173; Schlier, Römer, 221.

[54] Cf. also 6:18 (ἐλευθερωθέντες δὲ ἀπὸ τῆς ἁμαρτίας ἐδουλώθητε τῇ δικαιοσύνῃ). Similarly, 8:9 (Ὑμεῖς δὲ οὐκ ἐστὲ ἐν σαρκὶ ἀλλὰ ἐν πνεύματι) and 5:5 (ὅτε γὰρ ἦμεν ἐν τῇ σαρκί) imply that "we" are no longer "in the flesh."

moreover, serves an evident purpose as a basis for exhortation, here the general exhortation of 6:15-23 not to sin.[55]

It should not be necessary to demonstrate that Paul considers sin to be an actual issue for his audiences, whatever he may say on occasion about their freedom from sin; for my present purposes I think 6:15-23 adequately establishes the point. In the same way, any escape from flesh to spirit must be taken as provisional at best; that is the premise of Paul's question in Gal 3:3, ἐναρξάμενοι πνεύματι νῦν σαρκὶ ἐπιτελεῖσθε;[56] Paul's expressions about freedom from sin and flesh accordingly do not suffice to rule out the literal meaning of the person and tense chosen by Paul in 7:14-25. Nor do the various supposed examples of rhetorical usage make a strong case for such a usage here. Kümmel collects a handful of cases where he considers the first person to be used as a stylistic device;[57] but these are not apposite. His three rabbinic examples[58] each involve specific anecdotes which Kümmel considers fictitious, told simply to illustrate a point. In each of these cases, however, the first person is incidental to the anecdote, which would be equally fictitious if it were told in the third person; and I do not see what is gained by showing that fictions are possible. Neither Kümmel nor anyone else suggests that the picture Paul draws in 7:14-25 is not true of anyone; the question is rather, of whom is it true?

Kümmel's Greek examples are of a different kind.[59] Each involves a conditional sentence; but a conditional sentence does not represent its condition to be true. Moreover, a general conditional sentence, like those Kümmel cites, has the same meaning whether in the first, second or third person; it does not represent that it refers peculiarly to any individual. But a declarative sentence does make that representation.[60]

---

[55] Also noteworthy in 6:15-23 is Paul's concession that he speaks in human terms "because of the weakness of your flesh" (διὰ τὴν ἀσθένειαν τῆς σαρκὸς ὑμῶν).

[56] Cf. also 2 Cor 1:22, according to which πνεῦμα is received by Paul and his congregations only as an ἀρραβών. In Greek law an ἀρραβών is given before a transaction is completed; if the party receiving the ἀρραβών does not carry out the contract, the ἀρραβών must be returned two-fold. See Pringsheim, Sale, 351; Taubenschlag, Law, 375, 410.

[57] Kümmel, Römer 7, 126-31.

[58] M. Ber. 1.3 (tr. Danby): "R. Tarfon said: I was once on a journey and I reclined to recite [the Shema`] in accordance with the School of Shammai, and so put myself in jeopardy by reason of robbers." Kümmel's other rabbinic examples, similar in kind, are m. Abot 6.9; b. Ber. 3a.

[59] Demosthenes, Orations, 9.17; Pseudo-Xenophon, Athenian Constitution, 1.11; 2.11-12; Philo, De Somniis, 1.29 §177.

[60] Kümmel's analysis leads him (along with most German commentators) to refer to the speaker of Romans 7 as "das Ich": e.g., on Rom 7:18, "Das Ich ist sich bewußt, das . . ." (Römer 7, 60). This objectification of the first person would not be plausible in discussing

Kuss, in contrast, tries to show precedents from within Paul's own writings, but to no greater effect.[61] He too relies on conditional sentences,[62] and on 1 Cor 6:12, 15, which use the first person by way of example, not as part of a declaration. There remains 1 Cor 13:11: ὅτε ἤμην νήπιος, ἐλάλουν ὡς νήπιος κ.τ.λ. Here I allow the parallel; but this is merely a case of Paul reporting of himself what is *also* true of others; it is still true of himself.

Finally, Romans 7 contrasts with the psalms (canonical and extra-canonical) sometimes offered as parallels: for example, Pss 69, 77; Pss Sol 5, 8; 1 QH 3.19 ff.; 11:3 ff.[63] The similarity in expression may be conceded, but the difference between psalms and epistles is critical. If a friend writes to me in the style of one of these psalms, and without indicating that it is someone else's tribulation she expresses, I will presume that she expresses her own. I will not take her use of psalmic forms to transform her own statement into a literary exercise.

I propose therefore to begin my analysis of Rom 7:14-25 with the assumption that when Paul says ἐγώ he means himself, and when he uses the present tense he means that also. At the same time I presume that Paul expects his account to be recognizable to his readers, for otherwise the account serves no purpose.[64] Therefore, in paraphrasing Paul I shall use the first person plural; Paul's first person singular places a greater emphasis on his sharing in the difficulties of his audience, but for my purposes as an observer the plural seems to me to offer greater clarity.

I grant that if Paul's chief purpose in vv. 14-25 is to describe his hearers' condition, it is possible that Paul himself—despite his first person singular—does not actually share that condition. Perhaps Paul has been freed by the spirit (cf. 8:2) from the condition he describes, to which his hearers, at a less advanced level, yet remain subject; in this case Paul only pretends to be like his hearers as a way of gaining a better hearing from them. This interpretation smooths over the evident contrast between 7:14-25 and 8:1-11, but I think the

---

the passages Kümmel uses for examples of the rhetorical use of the first person (as, in *m. Ber.* 1.3, "The 'I' was on a journey, and reclined to recite the Shema," etc.), a further indication that these passages provide doubtful support for this interpretation.

[61] Kuss, *Römer*, 2.442.

[62] Rom 3:7; 1 Cor 10:29, 30; 13:1-3; 14:11, 14, 15; Gal 2:18. (I have argued that Gal 2:18 does actually refer to Paul; see Chapter 5.)

[63] These parallels are proposed by Dunn, *Romans*, 1.382; cf. Käsemann, *Romans*, 193.

[64] Thus Nygren (*Romans*, 287): ". . . if the reader, without preconceived view, had let the text speak as it actually is, he would not have construed verses 14-25 as anything but a characterization of the present life of the Christian." A similar view is taken by Luther (*Romans*, 327), Calvin (*Romans*, 151), Barth (*Romans*, 257-70), Barrett (*Romans*, 152-53), Cranfield (*Romans*, 1.344-46), and Meyer ("Romans," 1151).

hypothesis that Paul was concealing something from his hearers is a perilous one. We have only what he told his hearers; if Paul tells us in chapter 8 that he had adopted a guise in chapter 7, it would seem that he told his original audience this also. In the absence of clear evidence that Paul does not mean what he says, I shall take him at face value.

Verse 14

Paul begins with a proposition about νόμος as contrasted to himself:

Οἴδαμεν γὰρ ὅτι ὁ νόμος πνευματικός ἐστιν, ἐγὼ δὲ σάρκινός εἰμι πεπραμένος ὑπὸ τὴν ἁμαρτίαν.[65]

As I have noted,[66] νόμος refers here to Jewish νόμος. Paul introduces his proposition with οἴδαμεν γὰρ. οἶδα I have discussed;[67] the term does not imply any particular source of knowledge, nor is any suggested here; rather, the proposition seems to be taken for granted.[68] This proposition is in two parts: νόμος on the one hand, ἐγώ on the other.[69] These two sides are put in opposition by the terms πνευματικός and σάρκινος.[70] Paul is drawing on his standard opposition of πνεῦμα and σάρξ, which appears most conspicuously in Gal 5:16-17:

Λέγω δέ, πνεύματι περιπατεῖτε καὶ ἐπιθυμίαν σαρκὸς οὐ μὴ τελέσητε. ἡ γὰρ σὰρξ ἐπιθυμεῖ κατὰ τοῦ πνεύματος, τὸ δὲ πνεῦμα κατὰ τῆς σαρκός, ταῦτα γὰρ ἀλλήλοις ἀντίκειται, ἵνα μὴ ἃ ἐὰν θέλητε ταῦτα ποιῆτε.

This opposition is also seen in Rom 8:4 (τοῖς μὴ κατὰ σάρκα περιπατοῦσιν ἀλλά κατὰ πνεῦμα), 8:9 (Ὑμεῖς δὲ οὐκ ἐστὲ ἐν σαρκὶ ἀλλὰ ἐν πνεύματι); and 1 Cor 3:1 (οὐκ ἠδυνήθην λαλῆσαι ὑμῖν ὡς πνευματικοῖς ἀλλ᾽ ὡς σαρκίνοις).[71]

---

[65] A rare variant reading is οἶδα μέν. This is unlikely; it produces a μέν which is not parallel to the subsequent δέ. See Metzger, *Textual Commentary*, 514.

[66] Above, at n. 21.

[67] See Chapter 5, at nn. 34-36 and following.

[68] Cf. Rom 2:2; 3:19; 1 Cor 8:4; 2 Cor 5:1.

[69] ἐγώ here does not seem to be particularly emphatic; it is true that one does not need both ἐγώ and εἰμι, but omission of the latter would be at least as likely as omission of the former. See below, n. 76.

[70] Some manuscripts have σάρκικος. On the difference, see n. 93 below.

[71] Other texts include Rom 8:5, 6; Gal 3:3; 4:29; 6:8. The note of *opposition* (as distinct from *contrast*) is not uniform in these texts; contrast is a general theme that can be seen in other, non-Christian literature, but opposition is distinctly Pauline. In the NT outside Paul, only John 3:6 (τὸ γεγεννημένον ἐκ τῆς σαρκὸς σάρξ ἐστιν, καὶ τὸ γεγεννημένον ἐκ τοῦ πνεύματος πνεῦμα ἐστιν) implies opposition, although Matt 26:41 = Mark 14:38 (τὸ μὲν πνεῦμα πρόθυμον, ἡ δὲ σὰρξ ἀσθενής) comes close. BAGD (s.v. σάρξ 7) cites no non-Christian literature for the opposition; LSJ cites a Jewish inscription (SIG 1181.1-3:

It follows that if νόμος is πνευματικός and ἐγώ is σάρκινος the two are in separate, mutually exclusive, warring realms. Paul does not elsewhere use the πνεῦμα/σάρξ disjunction in discussing νόμος; twice in Romans and once in 2 Corinthians he opposes πνεῦμα to something that seems to resemble νόμος, but in each case he is careful to say γράμμα rather than νόμος.[72] Delicacy might have prevented Paul from opposing νόμος and πνεῦμα, for he is always circumspect in casting doubt on the connection between νόμος and God.[73] But here Paul takes the sharply contrasting view that νόμος is of course (οἴδαμεν) πνευματικός.[74]

This fundamental distinction between νόμος and ἐγώ suggests why νόμος has not prevented sin from obtaining dominion over humans: not, as it were, that νόμος is too weak, but that it is too strong. Neither we nor sin attain to the realm where νόμος is found; how then can νόμος help us?[75] Paul will develop this idea of separate realms in 7:21-23.

Paul connects ἁμαρτία to σάρξ by the phrase πεπραμένος ὑπὸ τὴν ἁμαρτίαν, which he puts in apposition to σάρκινος.[76] The connection between σάρξ and ἁμαρτία, which supplies a necessary link in the argument, is presumed rather than asserted—as though to be "fleshly" were identical to being "sold under sin."[77] At any rate, under either formulation it is evidently a condition beyond one's control.[78]

ἐπικαλοῦμαι καὶ ἀξιῶ τὸν θεὸν τὸν ὕψιστον, τὸν κύριον τῶν πνευμάτων καὶ πάσης σαρκός), but this is distinction, not opposition. The distinction can be found in LXX texts such as Gen 6:17 (πᾶσαν σάρκα, ἐν ᾗ ἐστιν πνεῦμα ζωῆς), which show that the two, although distinct, are complementary and not opposed. Most of the Greek examples given by Schweizer under the title "The Corruptible σάρξ in Distinction from the Incorruptible Part of Man" (TDNT 7 (1971) 102-3) likewise show distinction rather than opposition; most of these examples also do not use the term πνεῦμα.

[72] Rom 2:29; 7:6; 2 Cor 3:6-7.

[73] See Chapter 4, at nn. 49-60.

[74] This supports my refusal in Chapters 2 and 4 to identify νόμος and γράμμα. Wilckens's remark (Römer, 2.86), "das pneumatische Wesen des Gesetzes widerspricht der Antithese in V 6," is therefore inaccurate.

Strictly speaking, the contrast in Rom 7:6 is not between πνεῦμα and γράμμα, which are adjectival, but between καινότης and παλαιότης. One might reconcile 7:14 and 7:6 by saying that νόμος is **παλαιότης** πνεύματος.

[75] That is, Jewish νόμος. In 8:2 Paul will say ὁ γὰρ νόμος τοῦ πνεύματος τῆς ζωῆς ἐν Χριστῷ Ἰησοῦ ἠλευθέρωσεν σε ἀπὸ τοῦ νόμου τῆς ἁμαρτίας καὶ τοῦ θανάτου. But the qualifying phrase τοῦ πνεύματος changes the reference; this is not Jewish νόμος, but something new. See below, at n. 179.

[76] εἰμι, which could have been omitted, is used to separate the two.

[77] In fact the connection between ἁμαρτία and σάρξ seems to be ad hoc; outside this passage it is found only in the adjacent verses 7:5 and 8:3.

Verse 15

We might expect here a demonstration of the second half of v. 14;[79] but this is not how Paul's argument works. Vv. 15-20 as a whole could be taken for such a demonstration, ending as they do with the conclusion that sin dwells in one, controlling what one does;[80] but so deferred a demonstration of the basic proposition would considerably weaken the argument. Instead, Paul must expect the whole of v. 14 to be accepted without argument.[81] V. 15 rather develops its consequence.

ὃ γὰρ κατεργάζομαι οὐ γινώσκω· οὐ γὰρ ὃ θέλω τοῦτο πράσσω, ἀλλ᾽ ὃ μισῶ τοῦτο ποιῶ.

Κατεργάζομαι appears in vv. 15-20 four times, together with ποιέω (five times, in vv. 15, 16, 19, 20, 21) and πράσσω (twice, in vv. 15, 19). The terms are not fundamentally different;[82] however, κατεργάζομαι here recalls the two expressions of vv. 8 and 13, already noted above.[83] These prior verses refer to sin "working" in me desire (v. 8) and death (v. 13); in v. 15 "I" is the subject, but in vv. 17 and 20 Paul will say that after all it is not "I" (emphatic in these verses) that "works," but ἡ οἰκοῦσα ἐν ἐμοὶ ἁμαρτία —a result prefigured by εἰμι πεπραμένος ὑπὸ τὴν ἁμαρτίαν in 7:14. The consistent association in these expressions of "I," sin and "working" carries with it also the desire and death which, according to vv. 8, 13, are what sin "works"; this suggests that desire and death are likewise what (according to v. 15) Paul "works."[84]

According to Käsemann (*Romans*, 200-01), πεπραμένος ὑπὸ τὴν ἁμαρτίαν "presents the theme of the sub-section [vv. 15-20]." So Käsemann interprets the passage; but I cannot see that anything in this verse suggests that the concluding phrase is decisive.

[78] This is made explicit by the term πεπραμένος, which (when applied to a person) ordinarily means slavery; cf. Matt 18:25; *Herm. Vis.* 1.1.1. (Although the term can be used of one who accepts a bribe [LSJ, s.v. πέρνημι II], nothing in this context suggests that meaning.)

[79] Οἴδαμεν implies that no demonstration is needed, but this could apply only to the first half of v. 14.

[80] So Schlier (*Römer*, 230).

[81] Notwithstanding v. 15's introductory γάρ. On γάρ, see Chapter 5, n. 114.

[82] So Käsemann (*Romans*, 202): "The variations of the verbs κατεργάζομαι, ποιῶ and πράσσω are undoubtedly rhetorical . . ." Cf. Kuss, *Römer*, 2.453; Schlier, *Römer*, 230. Those who see distinctions do not see the same ones; thus Cranfield (*Romans*, 1.358) suggests that κατεργάζομαι and ποιῶ are equivalent but differ from πράσσω, while Dunn (Romans, 1.389) equates κατεργάζομαι and πράσσω.

A πράσσω/ποιῶ distinction seems especially unlikely in view of the interchange of these terms in v. 19, contrasted with v. 15.

[83] At n. 33.

[84] Wilckens, *Römer*, 2.86-87.

Verse 15 also says that the speaker does not "know" (οὐ γινώσκω) what he "works". For γινώσκω various senses are possible: "know," "understand" or "comprehend," or even "decide."[85] The last, despite the backing of BAGD, is improbable on lexical grounds,[86] but it is difficult to choose between "know" and "understand, comprehend." If we read v. 15b-c (οὐ γὰρ ὃ θέλω τοῦτο πράσσω, ἀλλ᾽ ὃ μισῶ τοῦτο ποιῶ) as an explanation of 15a (ὃ γὰρ κατεργάζομαι οὐ γινώσκω), which seems plausible, then the point of 15a appears to be that Paul knows *what* he does—he does what he hates—but he does not know *why* he does this; we might paraphrase, "I don't understand why I do what I hate rather than what I want."

On the other hand, if we take it that κατεργάζομαι invokes the idea that sin within the speaker (v. 20) "works" desire and death (vv. 8, 13), then Paul does not know *what* he works; we might paraphrase, "I don't realize what I accomplish."[87] This second interpretation leaves the relation of 15a to 15b-c uncertain. Bultmann ("Romans 7," 150) draws a distinction between the sense of 15a and that of 15b-c, on the ground that γιγνώσκω refers to consciousness but θέλω to unconsciousness: "For man is not primarily viewed by Paul as a conscious subject; the propensities of man's willing and doing which give him his character are not at all the strivings of his subjectivity." This is not based on anything in 7:14-25, and in fact Paul's various verbs of knowledge in this passage make this idea very unlikely here.[88]

These two interpretations are analytically separate—the first depending on a general meaning for κατεργάζομαι, ποιέω and πράσσω, while the second

---

[85] "Experience" is also a possible rendering, mentioned by Bultmann in his TDNT article (1 [1964] 689-90; contrast LSJ, BAGD) although not in "Romans 7." But so far as I can determine γινώσκω is never divorced from consciousness. I think "know" and "understand" are therefore clearer than "experience," which leaves the connection to consciousness vague.

[86] BAGD, s.v. γινώσκω 6.a.a, says of Rom 7:15 "almost = *desire, want, decide . . .*" (emphasis in original). The passages cited, however, are limited to the sense "decide," and all but one involve the specific idiom γινώσκω + infinitive (cf. LSJ, s.v. II.1). The exception is Οὗτοι [Γαλάται] περὶ πολέμου βουλευόμενοι ταῖς γυναιξὶν ἀνακοινοῦνται, καὶ ὅ τι ἂν γνῶσιν αἱ γυναῖκες, τοῦτο κρατεῖ (*Paradoxigraphicus Vaticanus*, 46; see Keller, *Scriptores*). But an infinitive (ποιεῖν or the like) may be understood.

[87] This is Bultmann's view ("Romans 7," 155).

[88] Bornkamm ("Sin," 97), also interprets 15a independently of 15b-c; for him, "The 'it deceived me' [7:11] is the basis of 'I do not understand' (v. 15)." But if there is a connection between the arguments of vv. 11 and 15, Paul does not develop it; the basic thrust of 7:14-25 has to do with power, not deception.

Dunn (*Romans*, 1.389) sees in the division within Paul which appears in this verse the "eschatological tension" between the believer's actual life and "the possibilities and promise of a wholly Spirit-directed life . . ." which is still to come. However, the eschatological language which Paul employs elsewhere is absent here.

depends on taking all three to refer specifically to the actions of sin—but practically the interpretations overlap, both effecting a separation between Paul and his conduct.[89] Verse 15c essentially repeats 15b. Although μισῶ of 15c might be a stronger term than the οὐ . . . θέλω of 15b—excluding the possibility that the speaker is merely doing what he is indifferent to—the use of οὐ θέλω again in 16a is surely not intended to weaken 15b and c. More likely, Paul sees 15b, 15c and 16a as equivalent; the basic statement is thus emphasized by repetition.

Verse 16

Here a repetition of vv. 15b and c is followed by a new idea:

εἰ δὲ ὃ οὐ θέλω τοῦτο ποιῶ, σύμφημι τῷ νόμῳ ὅτι καλός.

The relation between the two halves of this verse is not explicit, but it can easily be inferred. The unstated presumption is that what Paul does is contrary to νόμος;[90] but because Paul does not wish to do this (v. 16a), it follows that he actually, and despite his conduct, agrees with νόμος (v. 16b).[91] This presumption of failure to comply with νόμος seems to conflict with what Paul

---

[89] See Wilckens (Römer, 2.87).

[90] ὁ νόμος is necessarily definite, and in this context it cannot be anything but Jewish νόμος. Käsemann (Romans, 202-3) interprets νόμος here in a novel sense, as "the will of God disclosed in the law," by which he apparently means not simply Jewish νόμος, but everything God requires of us. In this way Käsemann wishes to avoid the problem raised by Paul's declaration in 7:15 that he never (apparently) does what he wants; as Käsemann says, one does not in fact always fail to do what one wishes; but, Käsemann continues, "Verse 16b shows what sphere is in view. . . . The experience which Paul envisions consists in the fact that the pious, who alone come into the picture here, do not succeed in realizing the will of God as the true good so long as the Spirit of Christ is not given to them."

I think there is no basis for supposing that νόμος has here such an unexpected reference. The difficulty with the stark formulation of v. 15 must be solved in another way; I think Lagrange (Romains, 175) is right in observing, "Il est prudent de ne pas serrer de trop près des termes qui ne sont examples d'une certaine exagération littéraire." This, in substance, is the view of Calvin (Romans, 152) and Luther (Romans, 330).

[91] Strictly speaking, this follows only if there is no third course of conduct, different both from what Paul does and from what νόμος requires. Paul does not allow this possibility, at any rate not in this context. Cf. the two spirits of Qumran (1 QS 3.18-4.1).

Bultmann ("Romans 7," 156) understands σύμφημι τῷ νόμῳ ὅτι καλός to mean "not a specific agreement with [the law's] concrete demands, but an affirmation of its fundamental intention to lead to life." But this does not explain how the second half of the verse follows from the first, as the conditional form implies; in fact, Bultmann's conclusion is not derived from an exegesis of this verse at all, but as the result of a complex argument about Rom 7 as a whole, an argument which actually depends on Bultmann's reading of all that Paul says about sin, law, life and death.

says of himself elsewhere, especially in Phil 3:5-6, but here, following a discussion of enslavement to sin (7:14) and of sin's deadliness (7:10-11, 13), it is not surprising.[92]

Σύμφημι τῷ νόμῳ ὅτι καλός personalizes νόμος, as do all passages which ascribe speech to it. The first part of the clause, σύμφημι τῷ νόμῳ, might have stood alone; or alternatively, Paul could have made the second part clearer by writing σύμφημι τὸν νόμον καλὸν εἶναι.[93] Instead, Paul chooses to say both that he agrees with νόμος, and that νόμος is καλός. The first proposition complicates the picture presented in 7:14, according to which νόμος and πνεῦμα stand on one side, ἐγώ and ἁμαρτία on the other; now νόμος and ἐγώ are on the same side. This complication will be developed in the following verse. The second proposition attaches to νόμος yet another term of approbation, one which will figure in verses 18 and 21.

Verse 17

Paul draws a further conclusion here:

νυνὶ δὲ οὐκέτι ἐγὼ κατεργάζομαι αὐτὸ ἀλλὰ ἡ οἰκοῦσα ἐν ἐμοὶ ἁμαρτία.

From the separation between his wish and his conduct Paul infers that this conduct is not in fact his. Does αὐτὸ refer back to the τοῦτο ποιῶ of v. 16, or to ὅ . . . κατεργάζομαι in 7:15? As in the similar case of v. 15 (above, at n. 89), both possibilities are left open. ἐγώ is contrasted with ἡ οἰκοῦσα ἐν ἐμοὶ ἁμαρτία.[94] This last expression changes the metaphor of 7:14; according to that verse Paul is enslaved to sin, an external relation, but here sin is within Paul.[95] This is very similar in structure to Gal 2:20: ζῶ δὲ οὐκέτι ἐγώ, ζῇ δὲ ἐν

---

[92] One could eliminate the conflict with Paul's affirmation of νόμος-observance in Phil 3:5-6 if the τοῦτο ποιῶ here refers to the sin and death associated with κατεργάζομαι; in that case the point would be that Paul does things he is not aware of. On the other hand, the association of κατεργάζομαι with sin and death seems to depend on giving κατεργάζομαι a distinct sense, different from that of ποιῶ and πράσσω.

[93] LSJ, s.v. σύμφημι 3, gives this as Paul's meaning.

[94] Note Moulton-Turner, Syntax, 37: ἐγώ is often stated for antithesis.

[95] Besides the usual meaning of οἰκέω, "inhabit," (LSJ, s.v. I), it can also mean "manage, direct a household or estate" (ibid., s.v. II; e.g., Euripedes, Electra, 386-87: οἱ γὰρ τοιοίδε τὰς πόλεις οἰκοῦσιν εὖ καὶ δωμάθ, "for such [men] govern states and homes well"). LSJ does not report this sense with ἐν, but if this sense survives in Paul's time it could lie in the background here. The idea could then be the straightforward "sin ruling in me," rather than "sin within me," which leaves more ambivalence about my relation to sin. But this is uncertain.

If οἰκέω does mean "inhabit," and if there were here an idea that one owns one's dwelling, then the idea of ownership from 7:14 would be preserved here. But this is not

ἐμοὶ Χριστός.⁹⁶ The thoughts of these two verses, as expressed by the phrases ἡ οἰκοῦσα ἐν ἐμοὶ ἁμαρτία and ἐν ἐμοὶ Χριστός, are quite different, but they have this in common: what I do in fact is done by something else.⁹⁷ But we should recall from Chapter 5 that in Gal 2:20 Paul proceeds immediately to explain the sense in which "Christ lives in me"; Paul means that he himself lives "in the faith of the Son of God." Neither in Galatians nor here in Romans does Paul truly mean that he himself is only a cipher. After all, Paul insists here that his will is contrary to sin; this is the basis of the assertion that it is sin and *not himself* that acts.

With vv. 16-17 Paul has altered the framework he set up in vv. 14-15. In v. 14 πνεῦμα and σάρξ were contrasted; νόμος was allied with πνεῦμα on one side, and both ἐγώ and ἁμαρτία were allied with σάρξ on the other.⁹⁸ But now ἐγώ has been linked with νόμος (v. 16) and contrasted with ἁμαρτία (v. 17). These two views of oneself derive from two different perspectives: on the one hand, in terms of θέλειν and γινώσκειν, and on the other, in terms of ποιεῖν, πράσσειν and κατεργάζεσθαι. This distinction requires careful consideration; we might suppose, for example, that ἐπιθυμία would relate to θέλειν rather than to ποιεῖν, but in 7:8 Paul speaks of ἐπιθυμία as a product of sin.⁹⁹ In fact this follows from Paul's scheme: if ἐπιθυμία is counter to νόμος (7:7-8), but what I wish (θέλω) is in accord with νόμος (7:16), then desire and wish must be distinct.¹⁰⁰

All of the kinds of activity that Paul associates with sin in Rom 7:7-25—ἐπιθυμία, ποιέω and πράσσω¹⁰¹—are ones that relate to performing (or failing

---

integral to the verb οἰκέω; see, e.g., Isa 6:5 (LXX): ἐν μέσῳ λαοῦ ἀκάθαρτα ... ἐγὼ οἰκῶ ... It is not likely that the typical Roman Christian owned his or her dwelling.

⁹⁶ Strictly speaking the ἀλλά-clause of Rom 7:17 requires κατεργάζεται αὐτό, as Gal 2:20 has ζῇ, but Paul's meaning is clear without this. To have ἡ οἰκοῦσα ἐν ἐμοὶ ἁμαρτία appear as the subject of a verb in the first person singular only reinforces Paul's point: what I do in fact is done by sin.

⁹⁷ The slavery metaphor of Rom 7:14 is also paralleled by, e.g., Rom 1:1 (Παῦλος δοῦλος Χριστοῦ Ἰησοῦ) and 6:22 (δουλωθέντες δὲ τῷ θεῷ).

⁹⁸ Although ἐγώ and ἁμαρτία are each linked with σάρξ they are not identified with it; Paul is made of σάρξ (7:14) (according to Moulton-Howard, [Accidence, 378], the -ινος suffix generally means "made of," while -ικός means "-like"), but ἁμαρτία; Paul speaks of ἡ σάρξ μου, but not of ἡ ἁμαρτία μου.

⁹⁹ ἡ ἁμαρτία ... κατεργάσατο ἐν ἐμοὶ πᾶσαν ἐπιθυμίαν.

¹⁰⁰ Note that Paul does not always speak in this way; in Gal 5:17 he says that both σάρξ and πνεῦμα "desire" (ἐπιθυμέω).

¹⁰¹ κατεργάζομαι also, if we take the term to refer to activity, as a rough synonym for ποιέω and πράσσω. This meaning is suggested, as I have noted, by the probability that v. 15b-c is a gloss on v. 15a; but 7:8, 13 also suggest that κατεργάζομαι refers not simply to activity but to the result of activity: desire, and death.

to perform) what νόμος commands.[102] γινώσκω, οἶδα, θέλω and σύμφημι, in contrast, do not relate to what νόμος commands. This yields an odd result: one is in accord with νόμος just to the extent that performance is not in view. But the idea of performance is fundamental to the idea of νόμος, as we saw in our survey of its meaning in Chapter 2.[103] To speak of approving νόμος, only not doing it, is paradoxical. Once again, as in Romans 2,[104] Paul steps outside the ordinary scene invoked by νόμος, a scene in which we take it for granted not only that we are able to do νόμος (aspect 3), but that νόμος can compel us to do so (aspect 4).[105] Paul's portrayal of νόμος in these verses challenges not only its efficacy, but its meaning.[106]

Verse 18a

Here Paul develops the idea of οἰκεῖν ἐν ἐμοί:

Οἶδα[107] γὰρ ὅτι οὐκ οἰκεῖ ἐν ἐμοί, τοῦτ᾽ ἔστιν ἐν τῇ σαρκί μου, ἀγαθόν·

This raises four questions: (1) How does Paul "know" (οἶδα) what he says here? (2) What relation is implied between the speaker and the speaker's σάρξ? (3) What is meant by ἐν τῇ σαρκί μου? (4) to what does ἀγαθόν refer? It will be productive to treat these questions in reverse order.

---

102 For ποιεῖν νόμον, see Rom 2:14; Gal 5:3; cf. Rom 2:13 (ποιηταὶ νόμου). For πράσσειν νόμον, see Rom 2:25. As for ἐπιθυμία, νόμος itself says οὐκ ἐπιθυμήσεις (see Rom 7:7).

103 Performance underlies aspects 2 (judgment), 3 (guide), and 4 (command).

104 See Chapter 4, at nn. 94-104.

105 If these be removed, judgment (aspect 2) can still remain, but it takes on a new meaning. But Paul does not make direct use of the idea of judgment here (although v. 24 may allude to it).

106 Schlier (Römer, 231-32) sees in 7:17 not simply two views of oneself, but two different selves: "der Mensch als Geschöpf, der geschöpfliche Mensch als solche," and "der geschichtliche Mensch." I do not see how Paul invokes the ideas of Schöpfung or Geschichte, nor that he speaks here of different selves—especially if the αὐτὸς ἐγὼ of 7:25b be genuine (which Schlier denies; on this, see below, at n. 164).

Cf. Barth (Romans, 266): "I have no reason to suppose that the EGO which performs and the EGO which disapproves can escape identification . . . . within the four walls of the house of sin dwells but one man."

Dunn (Romans, 390) understands the two views of self eschatologically: "The fact that the 'I' can thus disown ὃ οὐ θέλω, ὃ μισῶ, is a consequence of its eschatological standing in the Already but also the Not-yet of eschatological grace." This tension undoubtedly underlies the passage as a whole, and explains why Paul can describe his situation so negatively, in contrast to his account in, e.g., Rom 8.

107 Capitalized in Nestle-Aland[26]; lower case in UBS[3].

ἀγαθόν. In 7:13 τὸ ἀγαθόν evidently refers to νόμος.[108] νόμος could also be the referent here in v. 18a, making this proposition a corollary of 7:14: since νόμος is πνευματικός, it does not dwell ἐν σαρκί.[109] But if Paul intended a specific reference, an anaphoric article would be expected: τὸ ἀγαθόν, as in 7:13. I take it that ἀγαθόν includes νόμος, and that in light of 7:13, 14 and 16[110] one will think especially of νόμος here; but ἀγαθόν encompasses more than νόμος; see vv. 18b-21, where ἀγαθόν and καλόν are each objects of verbs of action. Paul has in mind not only the good νόμος, but the good which νόμος requires.[111] In either sense, this good is not within Paul.[112]

ἐν τῇ σαρκί μου. σάρξ is an ambiguous term; on the one hand we have the clearly negative σάρκινος of 7:14; on the other hand, the precise phrase ἐν σαρκί seems to be a particular idiom. Although Paul speaks occasionally of himself not being ἐν σαρκί,[113] this either involves a special sense of ἐν σαρκί or is hyperbolic. A more restrained expression appears in 2 Cor 10:3: Ἐν σαρκὶ γὰρ περιπατοῦντες οὐ κατὰ σάρκα στρατευόμεθα . . . In a number of passages ἐν σαρκί seems to refer simply to human life: for example, τὸ δὲ ἐπιμένειν ἐν τῇ σαρκί (Phil 1:24) and ὃ δὲ νῦν ζῶ ἐν σαρκί (Gal 2:20), both of

---

108 Or to ἐντολή, or perhaps to νόμος viewed as ἐντολή. (Apparently these distinctions are not important to Paul at this point.)

109 Wilckens (Römer, 2.88) takes ἀγαθόν to refer to Gesetz; Dunn (Romans, 1.391) suggests that there may be an allusion.

110 σύμφημι τῷ νόμῳ ὅτι καλός.

111 Similarly van Dülmen, (Theologie, 114). Bornkamm ("Sin," 96) and Bultmann ("Romans 7," 155) take ἀγαθόν to mean "life" rather than νόμος. The argument turns on the phrase κατεργάζεσθαι τὸ καλόν in 7:18b, which suggests ζωή as a contrast with κατεργαζομένη θάνατον in 7:13. I think v. 18b does hint at this, but this hint does not exclude a reference to νόμος; 7:16b says explicitly that νόμος is καλός. Moreover, if νόμος is ἀγαθός (7:12-13; cf. 7:14 [ὁ νόμος πνευματικός ἐστιν]) and καλός (7:16), it may also be associated with ζωή—at least in so indirect a way as 7:18 makes that association. But even if τὸ καλόν in 7:18b is unrelated to νόμος, this does not mean that ἀγαθόν in 7:18a is similarly independent.

112 The reference to ἀγαθόν in 7:18 is best rendered, "Good does not dwell . . .," treating ἀγαθόν as a substantive, as in TEV, Cranfield (Romans, 1.340), Käsemann (Romans, 198-99), Schlier (Römer, 228). The more common translation is "Nothing good dwells . . .," treating ἀγαθόν strictly as an adjective; see JB, NASB, NEB, NJB, RSV, Kuss (Römer, 2.481); cf. AV, Barrett (Romans, 148), Dunn (Romans, 1.390): "no good thing"; NAB, Wilckens (Römer, 2.74): "no good". Either rendering is grammatically acceptable; the former is more literal and conveys a clearer suggestion that something in particular is thought of—νόμος, and things related to it.

113 Ἡμεῖς δὲ οὐκ ἐστὲ ἐν σαρκὶ ἀλλὰ ἐν πνεύματι . . . (Rom 8:9); cf. ὅτε γὰρ ἦμεν ἐν τῇ σαρκί. . . (7:5).

which say that Paul is himself ἐν σαρκί.[114] The reference to ἡ σάρξ μου in v. 18a fits with these latter expressions, and is therefore consistent with my thesis that Paul is speaking of his present self.

ἐγώ and ἡ σάρξ μου. The phrase τοῦτ᾽ ἔστιν ἐν τῇ σαρκί μου is sometimes taken to correct the preceding ἐν ἐμοί, distinguishing the σάρξ from the ἐγώ which, as Paul has just said, agrees with νόμος and wishes to do good.[115] But τοῦτ᾽ ἔστιν is an explanatory phrase, not a correcting one,[116] which in Paul typically introduces an interpretation of scripture.[117] I see no inconsistency in Paul saying that he wishes to do good and that good does not dwell in him; moreover, Paul has just declared specifically that he is σάρκινος (7:14) and, as we have just seen, he allows in many other places that he is ἐν σαρκί. There is nothing here to indicate that there is some other part or aspect of him in which good does dwell, especially if ἀγαθόν refers particularly, as I have suggested, to matters related to νόμος.[118]

οἶδα. I have noted already, in connection with Gal 2:16 and Rom 7:14, that οἶδα does not in itself imply knowledge from experience. Now, however, the first person singular following on the discussion of what Paul observes about himself suggests a ground for what he now says.

Verse 18a accordingly says that Paul perceives that good, and especially the good νόμος, does not dwell within him, because in fact he does other than the good.

---

114 Cf. 2 Cor 12:7 (ἐδόθη μοι σκόλοψ τῇ σαρκί). Passages which do not refer to Paul himself include Rom 6:19 (ἀνθρώπινον λέγω διὰ τὴν ἀσθένειαν τῆς σαρκὸς ὑμῶν . . .) and 1 Cor 7:28 (θλίψιν δὲ τῇ σαρκὶ ἕξουσιν οἱ τοιοῦτοι . . .).

115 So Barrett, Romans, 145; similarly Kümmel, Römer 7, 61; Sanday and Headlam, Romans, 182. Cranfield (Romans, 1.361) draws a similar conclusion from Rom 8:9, observing that "in the Christian the Holy Spirit dwells . . ."

116 Käsemann (Romans, 204-5), Bornkamm ("Sin," 98), Schlier (Römer, 232) and Wilckens (Römer, 2.87) all agree that τοῦτ᾽ ἔστιν is explanatory.

Kümmel (Römer 7, 61) cites two examples of a "Selbstkorrektur" usage, Phlm 12 and Rom 1:12. In the first of these τοῦτ᾽ ἔστιν introduces the metaphor of Philemon as Paul's σπλάγχνα, and I cannot see how this "corrects" anything. In Rom 1:12, with τοῦτό δέ ἐστιν Paul says that he and the Romans may encourage one another, and not simply (as he said in 1:11) that he will strengthen them; but this is a weak analogy, for here the δέ might be inserted precisely to indicate an element of contrast unusual to τοῦτ᾽ ἔστιν. In any case 1:12 does not modify the preceding verse, but only adds to it.

117 Rom 9:8; 10:6, 7, 8. Elsewhere in the New Testament the phrase always introduces an interpretation: Matt 27:46; Mark 7:2; Acts 1:19; 19:4; Heb 2:14; 7:5; 9:11; 10:20; 11:16; 13:15.

118 Cranfield's view (Romans, 1.361), that 7:18 conflicts with 8:9 unless τοῦτ᾽ ἔστιν corrects ἐν ἐμοί, takes ἀγαθόν too broadly. Here Paul is not thinking of good in the abstract, and certainly not of the πνεῦμα θεοῦ of 8:9, but of νόμος and the doing of νόμος.

Verse 18b

Here Paul develops the spatial imagery suggested by οἰκέω and ἐν ἐμοί: τὸ γὰρ θέλειν παράκειταί μοι, τὸ δὲ κατεργάζεσθαι τὸ καλὸν οὔ.

Even to wish good is not precisely in Paul, but it is next to him;[119] this spatial imagery may play on the Pauline idea of the two realms of spirit and flesh, for though Paul finds himself (he says) in the fleshly realm, the spiritual realm is at hand. But to do good is not present to him at all.[120] Paul's expression here is similar to v. 15, but now he speaks objectively rather than subjectively: not that he wills but can't work, but that willing is present and working is not. This impersonal way of speaking helps prepare the way for vv. 21-23, in which, as we shall see, Paul himself becomes merely the battleground for an array of νόμοι.

Verse 19

At this point, however, Paul balances the objective and subjective accounts; he now returns to the first-person language which dominates the passage as a whole, closely paraphrasing v.15:

οὐ γὰρ ὃ θέλω ποιῶ ἀγαθόν, ἀλλὰ ὃ οὐ θέλω κακὸν τοῦτο πράσσω.

The principal change here from v. 15 is the insertion of ἀγαθόν and the complementary κακόν.[121] This develops indirectly the connection between what Paul wishes and νόμος. As we saw, this connection was presumed but not stated in v. 16; ἀγαθόν alludes to it in v. 18; and now here ἀγαθόν is what one wishes to do but does not.

Verse 20

Here Paul repeats himself again, not approximately as in v. 19 but word-for-word:

---

[119] παράκειμαι has generally its literal sense, to lie near (NT, LXX; see LSJ, s.v.), and thus I assume that it is for the literal sense, with its contrast to οἰκέω and ἐν ἐμοί, that Paul has chosen this relatively rare term (in the NT, only here and in 7:21; in the LXX, only 10 times [all in the Apocrypha; nevertheless, the term is not late, appearing in Homer, Plato and Aristotle (LSJ, s.v.)]).

[120] Dunn (*Romans*, 1.391) thinks to the contrary that παράκειται is chosen "to stress the difficulty of doing good, not that it is impossible . . ." He thus places the stress on a supposed negative pregnant: "not present [but not too far away]." The most that can be said is that Paul does not expressly exclude this possibility. But I see no reason to think that he had it in mind.

[121] Paul also reverses ποιῶ and πράσσω, and (as in v. 16) he substitutes οὐ . . . θέλω for μισῶ.

εἰ δὲ ὃ οὐ θέλω ἐγὼ τοῦτο ποιῶ, οὐκέτι ἐγὼ κατεργάζομαι αὐτὸ ἀλλὰ ἡ οἰκοῦσα ἐν ἐμοὶ ἁμαρτία.

This is identical to vv. 16-17, with the insertion of ἐγώ following θέλω[122] and the omission of the reference to νόμος at the end of v. 16.[123] Paul is now recapitulating the argument of vv. 14-17 as a prelude to taking up the argument of vv. 21-25; what he omits is the treatment of νόμος in v. 16b and vv. 18-19 as καλός and ἀγαθός. This smoothes the transition to the argument about to come, in which καλός and its converse κακός both appear, but are associated with the term νόμος in a different way.

Here we have also, once again, sin "working": an allusion to ἡ ἁμαρτία . . . διὰ τοῦ ἀγαθοῦ μοι κατεργαζομένη θάνατον (v. 13). But the phrase διὰ τοῦ ἀγαθοῦ remains obscure. How is it that sin works "through the good [νόμος]"? This question Paul will answer in vv. 21-23; not in terms simply of νόμος, but of νόμοι.

Verse 21

Now the use of νόμος takes a sharp turn.

εὑρίσκω ἄρα τὸν νόμον, τῷ θέλοντι ἐμοὶ ποιεῖν τὸ καλόν, ὅτι ἐμοὶ τὸ κακὸν παράκειται.

To this point in chapter 7 (apart from 7:2a and 3) νόμος has evidently referred to Jewish νόμος; but the natural reading of v. 21 is, as I argued in Chapter 3,[124] that here Paul speaks of a different νόμος, the content of which is stated by the ὅτι-clause standing in apposition to τὸν νόμον: it is a νόμος that when Paul wishes to do good, evil is at hand.

Jewish νόμος is indeed referred to in this verse, but by the term τὸ καλόν, whose association with Jewish νόμος has been established in 7:16 and 18b.[125] The statement of the νόμος of 7:21 combines a subjective formulation of what Paul wishes (after the manner of 7:15, 16, 19) with an objective formulation of what he does (after the manner of 7:18); and it is the objective form which governs, supplying the main clause of the νόμος here stated. In fact there is no express reference to what Paul does; τὸ κακόν is ambivalent, perhaps referring

---

122 The ἐγώ conforms 20a to 20b. Whether it has been added by Paul or by later scribes is not clear; a number of manuscripts and traditions, including B C D F G latt sa, Clement and Epiphanius, omit ἐγώ in v. 20a. ℵ A Ψ Majority Text and bo have ἐγώ; either they added it to balance the ἐγώ in 20b, or the others omitted it to harmonize 20a with 16.

123 The introductory νυνὶ δὲ of v. 17 is also omitted.

124 See Chapter 3, n. 74.

125 See also 7:13, 18a (ἀγαθος).

to what Paul does,[126] perhaps to ἁμαρτία which causes him to do it[127] (in either case contrasted with Jewish νόμος). The ambivalence is probably intentional, reflecting the close association between sin and evil deeds. If τὸ κακόν does refer to deeds, the impersonal formulation of v. 21b is simply consistent with v. 20, which declares that Paul does not in fact do these deeds; sin does. If τὸ κακόν refers to sin, v. 21b essentially repeats the final phrase of v. 20. In either case, the substance of the νόμος of v. 21 is a restatement of what Paul has just said in vv. 15-20. What, then, does he "therefore discover" (εὑρίσκω ἄρα)?[128] He discovers that this association of good and evil is a νόμος. Of the various concepts associated with νόμος, in this context νόμος as control[129] is predominant. This aspect of νόμος is certainly in Paul's mind here, for he is about to present it expressly in 7:23b, c, 25a, b, and it meshes with 7:14-20 also. The disjunction between what Paul wills and what he does is on its face something beyond Paul's own power, as he has stressed in the twice repeated οὐκέτι ἐγὼ κατεργάζομαι αὐτὸ ἀλλὰ ἡ οἰκοῦσα ἐν ἐμοὶ ἁμαρτία. Now this alien power is given the tangible shape of νόμος; εὑρίσκω emphasizes this tangibility.

The use of νόμος in this way depends also, indirectly, on another aspect of the term's meaning, that νόμος relates to a people (aspect 5); for it follows from this that each νόμος has a realm in which it applies. A multiplicity of νόμοι, each with its own realm, is inherent in the term's ordinary meaning.[130] Paul draws on this in suggesting another νόμος in 7:21 and, as we shall see, he draws on it yet more extensively in 7:22-23.[131]

---

[126] Cf. κακὸν τοῦτο πράσσω in 7:19. The pattern of 7:15, 19 leads one to expect such a reference after θέλειν.

[127] Then ἐμοὶ τὸ κακὸν παράκειται would be parallel to οἰκ[εῖ] ἐν ἐμοὶ ἡ ἁμαρτία (7:17, 20).

[128] The meaning of εὑρίσκω as "discover," not "deduce," is illustrated consistently in Paul's use of the term: e.g., Rom 4:1; 7:10; 1 Cor 4:2; 15:15; 2 Cor 2:13; 9:4; Gal 2:17.

[129] Aspect 4; see appendix to Chapter 2.

[130] As Paul would have had good cause to know; a Jew and (if Acts is right) a citizen of Tarsus and a citizen of Rome, he was subject, under appropriate circumstances, to the νόμος of each. The situation is not much altered if one rejects Acts' account that Paul was a citizen of Rome and Tarsus. Any tradesman in the eastern Mediterranean would have done business under ordinary Greek commercial νόμος; anyone who encountered Roman authorities, as Paul certainly did (2 Cor 11:25a; Phil 1:13), would have encountered aspects of Roman νόμος as well.

[131] The idea that νόμος has a source (aspect 6) may be invoked by the close association of v. 21 with ἁμαρτία. As for the other aspects of νόμος, if I am right in contending that they describe the term's meaning then all lie latent here, but they do not appear to function in Paul's argument.

There is therefore a lexical connection between the νόμος of 7:21 and the Jewish νόμος which is Paul's concern in 7:14-25. In itself this connection would not necessarily be important to Paul's argument; a word can be used in different ways without the speaker intending to make relate the different uses, or even noticing them. But νόμος is so central a topic here that I doubt Paul ever uses it accidentally; moreover, I shall show that his multiple usage of νόμος in the next two verses (22-23) establishes a deliberate usage into which 7:21 also fits.

It is therefore appropriate to compare the νόμος of v. 21 with the Jewish νόμος which has been Paul's subject up to now. Where Jewish νόμος is ἀγαθός and καλός, the νόμος of v. 21 is evidently κακός. But the chief point comes from the keynote in 7:14: if Jewish νόμος is πνευματικός, what is the νόμος of 7:21? What can it be but σάρκινος?[132] The limitation of Jewish νόμος, which prevents its effectiveness over the flesh, is mirrored by the power of this other νόμος.

The effect of this argument is a relativization of Jewish νόμος. It is similar to the relativization which occurs in Galatians, where νόμος is treated as an artifact of the Jewish people, comparable in principle to the νόμοι of other peoples; here in Rom 7:21 Jewish νόμος is treated as comparable to the νόμος which decrees that Paul, despite his own wish, does not do Jewish νόμος. This relativization of Jewish νόμος amounts to a devaluation of it; for by presenting it as one νόμος among many Paul implicitly rules out viewing it as the unique command of God. Although νόμος is not dissociated from God here, precisely what might have seemed one of the favorable and even divine features of νόμος, that it is πνευματικός, also points to the limitation and weakness of νόμος: that there are many νόμοι, and if one of the spirit, then by the same token one of the flesh.

But what happens when there are many νόμοι, νόμοι in conflict? Paul develops this theme in vv. 22-23.

Verses 22-3

The νόμοι expand geometrically, from one to two, and now from two to four:

συνήδομαι γὰρ τῷ νόμῳ τοῦ θεοῦ κατὰ τὸν ἔσω ἄνθρωπον, βλέπω δὲ ἕτερον νόμον ἐν τοῖς μέλεσίν μου ἀντιστρατευόμενον τῷ νόμῳ τοῦ νοός μου καὶ αἰχμαλωτίζοντά με ἐν τῷ νόμῳ τῆς ἁμαρτίας τῷ ὄντι ἐν τοῖς μέλεσίν μου.

---

132 Note the link between σάρξ and ἁμαρτία in 7:14 and 25.

The four νόμος-expressions here are usually taken to refer to two νόμοι,[133] or only to one.[134] But this overlooks Paul's precise expressions. Since the ἕτερος νόμος of v. 23 captures one ἐν τῷ νόμῳ τῆς ἁμαρτίας, the natural reading is that these are distinct νόμοι.[135] The distinction between ὁ νόμος τοῦ θεοῦ and ὁ νόμος τοῦ νοός μου is not so directly expressed, but if it be granted that there are two bad νόμοι rather than one, two good νόμοι are an obvious parallel.[136] At any rate Paul, by the marked variations in his terminology, certainly suggests that he has four νόμοι in view.[137]

There is no great difficulty in this if my reading of v. 21 is correct. Verse 21 establishes the precedent for a metaphorical use of νόμος,[138] and vv. 22-23 simply extend this usage: it is as if the multiple forces battling about and within him were so many νόμοι.[139]

What are the purpose and effect of these multiple metaphors? In the first place, we have the impression that there are so many νόμοι that they can scarcely be kept straight; the very suggestion of multiplicity, without working out in detail what these multiple entities are and how they relate, accentuates the relativization of νόμος begun in v. 21. But some additional observations can be made about each separate νόμος.

ὁ νόμος τοῦ θεοῦ. This is presumably Jewish νόμος. Even if Paul is often circumspect about the standard Jewish association of νόμος with God,[140] there is no basis for supposing that any other νόμος is God's.[141] Moreover, in

---

[133] E.g., Barrett, *Romans*, 149-50; Cranfield, *Romans*, 1.364; van Dülmen, *Theologie*, 116-18; Kümmel, *Römer* 7, 62-63; Kuss, *Römer*, 2.456-57; Lagrange, *Romains*, 178-79; Schlier, *Römer*, 234.

[134] E.g., Dunn, *Romans*, 1.395; Wilckens, *Römer*, 2.90-91.

[135] To be sure, they are both located ἐν τοῖς μέλεσίν μου. But this does not mean that the νόμοι are identical.

[136] The discrepancy between τοῦ θεοῦ and τοῦ νοός μου further hints at a distinction. This problem is not solved by marking the first genitive as one of source and the second as one which specifies the realm in which the νόμος operates; could it be that God rules only my mind?

[137] Four νόμοι are seen by Calvin (*Romans*, 152), Jerome (see Lagrange, *Romains*, 178), and Kuhl (*Römer*, 240-41).

[138] Such a precedent may have been established earlier, in 3:27, a passage which I have not analyzed.

[139] Kuss (*Römer*, 2.456-57) and Lagrange (*Romains*, 178-79) both consider the possibility that Paul identifies four distinct νόμοι, but conclude that he is speaking imprecisely. I think they miss the point.

[140] See Chapter 4, at nn. 49-60. In Romans, however, Jewish νόμος and God are associated at least at 2:13, 15, 23.

[141] Käsemann (*Romans*, 205) takes νόμος τοῦ θεοῦ to be "God's will in a general sense" ("Gotteswillen in einer generellen Wise"). This raises questions that Käsemann does not

this context συνήδομαι γὰρ τῷ νόμῳ recalls σύμφημι τῷ νόμῳ (7:16), a reference to Jewish νόμος.[142]

In contrast to the three νόμοι of 7:23, which are each qualified by a reference to a part or aspect of Paul himself (ἐν τοῖς μέλεσίν μου, or τοῦ νοός μου), ὁ νόμος τοῦ θεοῦ is not. The superficially similar prepositional phrase κατὰ τὸν ἔσω ἄνθρωπον is most striking for its contrast with these other expressions; it modifies the implied "I" rather than νόμος.[143] Moreover, Paul says that the νόμος of sin is within him; he does not say this of the νόμος of God.

ἕτερος νόμος. Since another νόμος has already been identified in 7:21, that is a natural referent for ἕτερος νόμος here; βλέπω . . . νόμον also invokes εὑρίσκω . . . νόμον in 7:21. But Paul does not make this reference explicit, as he could have done by using τούτον or even τόν. Moreover, the phrase ἐν τοῖς μέλεσίν μου mars the parallel with 7:21, for the νόμος of 7:21 is stated in terms of both "willing" and "doing." The whole of 7:23 may thus be seen as an elaboration of 7:21; 7:21 summarizes the νόμοι described in 7:23, and states this summary in the form of a νόμος.

Specifically, Paul says of the ἕτερος νόμος (a) that it is ἐν τοῖς μέλεσίν μου, (b) that it wars against ὁ νόμος τοῦ νοός μου, and (c) that it captures Paul in ὁ νόμος τῆς ἁμαρτίας. τὰ μέλη μου are probably more-or-less equivalent to ἡ σάρξ μου (7:18);[144] this implies a connection between the members and sin which the concluding phrases of v. 23 confirm. The phrase also contrasts with both ὁ νοῦς μου and ὁ ἔσω ἄνθρωπος, both contextually and literally (it is the outer, opposed to the inner). Points (b) and (c), the connections to other νόμοι, must be briefly deferred as we take a preliminary look at those other νόμοι.

---

address. What is this "will of God"? How is it manifested? Does it include Jewish νόμος? What else does it include?

It is my thesis that to apply νόμος to "God's will in a general sense" would *mean* to treat this "will" as having all of the attributes of νόμος identified in Chapter 2: as verbal, as relating to judgment, as a guide, as a command, as tied to a people, as having a source, and as something which people can put themselves under. All this can be said—Paul says it—of Jewish νόμος; whether it can be said of God's will in some other sense is doubtful; whether Paul in fact said it (and whether he would have expected his audience to understand any such reference of ὁ νόμος τοῦ θεοῦ to "God's will in a general sense") is more doubtful still.

[142] συνήδομαι is sometimes rendered "rejoice *with*" (BAGD, s.v.), a personification of νόμος. But it can also mean "rejoice *in*"; see LSJ, s.v. I.2, and Moulton and Milligan, *Vocabulary*, s.v., with examples there cited.

[143] One may also take the expression adverbially, but the meaning is equivalent.

[144] μέλος and σάρξ in Paul, although not interchangeable, are usually related (see, e.g., Rom 7:5). The unusual μου with σάρξ in 7:18 brings the two much closer together.

ὁ νόμος τοῦ νοός μου. This is connected to the νόμος of God (v. 22) by (a) the phrase τοῦ νοός μου,[145] and (b) the statement that it battles ἕτερος νόμος. τοῦ νοός μου may specify the realm in which the νόμος operates, or its source; the former is common in general usage with νόμος,[146] but the latter is found in the parallel expressions ὁ νόμος τοῦ θεοῦ and ὁ νόμος τῆς ἁμαρτίας within vv. 22-23.[147] We can take ὁ νόμος τοῦ νοός μου as identical to ὁ νόμος τοῦ θεοῦ by regarding νοός μου as a specification of scope, although, as I have noted,[148] this imposes a striking limit on the scope of the νόμος of God. But if, as I have argued, these two νόμοι are distinguished, then νοός μου probably states source; the phrase can mean something like "the rule of my mind," that is, "what my mind wills"—as described in 7:15, 16, 19, 20, 21.[149] There is a close connection between this νόμος and Jewish νόμος, as Paul says in 7:16b and 7:22, but they are not the same.

ὁ νόμος τῆς ἁμαρτίας. Here, as I have said, the genitive is evidently one of source: "the rule of sin," in comparison to "the rule of my mind."[150] This fits the account of ἁμαρτία in 7:14, 17 and 20. This νόμος is found ἐν τοῖς μέλεσίν μου, which accords with the idea that sin "dwells in me" (7:17, 20) and the apparent equivalence of this "in me" to "in my flesh" (7:18).

The four νόμοι. These understandings of ὁ νόμος τοῦ νοός μου and ὁ νόμος τῆς ἁμαρτίας suggest an understanding of ἕτερος νόμος: that this is the

---

145 Since Paul agrees with νόμος (7:16, 22).

146 Note the following examples, all taken from Josephus, J.W.: νόμος ἱστορίας, "law of [writing] history" (1.1.4 §11); νόμος τῆς γραφῆς, "law of writing" (5.1.3 §20); νόμος πάντων ἀνθρώπων, "law of all humankind" (1.19.4 §378); νόμος πολέμου, "law of war" (2.6.2 §90; 3.8.5 §363; 4.4.3 §260; 4.6.3 §388; 5.8.1 §332; 6.4.3 §239, 6.6.2 §346, 6.6.3 §353); νόμος φύσεως, "law of nature" (3.8.1 §370); νόμος καταλήψεως, "law of capture" (4.2.5 §117); νόμοι στρατείας, "laws of campaign" (5.3.4 §123); νόμος ἁγνείας, "law of sanctity" (5.5.2 §194); νόμος κλήρου, "law of the lot" (7.9.1 §396).

147 These also are paralleled within Josephus: νόμος τοῦ θεοῦ, "law of God," Ant. 11.5.1 §§124, 130; νόμος δεσπότου, "law of the emperor," J.W. 2.10.4 §195.

148 See above, n. 136.

149 In this metaphorical usage the focus is on aspects 3, 4, 5 and 6 of the meaning of νόμος (guide, command, multiplicity of νόμοι and source). Aspect 1 may also be implied, if Paul assumes that the mind acts verbally; aspects 2 and 7 (judgment, subject to choice) are not particularly apposite.

150 Fitzmyer ("Pauline Theology," 1405) says, "'[T]he law of sin' is an appositional genitive . . ." I think this is nearly right, but the two terms are not simply equated; a particular character is ascribed to ἁμαρτία by saying that it has a νόμος. Probably the focus is on aspects 4, 5 and 6 (command, multiplicity and source), but 2 (judgment, especially punishment) may be implied. Aspects 1, 3 and 7 (verbal, guide, subject to choice) are not particularly apposite.

νόμος of my members, after the fashion of the νόμος of my mind.[151] The picture presented by 7:22-23 thus develops what was implied in 7:14, that νόμος, as πνευματικός, rules only in matters πνευματικός. According to 7:22-23, Paul's mind submits to Jewish νόμος, but Paul's members refuse to submit to Paul's mind (ἀντιστρατευόμενον τῷ νόμῳ τοῦ νοός μου); they submit instead to sin (αἰχμαλωτίζοντά με ἐν τῷ νόμῳ τῆς ἁμαρτίας τῷ ὄντι ἐν τοῖς μέλεσίν μου). Each of the actors in this drama is characterized as a νόμος, and the drama as a whole is summarized by yet another νόμος, the νόμος discovered in 7:21. The metaphor of νόμος is here carried to its conclusion. In 7:21 Paul introduced the idea that one νόμος is balanced by another, and here he develops this idea still farther. Even the νόμος of God cannot save effectively, caught as it is in the coils of these other νόμοι. Through these other νόμοι sin accomplishes the death of which Paul speaks in 7:13; or alternatively, because this happens as a result of the inherent weakness of νόμος which allows these other νόμοι to combat God's νόμος, we might say that sin accomplishes death through νόμος generically: νόμος as such leaves an opening through which sin enters to bring one to death.

In this argument everything focuses on two points, the power of νόμος,[152] and the limitation of νόμος to its realm. The power of one νόμος in its realm is insufficient to conquer the power of another in its realm; in matters of σάρξ, νόμος πνευματικός is helpless before νόμος σάρκινος.[153]

Verse 24

Paul breaks off this discussion with a lament and a cry for assistance:

Ταλαίπωρος ἐγὼ ἄνθρωπος· τίς με ῥύσεται ἐκ τοῦ σώματος τοῦ θανάτου τούτου;

Two phrases here summarize the situation just described, ταλαίπωρος ἄνθρωπος and τὸ σῶμα τοῦ θανάτου τούτου. The precise meaning of the second phrase has been debated, as the variety of English translations shows: "the body of this death" is popular among the versions in the King James tradition,[154] but "this body of death" is preferred by most of the commenta-

---

[151] Like ὁ νόμος τῆς ἁμαρτίας, this would be νόμος principally in its fourth, fifth and sixth aspects, and perhaps its second.

[152] On this point, compare van Dülmen (*Theologie*, 118): "Alles, was einer totalen Anspruch auf den ganzen Menschen erhebt, sei es der Wille Gottes, sei es die Sünde wird νόμος genannt." van Dülmen calls νόμος in this sense a "Herrschaftssystem."

[153] It would seem to follow, conversely, that in spiritual matters the fleshly νόμος must yield to the spiritual νόμος. I take this up below, in a brief discussion of Rom 8:1-11.

[154] AV, RV, RSV, NASB.

tors,[155] and a number of grammars and versions take τοῦ θανάτου to be equivalent to "mortal."[156] These variations reflect the ambiguous placement of τούτου,[157] but the ambiguity is largely formal. Whichever noun τούτου attaches to, the demonstrative itself must refer to the state of affairs just described, in vv. 22-23.[158] Inasmuch as these verses contain a more direct reference to "body" than to "death,"[159] "this body" seems clearer than "this death." As for "mortal" or an equivalent, that seems to me to imply a reference to physical death which is out of place in this passage. θάνατος is probably metaphorical here, as it evidently is in 7:5, 10 and 13 (twice), and "of death" has the advantage of suggesting this more clearly than mortal," and certainly than "doomed to death."

Thus the realm in which νόμοι oppose one another is characterized as a "body of death," from which one must be saved by someone else; νόμος is useless. "Salvation" (ῥύεσθαι) might in principle refer to what we usually call conversion,[160] or to eschatological deliverance,[161] or perhaps to no decisive

---

[155] Barrett, Romans, 151; Cranfield, Romans, 1.367; Dodd, Romans, 133. Dunn (Romans, 1.397) suggests this as an alternative to the AV. Foreign commentators use the equivalent expressions "diesem Todeslieb" (Käsemann, Römer, 191; Schlier, Römer, 228; Wilckens, Römer, 2.94), "diesem Leibe des Todes" (Kuss, Römer, 2.458), or "ce corps de la mort" (Lagrange, Romains, 179).

[156] Moule, Idiom Book, 38; Zerwick, Greek, §41; cf. Moulton-Howard, Accidence, 440. This idea underlies the translations "doomed to death" (JB, NEB, NJB), "under the power of death" (NAB), "that is taking me to death" (TEV) and "doomed to this death" (NEB margin). A variant is "dead body" (Moulton-Turner, Syntax, 214), which is a blend of the idiomatic (taking the noun for an adjective) with the literal ("dead" rather than "mortal"). Whether this use of the genitive depends on a Semitic pattern is debated; see the grammars cited in this note.

[157] E.g., Cranfield (Romans, 1.366-67). Zerwick (Greek, §41) argues that the demonstrative must be attached to the nomen regens, just as with a construct chain in the Semitic languages; but I do not think this nuance could govern the Greek, even if the Greek does have a Semitic background (which is uncertain). To avoid ambiguity Paul would have had to place τούτου immediately before one or the other τοῦ (demonstratives are ordinarily in the predicate position; see Smyth, Grammar, §1176); perhaps Paul's phrase is influenced by a desire to avoid this triple repetition of a syllable (τούτου τοῦ).

[158] Cf. Dodd (Romans, 133), although Dodd does not refer here to vv. 22-23): "The meaning of the phrase ['body of death'] is sufficiently clear if we recall the sinful body of vi. 6 in the light of vii. 9, 13; it is not the same as the mortal body of vi. 12." (emphasis in the original)

[159] μέλη, νοῦς. "Here . . . its [σῶμα's] range of meaning is close to that of σάρξ, precisely because the more neutral σῶμα is qualified as 'of death' . . ." Dunn, Romans, 1.397. See further Jewett, Anthropological Terms, 294-95 (seeing a gnostic background to Paul's language).

[160] This follows if vv. 14-25 refer to life as a Jew; it is ruled out if, as I have argued, Paul is speaking of his present condition.

moment, but to a process: in 2 Cor 1:10 Paul speaks in just this way of salvation from death, as something that happens over and over again.[162] This last possibility is the most likely, as we shall shortly see.

Verse 25

The first sentence of this verse underscores the answer to the rhetorical question of v. 24:

χάρις δὲ τῷ θεῷ διὰ Ἰησοῦ Χριστοῦ τοῦ κυρίου ἡμῶν.

It is the second half of the verse which has proved difficult, for it seems to contradict the first:

Ἄρα οὖν αὐτὸς ἐγὼ τῷ μὲν νοΐ δουλεύω νόμῳ θεοῦ τῇ δὲ σαρκὶ νόμῳ ἁμαρτίας.

If Christ has saved one from "the body of death," as v. 25a following v. 24 seems to say, how is it that one still serves the νόμος of sin? To eliminate this difficulty many have either (a) transposed v. 25b to precede v. 24,[163] or (b) deleted it altogether.[164] There is no textual evidence for either of these hypotheses.[165]

---

161 So Dunn (*Romans*, 1.397), on the ground that "the most characteristic sense of ῥύομαι within the NT writings is eschatological . . ." (but see the following note). This is consistent with my view of the referent for ἐγώ.

162 Paul writes that God ἐκ τηλικούτου θανάτου ἐρρύσατο ἡμᾶς καὶ ῥύσεται, εἰς ὃν ἠλπίκαμεν ὅτι καὶ ἔτι ῥύσεται . . . (So Nestle-Aland[26]; on the numerous textual variations, see Metzger [*Textual commentary*, 574-75] and Furnish [*II Corinthians*, 114-15]; the most significant of these, accepted by Furnish and *TEV*, has "death" in the plural.)

163 Dodd (*Romans*, 132).

164 Käsemann, *Romans*, 211-12; Kuss, *Römer*, 2.460-61; Schlier, *Römer*, 235; Wilckens, *Römer*, 2.96-97.

165 Käsemann (*Romans*, 211) states the case well:

> How precarious it is to assert there is a gloss here against the whole textual tradition merely on material grounds cannot be minimized in the slightest. There is no historical evidence for this. On the other hand, the price which has to be paid for assuming authenticity should not be underestimated. For in this case it is not just our interpretation of the context that falls. All that Paul says about baptism, law, and the justification of the ungodly, namely, all that he says about the break between the aeons, will have to be interpreted differently.

For Käsemann, as this quotation indicates, the difficulty with v. 25b is not merely a disruption in the flow of the argument; rather, v. 25b depicts a bifurcated self, which Käsemann has been at pains to argue is not Paul's view in vv. 14-23.

I do not read Rom 7:14-23 as Käsemann does; I further think that inconsistency is in general an indifferent argument for inauthenticity. Authors are often inconsistent; if we

But on the view that I have taken of 7:14-25 there is no particular problem with v. 25b. In my view, Paul discusses his present situation throughout this passage. It is true that this account is in some tension with some things he says elsewhere; as I have noted above (at nn. 47-64), however, this tension runs throughout 7:14-25. The natural way to read vv. 25a and b together, where all the manuscripts place them, is that Paul wishes here to make two separate points, contrasting but not contradictory. First: that God through Jesus Christ sustains Paul in the situation Paul has described.[166] Second: that Paul nevertheless remains in this situation.[167] Putting v. 25b before vv. 24-25a would have allowed the first point to submerge the second; omitting vv. 24-25a would have allowed the second to submerge the first. The text as we have it makes both points.[168]

It remains to consider the precise content of v. 25b. To begin with, the emphatic ἐγώ, seen five times before in this passage, is here further emphasized by αὐτός; the stress is probably on the point that the one who serves the νόμος of God is the same as the one who serves the νόμος of sin.[169] Each of the four νόμοι of vv. 22-23 appears here in v. 25b, but only two of them are here identified as νόμοι: νόμος θεοῦ and νόμος ἁμαρτίας.[170] In place of ὁ νόμος

---

find an inconsistency in a modern author we do not usually suppose that an editor has meddled; we just think that the author has been inconsistent.

[166] I say "sustain," but the only term Paul uses is ῥύσεται, which we usually translate "rescue" and take to imply a once-for-all event. But, as Cranfield observes (Romans, 1.367), Paul does not say in v. 25a that Christ *has* saved him; if Dunn is right in thinking that eschatological deliverance is meant, Paul evidently means that Christ *will* save him; this prospect sustains Paul. Or if—as I have suggested (at n. 162 above)—ῥύσεται in v. 25b is not eschatological, it may refer to a constantly repeated process. This is suggested in 2 Cor 1:10 (n. 162 above), and also in (a) Matthew's version of the Lord's Prayer (Matt 6:13): ῥῦσαι ἡμᾶς ἀπὸ τοῦ πονηροῦ, and (b) 1 Thess 1:10, using a present participle to describe Ἰησοῦν τὸν ῥυόμενον ἡμᾶς ἐκ τῆς ὀργῆς τῆς ἐρχομένης.

[167] So Nygren (Romans, 301): "As long as this life lasts, there continues the tension between the old aeon and the new, between the heart and the members, in the life of the Christian." Dunn (Romans, 1.397): "That this [Rom 7:24] can be the cry of one who already has the Spirit . . . is sufficiently evident from 8:23 and 2 Cor 5:2-5."

[168] So Lagrange (Romains, 180): "Au moment de conclure, Paul insiste sur l'unité de l'être humain déchiré par deux tendances contraire, exprimées cette fois avec une concision lapidaire."

[169] So Cranfield (Romans, 1.369 n. 4), Dunn (Romans, 1.398). Contrast Käsemann (Romans, 211): "αὐτὸς ἐγώ means the true I which can be separated from the flesh in non-Pauline fashion." This is a less natural reading; Käsemann, however, is arguing against the verse's authenticity.

[170] Notwithstanding the absence of the article, each surely has the same referent as the corresponding articular form in vv. 22-23. See Robertson, Grammar, 780; Bläser, Gesetz, 10.

τοῦ νοός μου we have simply ὁ νοῦς, and in place of ἕτερος νόμος ἐν τοῖς μέλεσίν μου simply ἡ σάρξ, which supports my view that these νόμοι are ways of referring to control exerted by mind and flesh; essentially the same thought can be conveyed, as it is here, without the term νόμος.[171]

The expression δουλεύω νόμῳ personalizes νόμος, as did the expression νόμον . . . ἀντιστρατευόμενον . . . καὶ αἰχμαλωτίζοντά με . . . in 7:23.[172] This creates an implicit contrast to the reference to Ἰησοῦ Χριστὸς ὁ κύριος ἡμῶν in v. 25a. Paul has called himself δοῦλος Χριστοῦ Ἰησοῦ at the very beginning of this letter (1:1), as he does elsewhere (Gal 1:10; Phil 1:1); indeed, the concepts of δουλεύω and κύριος suggest one another. The divided service of νόμος—according to this passage, an inevitably divided service—is contrasted with the undivided service of Christ.

Verses 14-25 Translated[173]

14 We all agree that the νόμος is part of the spiritual realm. But we are in the fleshly realm, suffering still under the enslaving power of sin.

15 [In this fleshly realm] we find that we neither understand our own actions—for so often we do exactly what we did not want to do—nor do we perceive the fruit those actions bear. 16 Thus it happens that we at the same time devote ourselves to νόμος, and yet disobey it; for our disobedience is not by our choice. 17 So the things we do, and the fruit our actions bear, are not in fact our own product; they are the product of sin, which rules the fleshly realm and us who are captive in that realm.

18 Thus the good [νόμος] and the good [deeds which νόμος commands] are not to be found in us, in the fleshly realm [which holds us captive]. Although we can wish to do the good things [required of citizens of the spiritual realm], we cannot actually accomplish those things.

19 So we desire the good [νόμος], but we do the very opposite. 20 Thus, since we do not do what we want to do nor bring about what

---

171 Similarly Kuhl (*Römer*, 241).

172 Cf. also πεπραμένος ὑπὸ τὴν ἁμαρτίαν in 7:14, which both personalizes sin and specifically invokes the idea of slavery.

173 In this paraphrase I attempt to stay as close as possible to the literal sense of Paul's words, marking my explanatory additions with brackets. Throughout, however, I render ἐγώ by "we"; I take it that Paul uses the first person to express solidarity with his hearers, not to distinguish himself from them.

we want to bring about, neither our actions nor the fruit of those actions is our own product; they are the product of sin, ruling us [who are still captive in the fleshly realm].

21 Thus we find it to be a νόμος [in the fleshly realm we inhabit] that although we wish to do the good [νόμος], we are actually surrounded by evil.

22-23 We should love to submit ourselves to God's νόμος! But we see our [fleshly] members seeking to exert their νόμος over the νόμος of our [spiritual] minds; and we find ourselves enslaved under the νόμος of sin. 24 Our condition is miserable! Who can save us from this [fleshly realm] of death?

25 Thanks be to God, for [he has given us] Jesus Christ [to lead us out of this dreadful condition]. [This knowledge sustains us as] we serve God's spiritual νόμος with our minds, yet remain subject to the power of sin's νόμος in our flesh.

Postscript: Romans 8:1-11

If I am right in concluding that 7:14-25 refers to Paul's present condition, then 8:1-11 does not refer to a newer condition but to a different aspect of the same condition; in this it follows the lead of 7:25a. Since 8:1-11 continues and develops the legal discussion of 7:14-25, a few comments are necessary. Whether κατάκριμα in 8:1 be "condemnation" or "punishment,"[174] it implies a legal process and invokes νόμος in aspect 2; the verse thus suggests a freedom from νόμος, and 8:2 makes this explicit, but by means of dual νόμοι:

ὁ γὰρ νόμος τοῦ πνεύματος τῆς ζωῆς ἐν Χριστῷ Ἰησοῦ ἠλευθέρωσέν σε ἀπὸ τοῦ νόμου τῆς ἁμαρτίας καὶ τοῦ θανάτου.[175]

As in 7:22-23, the identity of these νόμοι is not entirely clear; in fact Paul's terminology for them is not entirely clear, since ἐν Χριστῷ Ἰησοῦ may modify

---

[174] It is probably the latter; see Danker, "Under Contract," 105 n. 3 (concerning Rom 5:16); Moulton and Milligan, *Vocabulary*, s.v.; BAGD, s.v. LSJ cites one passage for the meaning "condemnation," Dionysius of Halicarnassus, *Ant. Rom.* 6.61, but there "punishment" is also possible.

[175] σε is disputed; there is significant authority for με and slight authority for ἡμᾶς and for no pronoun at all. σε is the more difficult reading; με harmonizes with chapter 7 and ἡμᾶς with 8:4. So Metzger, *Textual Commentary*, 516; Cranfield, *Romans*, 1.377; Dunn, *Romans*, 1.414; Käsemann, *Romans*, 214; Schlier, *Römer*, 236-37.

either τῆς ζωῆς or ἠλευθέρωσέν,[176] and καὶ τοῦ θανάτου may either attach to τοῦ νόμου or be separately dependent on ἀπό.[177] But there is no reason to doubt that ὁ νόμος τῆς ἁμαρτίας, with or without τοῦ θανάτου, refers to ὁ νόμος τῆς ἁμαρτίας of 7:23 and νόμος ἁμαρτίας of 7:25.

ὁ νόμος τοῦ πνεύματος τῆς ζωῆς is a new phrase. It recalls ὁ νόμος πνευματικός ἐστιν (7:14), which refers to Jewish νόμος. But the adjective πνευματικός and the phrase τὸ πνεῦμα τῆς ζωῆς do not necessarily have the same referent. Moreover, Rom 7:14-25 has demonstrated the inadequacy of Jewish νόμος to deal with the flesh—the point that Paul is about to summarize once again in 8:3. Although it is grammatically possible that Paul means in 8:2 that this very νόμος becomes efficacious when used by Christ, nothing in the preceding verses has prepared us for this, and the succeeding verses do not develop it; 8:3 appears to dismiss νόμος.

In analyzing 7:22-25 I concluded that each genitival expression with νόμος was a genitive of source, identifying the power whose control is in turn identified by the term νόμος.[178] I think it likely that the same principle operates here. ὁ νόμος τοῦ πνεύματος τῆς ζωῆς is then not Jewish νόμος, but a metaphorical expression, similar to those in 7:23 and 25, for a power: the power of τὸ πνεῦμα τῆς ζωῆς.[179]

In 8:3 ὁ νόμος, unadorned, evidently refers to Jewish νόμος, and so too in 8:4. Every "other νόμος" of 7:23 - 8:2 has been carefully described as such, and there is no comparable indication here that something other than Jewish

---

[176] The various possibilities are conveniently arranged by Cranfield (*Romans*, 1.374-75); he prefers the adverbial interpretation, which links the thought with that of 8:3.

[177] "Sin" and "death" are connected on either view, as in 7:9-10, and especially 13.

[178] Similarly, ὁ νόμος τοῦ ἀνδρός in 7:2 may refer to the rule of the husband. This understanding fits the analogy Paul implies between 7:2-3 and 4; as the wife is freed from the husband's rule, so the Christian is freed from the rule of Jewish νόμος. While most commentators take ὁ νόμος τοῦ ἀνδρός to mean "law of marriage" (e.g., Dodd, *Romans*, 119; Dunn, *Romans*, 1.368; Kuss, *Römer*, 2.435-36; Sanday and Headlam, *Romans*, 173; Schlier, *Römer*, 216; Zahn, *Römer*, 329), this is not an obvious term for that law, and no one has cited its use elsewhere. Moreover, it would be odd to say that the husband's death releases the woman from the law of marriage; it is actually that very law which provides that she is now free to be with another man.

[179] As with ὁ νόμος τῆς ἁμαρτίας (see n. 150 above), Fitzmyer ("Pauline Theology," 1403) sees νόμος here as figuratively equated with the noun in the appendant genitive: that is, νόμος is πνεῦμα (here Fitzmyer terms the expression an oxymoron, like νόμος πίστεως in Rom 3:27 and ὁ νόμος τοῦ Χριστοῦ in Gal 6:2). Käsemann (*Romans*, 215-16) says: "The law of the Spirit is nothing other than the Spirit himself in his ruling function in the sphere of Christ."

Paul does not explain τῆς ζωῆς. It may identify the spirit as life-giving (so Barrett, *Romans*, 155; Cranfield, *Romans*, 1.376; Dodd, *Romans*, 134-35; Käsemann, *Romans*, 215-16).

νόμος is meant. In 8:7 ὁ νόμος τοῦ θεοῦ means Jewish νόμος, like the parallel expressions in 7:22 and 25; Paul's argument depends on the same incompatibility between Jewish νόμος and σάρξ found in 7:14-15 and 8:3.

Results

As I acknowledged at the outset, my interpretation of Rom 7:14-25 differs from that usual in modern times; this appears chiefly in my view that Paul here discusses the condition of Christians. I do not wish to stress this point, however, for it is not critical to my understanding of νόμος.

I have concluded that in Romans 7-8 νόμος generally means Jewish νόμος, as it does in Galatians 2; the uses of the term in other ways, as in 7:23, 25; 8:2, 7, and perhaps 7:2-3,[180] are adopted because of points Paul wishes to make about Jewish νόμος. Paul's treatment of Jewish νόμος in Romans 7-8 is very different from his treatment of it in Galatians 2: not, however, because the term has a different meaning in the two letters, but because different aspects of its meaning are emphasized. In Galatians 2, the emphasis is placed on aspect 5, its relation to the Jewish people. In Romans 7-8, this aspect underlies Paul's treatment, for it allows him to speak of multiple νόμοι; but Paul's principal emphasis is on aspect 4, the controlling force of νόμος. This emerges first in 7:7-13, where νόμος is treated substantially as command (ἐντολή), and it is the point of the picture of multiple νόμοι with which Paul concludes chapter 7 and opens chapter 8.

The arguments of Galatians 2 and Romans 7-8 have in common their relativization of νόμος. In Galatians 2 this was implicit in the identification of Jewish νόμος with the Jewish people, and finally (in vv. 17-18) the subordination of the authority of νόμος to the authority of Jews, Ἰουδαῖοι φύσει such as Paul himself. In Romans 7-8 the relativization is explicit. There are many νόμοι. But there is only one God, and one Jesus Christ.

---

[180] See n. 178.

Chapter 7

ΔΙΑ ΠΟΙΟΥ ΝΟΜΟΥ;

The writings of the New Testament, like the communities in which those writings were composed and preserved, are fashioned out of diverse elements. St. Paul is a Jew; he not only avows his Jewish background (e.g., Rom 9:3; Gal 1:13-14; Phil 3:5-6), but the voices of Jewish scripture echo through his letters.[1] Paul is, however, also a citizen of the Diaspora, living and writing in a Roman and Greek world, subject to Roman and Greek law. He writes in Greek; even the echoes of Jewish scripture to which I have just referred are Greek echoes.

When Paul takes up the term νόμος to speak of Jewish matters, it is a Greek term he takes up. It has a special usage among Jews, and Paul's letters are evidence of this usage; but it is still Greek, with a meaning and significance tied to the Greek. The Jewish usage does not break free from the Greek meaning; it rather exploits it.

Thus νόμος in Paul's letters has a consistent meaning independent of whether or not in a particular passage it refers to Jewish νόμος. This meaning I have defined, in Chapter 2, by seven components: (1) νόμος is verbal;[2] (2) it is a standard for judgment; (3) it is a guide; (4) it controls; (5) it is tied to a particular people; (6) it has a source; and (7) people put themselves under it.

This meaning is evidenced chiefly for Jewish νόμος, for νόμος in Paul's letters usually refers to Jewish νόμος. But not always: in Chapter 3 I showed

---

[1] Hays, *Echoes*.

[2] Probably this is a supplementary component, an ordinary part of the term's meaning but not essential to it. Sometimes νόμος is only perceptible.

that, besides its usual definite reference to Jewish νόμος, νόμος also refers, from time to time, to a definite non-Jewish νόμος; to νόμος indefinitely; to νόμος generally; and to νόμος generically. All of these references show that Paul not only is aware—as he had to be—of broader senses of νόμος; he employs them.

In Chapters 4 and 5 I showed how this is reflected precisely in the relationship between Judaism and νόμος. As Greek νόμος is the νόμος of the Greeks and Roman νόμος is the νόμος of the Romans, so Jewish νόμος is the νόμος of the Jews. This goes beyond even Räisänen's formulation that νόμος is "the whole of Israel's sacred tradition,"[3] for on my analysis "sacred" is not part of the term's meaning, even though the traditions regarded by Jews as sacred are included (and indeed have pride of place). The relationship between νόμος and the Jewish people is fundamental, a matter of definition; in contrast, the relationship between νόμος and God is a matter of belief and assertion—and also, on occasion, for equivocation.

One νόμος among others: this theme is displayed not only in the tie between Jewish νόμος and the Jewish people, but also in the usage "νόμος of ____," found in 1 Corinthians 9, Galatians 6, Romans 3, and especially Romans 7. In itself this usage implies a variety of νόμοι; in Chapter 6 I showed how Paul employs this idea of various νόμοι in Romans 7 to show the weakness of νόμος. There, in contrast to Galatians, νόμος is explicitly linked to God; but the very expression of this link in the phrase ὁ νόμος τοῦ θεοῦ implies the existence of ὁ νόμος which is not τοῦ θεοῦ: if there were not such another νόμος, the phrase τοῦ θεοῦ would be superfluous. Paul proceeds to spell out this implication in the phrase ὁ νόμος τῆς ἁμαρτίας, together with the variety of other similar phrases found in Rom 7:21-23.

In all of these phrases we see νόμος presented as the νόμος of a particular realm. To speak of νόμος is thus to ask the question: which νόμος? ποῖος νόμος, or, as Paul says in Rom 3:27, διὰ ποίου νόμου; Even the νόμος of God, good and spiritual as Paul affirms it to be, is only the νόμος of the realm of the good and spiritual. Both nouns in the phrase ὁ νόμος τοῦ θεοῦ require attention; this νόμος is God's, but it is still only νόμος.

My chief result has thus been to place νόμος in the context of νόμοι. I hold that the term νόμος carries with it into Paul's writings the multiplicity of νόμοι which was a feature of Paul's life.

This philological proposition informs our understanding of Paul's theology, and perhaps of his history. When Paul uses νόμος to refer to the Jewish way of life, as I argue in Chapters 4 and 5, that term implies a

---

[3] Räisänen, Paul, 16.

particular understanding of Judaism. I should like to go further, for I consider it likely that the term νόμος, whose link to Judaism is certainly not original to Paul, has helped to shape Paul's understanding of Judaism. I suspect that the ordinary political significance of νόμος, linking any particular νόμος to a particular people, prompts Paul to see his ancestral traditions in terms of their relation to his ancestors rather than in terms of their relation to God. But this takes us beyond the results of my study; although I think my work suggests a causal link it does not demonstrate one.

This is of secondary importance. If the history of Paul's thought cannot be written, still I believe I have clarified an aspect of Paul's theology, Paul's view of Judaism. Jewish νόμος and the Jewish people define one another. Therefore if there is a gospel for the Gentiles, it follows as a matter of course that this gospel is free of Jewish νόμος. Jewish νόμος is for the Jews; Christ, however, is for everyone.

E. P. Sanders's explanation of Paul's attitude to νόμος makes the central point; only Sanders does not take this point far enough. Sanders writes: "If salvation is by Christ and is intended for Gentile as well as Jew, it is not by the Jewish law in any case . . ."[4] Sanders is right in tying the rejection of νόμος to the inclusion of Gentiles, but wrong in limiting the rejection of νόμος to the question of salvation. The matter is simpler than this: Jewish νόμος, because it is Jewish νόμος, is not Gentile νόμος.

Sanders's argument that Paul considers Gentile Christians to be bound by Jewish νόμος[5] is not persuasive. It has two defects. First, the texts on which Sanders relies to show that Gentile Christians are subject to νόμος generally do not mention νόμος.[6] I cannot regard this as an incidental omission. It goes to the central question: is there a connection between νόμος and the principles Paul invokes by language as broad as εἰς τὸ στηρίξαι ὑμῶν τὰς καρδίας ἀμέμπτους ἐν ἁγιωσύνῃ ἔμπροσθεν τοῦ θεοῦ (1 Thess 3:13)?[7]

Second, Sanders arrives at his conclusion by dispensing with certain difficult provisions of νόμος: "the requirement of circumcision, special days, and special food."[8] But can one take so free a hand with νόμος and still accept it as νόμος? Not according to Paul: Ἴδε ἐγὼ Παῦλος . . . μαρτύρομαι δὲ πάλιν

---

[4] Sanders, *Paul, the Law*, 152 (emphasis in the original).

[5] Ibid., 93-122.

[6] Ibid., 94. Seventeen texts are listed, only three with νόμος: Gal 6:2, which, however, speaks of ὁ νόμος τοῦ Χριστοῦ; and Gal 5:14 and Rom 13:8-10, both of which reduce νόμος to the single command ἀγαπήσεις τὸν πλησίον σου ὡς σεαυτόν. Significance is thus attached to a text from scripture, but precisely by casting aside every particular provision of νόμος.

[7] This is one of Sanders's examples (ibid., 94).

[8] Ibid., 114.

παντὶ ἀνθρώπῳ περιτεμνομένῳ ὅτι ὀφειλέτης ὅλον τὸν νόμον ποιῆσαι (Gal 5:2-3). One does not pick and choose among the provisions of νόμος.[9] Sanders's position is not Paul's, but that of the Teachers in Galatia; they evidently preach obedience to some parts of νόμος but excuse their hearers from obedience to other parts,[10] and in 5:3 Paul takes them to task for this. Paul has a different understanding of νόμος-observance, and in his view Jewish νόμος is not something to be observed by Gentiles.

This does not mean that Paul's expectations for Gentiles are unrelated to Jewish morality, or to Scripture. Certainly there are many connections; Paul does not proclaim a new morality. But he does not treat Jewish moral practice as νόμος, nor does he even appeal specifically to Jewish practice. When Paul rebukes the Corinthians over the man who lives with his stepmother, it is actually Gentile practice he refers to.[11] In Romans 2, where Paul does speak of Gentile νόμος-observance, he deliberately alters the concept of νόμος, making it a νόμος "of the heart" (2:29) which can be observed by Gentiles who yet remain Gentile.[12] This idea of a νόμος καρδίας, a νόμος which is not exactly νόμος, serves a particular function in the argument of Romans 2,[13] and does not appear elsewhere in Paul's letters.

If Paul considers that a gospel for non-Jews is inherently a gospel without Jewish νόμος, there remains the question of why there should be such a non-Jewish gospel. Perhaps Christ came only for the Jews—this would not have been a radical idea. To say that Paul abandoned νόμος because he preached to the Gentiles may seem to beg the question: why did Paul preach to the Gentiles? Which came first, the turn away from Judaism or the turn away from νόμος?

Francis Watson argues in his recent book that Paul turns to Gentiles because he has failed among Jews; Watson then proceeds to explain the abandonment of νόμος on the ground that its peculiar requirements (circumcision,

---

[9] George Foot Moore reports: "Shammai would have nothing to do with one who was not prepared to give implicit assent, before knowing its contents, to the unwritten law as well as the written." (*Judaism*, 1.341). Moore seems to regard this as an extreme view, but if the rule were otherwise, law would not be law. Consent to law is not a matter of approving individual prescriptions, but of recognizing the authority of the lawgiver.

[10] According to Gal 6:13 the Teachers themselves do not keep νόμος. Certainly they preach circumcision. Probably they do not preach the food laws, for if they did one would expect a more pointed discussion of such laws by Paul—especially when he discusses the Antiochene incident, which did involve food laws (Gal 2:11-14).

[11] . . . τοιαύτη πορνεία ἥτις οὐδὲ ἐν τοῖς ἔθνεσιν . . . (1 Cor 5:1) (οὐδέ, "not even" [BDF §445.2; BAG s.v. 3], makes an implicit reference to Jewish practice).

[12] That is, uncircumcised.

[13] See Chapter 4, at nn. 91-104.

food laws, the Sabbath and fast days) were a practical hindrance to Gentile conversion.[14] If my interpretation of Paul is correct, the second half of Watson's thesis is superfluous; once Paul turns to Gentiles he drops νόμος as a matter of course. Against Watson, 1 Cor 9:21 does not show that Paul excuses Gentiles from observing Jewish νόμος "as a matter of . . . practical expediency,"[15] for in that passage the issue is observance of Jewish νόμος by Paul, a Jew.[16]

I think that the basic question of why Paul turned to the Gentiles remains open. Watson's explanation is plausible, but there are other possibilities. The turn from νόμος might have come first, prompted perhaps by the perception that νόμος cursed Christ (Gal 3:13); this could explain why Χριστὸς ἐσταυρωμένος is a scandal to Jews (1 Cor 1:23).[17] Paul's own account in Gal 1:16 implies that he had from the beginning a divine commission to the Gentiles; the principal evidence that Paul began by preaching to Jews comes from Acts (e.g., 13:46-48), whose authority Watson rejects.[18]

Whatever the sequence of Paul's thought, the point remains that the turn to Gentiles and the turn from νόμος imply each other.[19] It is also the case that the question of νόμος for Jews remains open. Paul himself certainly dispenses with νόμος on some occasions, as 1 Cor 9:21 and Gal 2:11-14 testify; but he is apostle to the Gentiles, and it does not follow that all Jews should ignore νόμος at all times, nor even that Paul himself does so (cf. 1 Cor 9:20).

What is plain is that this question has no great importance for Paul. In setting Jewish νόμος against the background of the many νόμοι which are to be found in the world Paul makes Jewish νόμος—like every νόμος, like νόμος as such—one of those things τοῦ κόσμου against which, according to 1 Corinthians 1, things τοῦ θεοῦ are to be contrasted.

---

14 Watson, Paul, 28-38.

15 Ibid., 36.

16 Watson also refers (ibid.) to 1 Cor 10:32-11:1; if this passage deals with νόμος-observance it evidently applies the same principle as 1 Cor 9:21.

17 However, there is no reference to νόμος in 1 Cor 1.

18 Watson, Paul, 32, 188 n.55. See also Sanders, Paul, the Law, 179-82.

In 1 Cor 9:20 Paul speaks of preaching to Jews, but does not assign this to any particular period.

19 At least, in Paul's thought as reflected in the letters we have. It is possible that at an earlier time he held a different view.

BIBLIOGRAPHY

Abbott-Smith, G. *A Manual Greek Lexicon of the New Testament*. 3d ed. Edinburgh: Clark, 1937.

Achelis, E. "Über das Subject in Röm. 7. Eine biblisch-theologische Untersuchung." *Theologische Studien und Kritiken* 36 (1863) 670-704.

Achtemeier, P. *Romans*. Atlanta: John Knox, 1985.

Aland, K. and B. *The Text of the New Testament*. Grand Rapids: Eerdmans, 1987.

Aland, K., ed. *Vollstandige Konkordanz zum Griechischen Neuen Testament*. Berlin: de Gruyter, 1983.

Allegro, J.M. "Fragments of a Qumran Scroll of Eschatological Midrashim." *JBL* 77 (1958) 350-54.

Althaus, P. "Zur Auslegung von Röm. 7,14 ff. Antwort an Anders Nygren." *TLZ* 77 (1952) 475-80.

Anderson, F. L. "How God Gets the Law Fulfilled: Rom. 8:1-4." *Biblical World* 30 (1907) 118-22.

Aquinas, Thomas. *Commentary on St. Paul's Epistle to the Galatians*. Tr. F. R. Larcher. Albany: Magi, 1966.

Arndt, W. F. "Brief Studies: On Gal. 2:17-19." *Concordia Theological Monthly* 27 (1956) 128-32.

Augustine. *Propositions from the Epistle to the Romans, Unfinished Commentary on the Epistle to the Romans*. Atlanta: Scholars Press, 1987.

Baarda, T. "Het einde van de wet is Christus. Rom. 10:4-15, een Midrasj van Paulus over Deut. 30:11-14." *Gereformeerd Theologisch Tijdschrift* 88 (1988) 208-48.

Badenas, Robert. *Christ the End of the Law*. Sheffield: JSOT, 1985.

Bammel, E. νόμος Χριστοῦ. *SE* 3 (1964) 120-28.

Bandstra, A. J. *The Law and the Elements of the World.* Kampen: Kok, 1964.

Barclay, J. M. G. "Paul and the law: observations on some recent debates." *Themelios* 12 (1986) 5-15.

Bardy, G. "Saint Paul juriste." *Recherches de Science Religieuse* 31 (1943) 209-10.

Barr, J. *The Semantics of Biblical Language.* Oxford: Oxford University Press, 1961.

Barrett, C. K. *A Commentary on the Epistle to the Romans.* HNTC. New York: Harper & Row, 1957.

Barrett, C. K. *Freedom and Obligation. A Study of the Epistle to the Galatians.* London: SPCK, 1985.

Bartels, R. A. "Law and Sin in Fourth Esdras and Saint Paul." *LQ* 1 (1949) 319-29.

Barth, K. *The Epistle to the Romans.* 6th ed. Oxford: University Press, 1933.

Barth, M. "'The Faith of the Messiah.'" *HeyJ* 10 (1969) 363-70.

Barth, M. "Die Stellung des Paulus zu Gesetz und Ordnung." *EvT* 33 (1973) 496-526.

Barth, M. "Jews and Gentiles: The Social Character of Justification in Paul." *JES* 5 (1968) 241-67.

Barth, M. "Justification. From Text to Sermon on Galatians 2:11-21." *Int* 22 (1968) 147-57.

Barth, M. "St. Paul - A Good Jew." *Horizons in Biblical Theology* 1 (1979) 7-45.

Barth, M. *Ephesians. AB.* 2 vols. Garden City: Doubleday, 1974

Beck, I. "Altes und neues Gesetz. Eine Untersuchung über die Kompromisslosigkeit des paulinischen Denkens." *Münchener Theologische Zeitschrift* 15 (1964) 127-42.

Beker, J. C. *Paul the Apostle.* Philadelphia: Fortress, 1980.

Belleville, L. L. "'Under Law': Structural Analysis and the Pauline Concept of Law in Galatians 3.21 - 4.11." *JSNT* 26 (1986) 53-78.

Benoit, P. "La loi et la croix d'après saint Paul." *RB* 47 (1938) 481-509.

Berényi, G. "Gal 2,20: a Pre-Pauline or a Pauline Text?" *Bib* 65 (1984) 490-97.

Bergmeier, R. "Röm 7,7-25a (8,2): Der Mensch - das Gesetz - Gott - Paulus - die Exegese im Widerspruch?" *KD* 31 (1985) 162-72.

Betz, H. D. *Galatians.* Hermeneia. Philadelphia: Fortress, 1979.

Black, M. "Pharisees." *IDB* 3 (1965) 774-81.

Blank, J. "Der gespaltene Mensch. Zur Exegese von Röm 7,7-25." *Bibel und Leben* 9 (1968) 10-20.

Blank, J. "Evangelium und Gesetz. Zur theologischen Relativierung und Begründung ethischer Normen." *Diakonia* 5 (1974) 363-75.

Blank, J. "Warum sagt Paulus: 'Aus Werkem des Gesetzes wird niemand gerecht'?" *EKK* 1 (1969) 79-95.

Bläser, P. P. *Das Gesetz bei Paulus.* Münster: Aschendorff, 1941.

Boers, H. "The Problem of Jews and Gentiles in the Macro-Structure of Romans." *Neot* 15 (1981) 1-11.

Bonwetsch, D. "Römer 7,14 ff. in der alten Kirche und in Luthers Vorlesungen über den Römerbrief." *NKZ* 30 (1919) 135-56.

Bornkamm, G. "Gesetz und Natur (Röm 2:14-16)." In *Studien zu Antike und Christentum*, 93-118. Gesammelte Aufsätze Band II. München: Kaiser, 1959.

Bornkamm, G. "Sin, Law and Death. An Exegetical Study of Romans 7." 1950. In *Early Christian Experience*, 87-104. London: SCM, 1969.

Bornkamm, G. *Das Ende des Gesetzes*. München: Kaiser, 1963.

Bornkamm, G. "Sünde, Gesetz und Tod, Das Ende des Gesetzes." BEvT 16 5(1966) 51-69.

Boschi, B. "Legge e grazia in San Paolo. Loro momento dialettico nelle epistole ai Galatai e ai Romani." *Sacra Doctrina* 14 (1969) 591-614.

Bouwman, G. "'Christus Diener der Sünde.' Auslegung von Galater 2,14b-18." *Bijdragen* 40 (1979) 44-54.

Bover, J. M. "Valor do los terminos 'Ley', 'Yo', 'Pecado', en Rom. 7." *Bib* 5 (1924) 192-96.

Braun, H. "Römer 7,7-25 und das Selbstverständnis des Qumran-Frommen." *ZTK* 56 (1959) 1-18.

Bring, R. "Das Gesetz und die Gerechtigkeit Gottes. Eine Studie zur Frage nach der Bedeutung des Ausdruckes *telos nomou* in Röm. 10:4." *ST* 20 (1966) 1-36.

Bring, R. "Der Mittler und das Gesetz. Eine Studie zu Gal. 3,20." *KD* 12 (1966) 292-309.

Bring, R. "Die Erfüllung des Gesetzes durch Christus." *KD* 5 (1959) 1-22.

Bring, R. "Paul and the Old Testament. A Study of the ideas of Election, Faith and Law in Paul, with special reference to Romans 9:30 - 10:30." *ST* 25 (1971) 21-60.

Bring, R. *Christus und das Gesetz. Die Bedeutung des Gesetzes des Alten Testaments nach Paulus und sein Glauben an Christus*. Leiden: Brill, 1969.

Browning, W. "Studies in Texts—Rom. 7:18 f." *Theology* 52 (1949) 22-25.

Bruce, F. F. "Paul and the Law of Moses." *BJRL* 57 (1975) 259-79.

Bruce, F. F. "The Romans Debate - Continued." *BJRL* 64 (1982) 334-59.

Bruce, F. F. *The Epistle to the Galatians*. NIGTC. Grand Rapids: Eerdmans, 1982.

Bultmann, R. "Christus des Gesetzes Ende." In *Glaube und Verstehen* 2:32-58. 4 vols. Tübingen: Mohr, 1968.

Bultmann, R. "Romans 7 and the Anthropology of Paul." 1932. In *Existence and Faith*, 147-57. New York: Meridian, 1960.

Bultmann, R. "Zur Auslegung von Galater 2,15-18." 1952. In *Exegetica*, 394-99. Tubingen: Mohr, 1967.

Bultmann, R. *Theology of the New Testament*. 2 vols. New York: Scribner's, 1955.

Burton, E. D. "Detached Notes: νόμος." In id., *Galatians*, 443-60.

Burton, E. D. *A Critical and Exegetical Commentary on the Epistle to the Galatians*. ICC. Edinburgh: Clark, 1920.

Burton, E. D. *Notes on New Testament Grammar*. Chicago: University of Chicago Press, 1904.

Burton, E. D. *Syntax of the Moods and Testaments in New Testament Greek*. 3d ed. Chicago: University of Chicago Press, 1900.

Buscemi, A. "La struttura litteraria di Gal 2,14b-21." *Studii Biblici Franciscani Liber Annuus* 31 (1981) 59-74.

Bushell, G. "Law and Christian Spirituality According to St. Paul." *Australian Biblical Review* 5 (1956) 99-117.

Caird, G. B. *The Language and Imagery of the Bible.* Philadelphia: Westminster, 1980.

Callan, T. "Pauline Midrash: The Exegetical Background of Gal 3:19b." *JBL* 99 (1980) 549-67.

Calvin, J. *The Epistles of Paul the Apostle to the Galatians, Ephesians, Philippians and Colossians.* Edinburgh: Oliver & Boyd, 1965.

Calvin, J. *The Epistles of Paul the Apostle to the Romans and to the Thessalonians.* Edinburgh: Oliver & Boyd, 1960.

Campbell, W. S. "Christ the End of the Law: Rom 10:4." *Papers on Paul and Other New Testament Authors.* JSNTSupp 3. Sheffield: JSOT, 1980.

Carnap, R. *Introduction to Semantics.* Cambridge, Mass.: Harvard University Press, 1942.

Carney, Frederick S. "The Virtue-Obligation Controversy." *Journal of Religious Ethics* 1 (1973) 5-19.

Carpus. "Heaven." *The Expositor* 1st ser., 3 (1876) 62-73 [Gal 2:20].

Case, S. J. "The Jewish Bias of Paul." *JBL* 47 (1928) 20-31.

Case, S. J. "The Legalistic Element in Paul's Religion." *BW* 35 (1910) 151-58.

Cassirer, H. W. *Grace and the Law: St. Paul, Kant and the Hebrew Prophets.* Grand Rapids: Eerdmans, 1988.

Chrysostom, John. *Homilies on Galatians, Ephesians, Philippians, Colossians, Thessalonians, Timothy, Titus and Philemon.* n.d. Reprint. NPNF (1st ser.) 13. Grand Rapids: Eerdmans, 1979.

Chrysostom, John. *Homilies on the Acts of the Apostles and the Epistle to the Romans.* 1889. Reprint. NPNF (1st ser.) 11. Grand Rapids: Eerdmans, 1980.

Cohn-Sherbok, D. "Some Reflections on James Dunn's 'The Incident at Antioch.'" *JSNT* 18 (1983) 68-74.

Cosgrove, C. H. "Justification in Paul: A Linguistic and Theological Reflection." *JBL* 106 (1987) 653-70.

Cosgrove, C. H. "The Mosaic Law Preaches Faith: A Study in Galatians 3." *WJT* 41 (1978) 146-64.

Cranfield, C. E. B. "Some Notes on Romans 9:30-33." In *Jesus and Paulus, Festschrift W.G. Kümmel,* 35-43. Göttingen: Vandenhoeck & Ruprecht, 1975.

Cranfield, C. E. B. "St. Paul and the Law." *SJT* 17 (1964) 43-68.

Cranfield, C. E. B. *A Critical and Exegetical Commentary on the Epistle to the Romans.* ICC. 2 vols. Edinburgh: Clark, 1975-79.

Cremer, H. *Biblico-Theological Lexicon of New Testament Greek.* 4th ed. Edinburgh: Clark, 1895.

Crook, J. A. *Law and Life of Rome, 90 B.C.—A.D. 212.* Ithaca, N.Y.: Cornell University Press, 1967.

Crowther, C. "Works, Work and Good Works." *ExpTim* 81 (1970) 166-71.

Culler, M. L. "Exposition of Rom. 7:19." *LQ* 33 (1903) 98-105.

Dahl, N. A. *Studies in Paul.* Minneapolis: Augsburg, 1977.

Danker, F. W. "Romans v. 12: Sin under Law." *NTS* 14 (1967-68) 424-39.

Danker, F. W. "Under Contract: A Form-Critical Study of Linguistic Adaptation in Romans." In *Festschrift to Honor W. Wilbur Gingrich,* ed. E. H. Barth and R. E. Cocroft, 91-114. Leiden: Brill, 1972.

Daube, D. *Ancient Jewish Law.* Leiden: Brill, 1981.

Davies, D. M. "Free from the Law; an Exposition of the Seventh Chapter of Romans." *Int* 7 (1953) 156-62.

Davies, W. D. "Paul and the Law: Reflections on Pitfalls in Interpretation." *Hastings Law Journal* 29 (1978) 1459. Reprinted in W. D. Davies, *Jewish and Pauline Studies,* 91-122. Philadelphia: Fortress, 1984.

Davies, W. D. *Paul and Rabbinic Judaism.* 4th ed. Philadelphia: Fortress, 1980.

Davies, W. D. *Torah in the Messianic Age and/or the Age to Come.* JBL Monograph Series 7. Philadelphia: Society of Biblical Literature, 1952.

de los Rios, E. "Peccatum et Lex: Animadversiones in Rom. 7,7-25." *VD* 11 (1931) 23-28.

Démann, P. "Moses und das Gesetz bei Paulus." In *Moses in Schrift und Überlieferung,* 204-64. Düsseldorf: 1963.

Denniston, J. D. *The Greek Particles.* 2d ed. Oxford: Clarendon, 1954.

Dieterlé, C. "Etre juste ou vivre (Galates 1,11 - 2,21)." *Foi et Vie* 84/5 (1985) 5-18.

Dockery, D. S. "Romans 7:14-25: Pauline Tension in the Christian Life." *Grace Theological Journal* 2 (1981) 239-57.

Dodd, C. H. "ΕΝΝΟΜΟΣ ΧΡΙΣΤΟΥ." In *Studia Paulina, in hon. J. de Zwaan,* 96-110. Haarlem: Bohn, 1953.

Dodd, C. H. "The Law." In *The Bible and the Greeks,* 25-41. 1935. 3d impression (corrected). London: Hodder & Stoughton, 1964.

Dodd, C. H. *The Epistle of Paul to the Romans.* 1932. Reprint. London: Fontana, 1959.

Donaldson, D. L. "The 'Curse of the Law' and the Inclusion of the Gentiles: Galatians 3:13-14." *NTS* 32 (1986) 94-112.

Donfried, K. P., ed. *The Romans Debate.* Minneapolis: Augsburg, 1977.

Drane, J. W. "Tradition, Law and Ethics in Pauline Theology." *NovT* 16 (1974) 167-78.

Drane, J. W. *Paul—Libertine or Legalist?* London: SPCK, 1975.

Ducrot, O. and T. Todorov. *Encyclopedic Dictionary of the Science of Language.* Baltimore: Johns Hopkins University Press, 1979.

Dülmen, A. van. *Die Theologie des Gesetzes bei Paulus.* SBM 5. Stuttgart: Katholisches Bibelwerk, 1968.

Dunn, J. D. G. *Jesus, Paul and the Law.* Louisville: Westminster/John Knox, 1990.

Dunn, J. D. G. "Mark 2.1-3.6; a Bridge between Jesus and Paul on the Question of Law." *NTS* 30 (1984) 395-415.

Dunn, J. D. G. "Rom. 7,14-25 in the Theology of Paul." *TZ* 31 (1975) 257-73.

Dunn, J. D. G. "The Incident at Antioch (Gal. 2:11-18)." *JSNT* 18 (1983) 3-57.

Dunn, J. D. G. "The New Perspective on Paul." *BJRL* 65 (1983) 95-122.

Dunn, J. D. G. "Works of Law and the Curse of the Law (Galatians 3.10-14)." *NTS* 31 (1985) 523-42.

Dunn, J. D. G. *Romans.* Word Biblical Commentary. 2 vols. Dallas: Word, 1988.

Dupont-Sommer, A. *The Essene Writings from Qumran.* Oxford: Oxford University Press, 1961.

Ebeling, G. "Erwägungen zur Lehre vom Gesetz." *ZTK* 55 (1958) 270-306.

Ellis, E. E. *Paul's Use of the Old Testament.* Edinburgh: Oliver & Boyd, 1957.

Ellwein, E. "Das Rätsel von Römer 7." *KD* 1 (1955) 247-68.

Evers, F. O. "The Law with Jesus and Paul." *LCR* 31 (1912) 438-50, 709-20.

Fahy, T. "Faith and the Law. Epistle to the Romans, Ch. 4." *ITQ* 28 (1961) 207-14.

Fee, G. *The First Epistle to the Corinthians.* NICNT. Grand Rapids: Eerdmans, 1987.

Feine, P. *Das gesetzesfreie Evangelium des Paulus nach seinem Werdegang dargestellt.* Leipzig: Hinrichs, 1899.

Feuillet, A. "Loi ancienne et Morale chrétienne d'après l'Épître aux Romains." *NRT* 92 (1970) 785-805.

Feuillet, A. "Loi de Dieu, loi du Christ et loi de l'Esprit d'après les epîtres pauliniennes. Les rapports des ces trois lois avec la Loi Mosaique." *NT* 22 (1980) 29-65.

Fillmore, C. J. "Topics in Lexical Semantics." *Current Issues in Linguistic Theory,* edited by R. W. Cole, 76-118. Bloomington, Ind.: Indiana University Press, 1975.

Fitzmyer, J. A. "Paul and the Law." In *To Advance the Gospel,* 186-201. New York: Crossroad, 1981.

Fitzmyer, J. A. "The Letter to the Galatians." In *The New Jerome Biblical Commentary,* R. E. Brown, J. A. Fitzmyer, R. E. Murphy, eds., 780-90. Englewood Cliffs, N.J.: Prentice Hall, 1990.

Fitzmyer, J. A. "The Letter to the Romans." In *The New Jerome Biblical Commentary,* R. E. Brown, J. A. Fitzmyer, R. E. Murphy, eds., 730-68. Englewood Cliffs, N.J.: Prentice Hall, 1990.

Fitzmyer, J. A. "Pauline Theology." In *The New Jerome Biblical Commentary,* R. E. Brown, J. A. Fitzmyer, R. E. Murphy, eds., 1392-416. Englewood Cliffs, N.J.: Prentice Hall, 1990.

Fleischhauer. "Die paulinische Lehre vom Gesetz." *ThSW* 4 (1883) 37-71.

Flückiger, F. "Christus, des Gesetzes telos." *TZ* 11 (1955) 153-57.

Flückiger, F. "Die Werke des Gesetzes bei den Heiden (nach Röm 2, 14 ff.)." *TZ* 8 (1952) 17-42.

Flusser, D. "Durch das Gesetz dem Gesetz gestorben." *Judaica* 43 (1987) 30-46.

Friedländer, M. "The 'Pauline' Emancipation from the Law a Product of the Pre-Christian Jewish Diaspora." *JQR* 14 (1902) 265-301.

Friedrich, G. "Das Gesetz des Glaubens, Röm 3,27." *TZ* 10 (1954) 401-17.

Fuchs, E. "Existentiale Interpretation von Römer 7,7-12 und 21-23." *ZTK* 59 (1962) 285-314.

Fuller, D. P. "Paul and 'the Works of the Law.'" *WTJ* 38 (1975-76) 28-42.

Funk, R. W. "The Syntax of the Greek Article: Its Importance for Critical Pauline Problems." Ph.D. dissertation, Vanderbilt University, 1953.

Furnish, V. P. "Development in Paul's Thought." *JAAR* 38 (1970) 289-303.

Furnish, V. P. *II Corinthians.* AB. Garden City, N.Y.: Doubleday, 1984.

Gagarin, M. *Early Greek Law.* Berkeley: University of California Press, 1986.

Gager, J. G. "Some Notes on Paul's Conversion." *NTS* 27 (1981) 697-704.

Gaius. *The Institutes of Gaius.* Tr. F. De Zulueta. Oxford: Clarendon Press, 1946.

Gaston, L. "Paul and the Law in Galatians 2-3." In *Anti-Judaism in Early Christianity*; vol. 1; *Paul and the Gospels*, ed. P. Richardson, 37-57. Waterloo, Ont.: Laurier University Press, 1986.

Gaston, L. "Paul and the Torah." In *Antisemitism and the Foundations of Christianity*, edited by A. Davies, 48-71. New York: Paulist, 1979.

Gaston, L. "Works of Law as a subjective genitive." *SR* 13 (1984) 39-46.

Gaston, L. *Paul and the Torah.* Vancouver: University of British Columbia Press, 1987.

Gaventa, B. R. "Galatians 1 and 2: Autobiography as Paradigm." *NovTes* 28 (1986) 309-26.

Getty, M. A. "An Apocalyptic Perspective on Rom 10:4." *Horizons in Biblical Theology* 4/5 (1982-83) 79-131.

Glock, J. P. *Die Gesetzefrage im Leben Jesu und in der Lehre des Paulus.* Karlsruhe: 1885.

Goodenough, E. R. "Paul and the Hellenization of Christianity." In *Religions in Antiquity. Essays in Memory of E. R. Goodenough,* edited by Jacob Neusner, 23-68. Leiden: Brill, 1968.

Goodwin, D. R. "Ἐάν μή, Gal. ii. 16." *JBL* (June, 1886) 122-27.

Gordon, T. D. "A Note on ΠΑΙΔΑΓΩΓΟΣ in Galatians 3.24-25." *NTS* 35 (1989) 150-54.

Gordon, T. D. "The Problem at Galatia." *Int* 41 (1987) 32-43.

Grafe, E. *Die paulinische Lehre vom Gesetz nach den vier Hauptbriefen.* 2d ed. Leipzig: Mohr, 1893.

Greenwood, D. "Saint Paul and Natural Law." *Biblical Theology Bulletin* 1 (1971) 262-79.

Gronemeyer, R. "Zur Frage nach dem paulinischen Antinomismus." Ph.D. dissertation, Hamburg: 1970.

Grundmann, W. "Gesetz, Rechtfertigung und Mystik bei Paulus." *ZNW* 32 (1933) 52-65.

Gundry, R. H. "The Moral Frustration of Paul before his Conversion." In *Pauline Studies. Essays presented to F. F. Bruce,* edited by D. A. Hagner and M. A. Harris, 228-45. Grand Rapids: Eerdmans, 1980.

Gunther, J. J. *St. Paul's Opponents and their Background.* Leiden: Brill, 1973.

Gutbrod, W. "νόμος κ.τ.λ." *TDNT* 4 (1967) 1022-91.

Hafemann, S. J. "Presuppositions for a Study of Paul's View of the Law." *Tantur Yearbook* 1981-82: 155-67.

Hahn, F. "Das Gesetzverständnis im Römer- und Galaterbrief." *ZNW* 67 (1976) 29-63.

Hall, J. "Paul, the Lawyer, on Law." *Journal of Law and Religion* 3 (1985) 331-79.

Hanson, A.T. "The Origin of Paul's use of ΠΑΙΔΑΓΩΓΟΣ for the Law." *JSNT* 34 (1988) 71-76.

Harrington, W. J. "Christian Freedom." *Doctrine and Life* 25 (1975) 627-37.

Hasler, V. "Glaube und Existence. Hermeneutische Erwägungen zu Gal. 2,15-21." *TZ* 25 (1969) 241-51.

Hasler, V. E. *Gesetz und Evangelium in der alten Kirche bis Origenes.* Zürich: Gotthelf, 1953.

Haufe, C. "Die Stellung Paulus zum Gesetz." *TLZ* 91 (1966) 171-78.

Hays, R. B. "Psalm 143 and the Logic of Romans 3." *JBL* 99 (1980) 107-15.

Hays, R. B. *Echoes of Scripture in the Letters of Paul.* New Haven: Yale University Press, 1989.

Hays, R. B. *The Faith of Jesus Christ: An Investigation of the Narrative Substructure of Galatians 3:1 - 4:11.* SBL Dissertation Series. Chico, Cal.: Scholars, 1983.

Heiligenthal, R. "Soziologische Implikationem der paulinischen Rechtfertigunslehre im Galaterbrief am Biespiel der 'Werke des Gesetzes.' Beobachtungen zur Identitäts: findung einer frühchristlichen Gemeinde." *Kairos* 26 (1984) 38-53.

Heinemann, I. *La loi dans la pensée juive.* Paris: Michel, 1963.

Hill, D. *Greek Words and Hebrew Meanings: Studies in the Semantics of Soteriological Terms.* Cambridge: Cambridge University Press, 1967.

Hofius, O. "Das Gesetz des Mose und das Gesetz Christi." *ZTK* 80 (1983) 262-86.

Hofius, O. "Gesetz und Evangelium nach 2. Korinther 2." In *Paulusstudien,* 75-120. Tubingen: Mohr/Siebeck, 1989.

Hommel, H. "Das 7. Kapitel des Römerbriefs im Licht antiker Überlieferung." *ThViat* 8 (1961-62) 90-116.

Hoogt, M. J. van de. "Het ware leven." *Gereformeerd theologisch tijdschrift* 6 (1905) 10-12, 48-53 [Gal 2:20].

Hooker, M. D. "ΠΙΣΤΙΣ ΧΡΙΣΤΟΥ." *NTS* 35 (1989) 321-42.

Houlden, J. L. "A Response to James D. G. Dunn." *JSNT* 18 (1983) 58-67.

Howard, G. E. "Christ the End of the Law. The Meaning of Romans 10:4 ff." *JBL* 88 (1969) 331-37.

Howard, G. E. "On the 'Faith of Christ'." *HTR* 60 (1967) 459-65.

Howard, G. E. "Romans 3.21-31 and the Inclusion of the Gentiles." *HTR* 63 (1970) 223-33.

Howard, G. E. "The 'Faith of Christ'." *ET* 85 (1973-74) 212-15.

Hübner, H. "Das ganze und das eine Gesetz. Zum Problemkreis Paulus und die Stoa." *KD* 21 (1975) 239-56.

Hübner, H. "Gal 3,10 und die Herkunft des Paulus." *KD* 19 (1973) 215-31.

Hübner, H. *Law in Paul's Thought.* Edinburgh: Clark, 1984.

Hübner, H. "Identitätsverlust und paulinische Theologie. Anmerkung zum Galaterbrief." *KD* 24 (1978) 181-93.

Hultgren, A. J. "The Pistis Christou Formulation in Paul," *NT* 22 (1980) 248-63.

Hunt, A. S., and C. C. Edgar. *Select Papyri*. LCL. 2 vols. Cambridge, Mass: Harvard University Press, 1932, 1934.

Jackson, B. S. "Legalism." *JJS* 30 (1979) 1-22.

Jarrell, W. A. "Romans 7:7-25: The Experience of Sinners." *RevExp* 5 (1908) 586-97.

Jeremias, J. "Paulus als Hillelit." In *Neotestamenta et Semetica. In honor of M. Black,* edited by E. E. Ellis and M. Wilcox, 88-94. Edinburgh: Clark, 1969.

Jervell, J. "Paul in the Acts of the Apostles." In *Les Actes des Apôtres,* edited by J. Kremer *et al.,* 297-306. Leuven: Leuven University Press, 1979.

Jewett, R. "Romans as an Ambassadorial Letter." *Int* 36 (1982) 5-20.

Jewett, R. "The Law and the Coexistence of Jews and Gentiles in Romans." *Int* 39 (1985) 341-56.

Jewett, R. *A Chronology of Paul's Life.* Philadelphia: Fortress, 1979.

Jewett, R. *Paul's Anthropological Terms.* Leiden: Brill, 1971.

Joest, W. *Gesetz und Freiheit. Das Problem des tertius usus legis bei Luther und die neutestamentliche Parainese.* Göttingen: Vandenhoeck Y Ruprecht, 1951.

Johnson, L. T. "Rom 3:21-26 and the Faith of Jesus." *CBQ* 44 (1982) 77-90.

Johnson, S. E. "Tarsus and the Apostle Paul." *Lexington Theological Quarterly* 15 (1980) 105-13.

Johnston, G. "Paul's Certainties: IV. The Validity of Moral Standards and the Sinfulness of Man." *ExpTim* 69 (1958) 240-43.

Joos, M. P. "Semantic Axiom Number One." *Language* 48 (1972) 257-65.

Jüngel, E. "Das Gesetz zwischen Adam und Christus. Eine Theologische Studie zu Röm 5,12-21." *ZTK* 60 (1963) 42-79.

Kapteijn, K. J. "Het lichaam dezes doods." *Gereformeerd theologisch tijdschrift* 10 (1909) 113-26 [Rom 7:24].

Käsemann, E. *Commentary on Romans.* Grand Rapids: Eerdmans, 1980.

Käsemann, E. "The Spirit and the Letter." In *Perspectives on Paul,* 138-66. London and Philadelphia: SCM and Fortress, 1971.

Keck, L. E. "The Function of Rom 3:10-18." In *God's Christ and His People. In honor of N. A. Dahl,* edited by J. Jervell and W. A. Meeks, 141-57. Oslo: Universitats Forlaget, 1977.

Keck, L. E. "The Law and 'The Law of Sin and Death' (Rom 8:1-4)." In *The Divine Helmsman. Presented to Lou H. Silberman,* edited by J. L. Crenshaw and S. Sandmel, 41-57. New York: Ktav, 1980.

Kelber, W. H. *The Oral and the Written Gospel.* Philadelphia: Fortress, 1983.

Kennedy, H. A. A. "St. Paul and the Law." *The Expositor* (8th series) 13 (1917) 338-66.

Kertelge, K. "Exegetische Überlegungen zum Verständnis der paulinischen Anthropologie nach Römer 7." *ZNTW* 62 (1971) 105-14.

Kertelge, K. "Gesetz und Freiheit im Galaterbrief." *NTS* 30 (1984) 382-94.

Kilpatrick, G. D. "Peter, Jerusalem and Galatians 1:13 - 2:14." *NovT* 25 (1983) 318-26.

Klöpper, A. "Zur Erläuterung von Gal. II, 14-21." *ZWT* 37 (1894) 373-95.

Klumbies, P.-G. "Zwischen Pneuma und Nomos. Neuorientierung in den galatischen Gemeinden." *Wort und Dienst* 19 (1987) 109-35.

König, A. "Gentiles or Gentile Christians? On the meaning of Romans 2:12-16." *Journal of Theology for Southern Africa* 15 (1976) 53-60.

Kripke, S. A. *Naming and Necessity*. Cambridge, Mass.: Harvard University Press, 1980.

Krummacher, E. W. "Über das Subject in Röm. 7. Einer exegetisch-psychologische Untersuchung." *Theologische Studien und Kritiken* 35 (1862) 119-36.

Kuech, W. "Dienst des Geistes und des Fleisches. Zur Auslegungsgeschichte und Auslegung von Rom 7,25b." *TQ* 141 (1961) 257-80.

Kuhl, E. *Der Brief des Paulus an die Römer*. Leipzig: Quelle & Meyer, 1913.

Kühner, R. *Ausführliche Grammatik der Griechischen Sprache*. Vol. 2. *Satzlehre*. Rev. B. Gerth. 2 pts. Hanover and Leipzig: Hahnsche, 1898-1904.

Kümmel, W. G. *Introduction to the New Testament*. Nashville: Abingdon, 1975.

Kümmel, W. G. *Römer 7 und die Bekehrung des Paulus*. 1929. In *Römer 7 und das Bild das Menschen im Neuen Testament*, ix-160. München: Chr. Kaiser, 1974.

Kürzinger, J. "Der Schlüssel zum Verständnis von Röm 7." *BZ* 7 (1963) 270-74.

Kuss, O. "Die Heiden und die Werke des Gesetzes (nach Röm. 2,14-16)." *MTZ* 5 (1954) 77-98.

Kuss, O. "Nomos bei Paulus." *MTZ* 17 (1966) 173-227.

Kuss, O. *Der Römerbrief*. 3 Lfg. to date. Regensburg: Pusket, 1957-.

Lackmann, M. "Beiträge sum Amt des Petrus im Neuen Testament." *Bausteine* 3 (1963) 1-7.

Ladd, G.E. "Paul and the Law." In *Sola Dei Gloria. In honor of W. C. Robinson*, edited by J. H. Richards, 50-67. Richmond: John Knox, 1968.

Lafon, G. "Les poètes de la loi. Un commentaire de *Romains 2,12-27*." *Christus* 134 (1987) 205-14.

Lafon, G. "Une loi de foi. La pensée de la loi en *Romains 3,19-31*." *RevScRel* 61 (1987) 32-53.

Lagrange, M.-J. *Saint Paul, Épître aux Romains*. Paris: Libraire Lecoffre, 1950.

Lagrange, M.-J. *Saint Paul, Épître aux Galates*. 2d ed. Paris: Lecoffre, 1925.

Lambrecht, J. "Man Before and Without Christ: Rom 7 and Pauline Anthropology." *Louvain Studies* 5 (1974) 18-33.

Lambrecht, J. "Gesetzesverständnis bei Paulus." In *Das Gesetz im Neuen Testament*, hg. K. Kertelge (Freiburg: Herder, 1986), 88-127.

Lambrecht, J. "Once Again Gal 2,17-18 and 3,21." *ETL* 63 (1987) 148-53.

Lambrecht, J. "The Line of Thought in Gal 2:14b-21." *NTS* 24 (1977-78) 484-95.

Lambrecht, J. "Why is Boasting Excluded? A Note on Rom 3,27 and 4,2." *ETL* 61 (1985) 365-69.

Lambrecht, J., and R. W. Thompson. *Justification by Faith. The Implications of Romans 3:27-31*. Wilmington, Del.: Glazier, 1989.

Lampe, G. W. H. *A Patristic Greek Lexicon*. Oxford: Oxford University Press, 1961.

Lang, F. "Gesetz und Bund bei Paulus." In *Rechtfertigung. Festschrift E. Käsemann,* edited by J. Friedrich, W. Pühlmann and P. Stuhlmacher, 305-20. Tübingen: Mohr, 1976.

Larsson, E. "Paul: Law and Salvation." *NTS* 31 (1985) 425-36.

Lategan, B. "Is Paul Defending his Apostleship in Galatians? The Function of Galatians 1. 11-12 and 2. 19-20 in the Development of Paul's Argument." *NTS* 34 (1988) 411-30.

Leal, J. "'Christo confixus sum cruci' (Gal 2,19)." *VD* 19 (1939) 76-80, 98-105.

Lekkerkerker, A. F. N. "Romeinen 7, een belijdenis der gemeente." *Nieuwe Theologische studiën* 23 (1940) 99-109.

Levinson, S. C. *Pragmatics.* Cambridge: Cambridge University Press, 1983.

Lightfoot, J. B. *The Epistle of St. Paul to the Galatians.* 1865. Reprint. Grand Rapids, Mich.: Zondervan, 1957.

Lipsius, D. "Über Gal. 2,17 f." *ZWT* 4 (1861) 72-82.

Lohmeyer, E. "Gesetzeswerke." In *idem., Probleme Paulinischer Theologie* (Stuttgart: Kohlhammer, n.d.), 31-74. Reprinted from *ZNW* 28 (1929) 177-207.

Lohmeyer, E. "Probleme paulinischer Theologie; II, 'Gesetzeswerke.'" *ZNW* 28 (1929) 177-207.

Lohse, E. "ὁ νόμος τοῦ πνεύματος τῆς ζωῆς. Exegetische Anmerkungen zu Röm 8,2." In *Neues Testament und christliche Existenz. Festschrift H. Braun,* edited by H. D. Betz and L. Schottroff, 279-87. Tübingen: Mohr, 1973.

Louw, J. P. *Semantics of New Testament Greek.* Atlanta: Scholars Press, 1982.

Louw, J. P., and Eugene Nida. *Greek-English Lexicon of the New Testament Based on Semantic Domains.* New York: United Bible Societies, 1988.

Louw, J. P., and Eugene Nida. *Lexical Semantics of the Greek New Testament.* Forthcoming.

Lowe, J. "An Examination of Attempts to Detect Development in St. Paul's Theology." *JTS* 42 (1941) 129-42.

Löwy, M. "Die Paulinische Lehre vom Gesetz." *MGWJ* 47 (1903) 322-39, 417-33, 534-44; 48 (1904) 268-76, 321-27, 400-16.

Luck, U. "Der Jakobusbriefe und die Theologie des Paulus." *TGl* 61 (1971) 161-79.

Lüdemann, G. *Paul, Apostle to the Gentiles.* Philadelphia: Fortress, 1984.

Lührmann, D. "Die 430 Jahre zwischen den Verheissungen und dem Gesetz (Gal 3,17)." *ZAW* 100 (1988) 420-23.

Lull, D. J. "'The Law Was Our Pedagogue': A Study in Galatians 3:19-25." *JBL* 105 (1986) 481-98.

Lull, D. J. *The Spirit in Galatia.* Chico, Cal.: Scholars Press, 1980

Lütgert, W. *Gesetz und Geist.* Gütersloh: Bertelsmann, 1919.

Luther, M. *Lectures on Galatians.* Luther's Works, vols. 26-27. St. Louis: Concordia, 1963.

Luther, M. *Lectures on Romans.* Luther's Works, vol. 25. St. Louis: Concordia, 1972.

Lutz, C. E. *Musonius Rufus: "The Roman Socrates".* Yale Classical Studies 10. New Haven: Yale University Press, 1947.

Luz, U. *Das Geschichtsverständnis des Paulus.* BEvT 49. München: Kaiser, 1968.

Lyall, F. "Legal Metaphors in the Epistles." *Tyndale Bulletin* 32 (1981) 81-95.

Lyall, F. "Roman law in the writings of Paul—Aliens and Citizens." *EvQ* 48 (1976) 3-14.

Lyall, F. "Roman Law in the Writings of Paul—The Slave and the Freedman." *NTS* 17 (1970) 73-79.

Lyall, F. "Roman Law in the Writings of Paul—Adoption." *JBL* 88 (1969) 458-66.

Lyonnet, S. "L'histoire du salut selon le chapitre VII de L'épître aux Romains." *Biblica* 43 (1962) 117-51.

Lyonnet, S. "Quaestiones ad Rom 7,7-13." *Verbum Domini* 40 (1962) 163-83.

Lyonnet, S. "St. Paul: Liberty and Law." *Bridge* 4 (1961-62) 229-51.

Lyons, J. *Semantics.* 2 vols. Cambridge: Cambridge University Press, 1977.

Lyons, J. *Structural Semantics.* Oxford: Blackwell, 1963.

MacDowell, D. M. *The Law in Classical Athens.* Ithaca: Cornell University Press, 1978.

MacGorman, J. W. "Romans 7 Once More." *Southwestern Journal of Theology* 19 (1976) 31-41.

Malina, B. J. "The Apostle Paul and the Law: Prolegomena for a Hermeneutic." *Creighton Law Review* 14 (1981) 1305-39.

Malina, B. J. *Christian Origins and Cultural Anthropology.* Atlanta: John Knox, 1986.

Marcus, J. "The Circumcision and the Uncircumcision in Rome." *NTS* 35 (1989) 67-81.

Marcus, R. *Law in the Apocrypha.* New York: Columbia University Press, 1927.

Martin, B. L. "Paul on Christ and the Law." *Journal of the Evangelical Theological Society* 26 (1983) 271-82.

Martin, B.L. "Some Reflections on the Identity of *ego* in Rom. 7:14-25." *SJT* 34 (1981) 39-47.

Martyn, J. L. "A Law-Observant Mission to Gentiles: the Background of Galatians." *Michigan Quarterly Review* 22 (1983) 221-36. Reprinted in *SJT* 38 (1985) 307-24.

Martyn, J. L. "Apocalyptic Antinomies in Paul's Letter to the Galatians." *NTS* 31 (1985) 410-24.

Maultsby, H. D. *Paul and the American Nomos: An Exegetical Study of Romans 7 and a Hermeneutic for Biblical Theology.* Washington, D.C.: University Press of America, 1977.

Maurer, C. *Die Gesetzlehre des Paulus nach ihrem Ursprung und in ihrer Entfaltung.* Zurich: Evangelischer Verlag, 1941.

McEleney, N. J. "Conversion, Circumcision and the Law." *NTS* 20 (1973-74) 319-41.

Metzger, B. M. *A Textual Commentary on the Greek New Testament.* Corrected ed. London: United Bible Societies, 1975.

Meyer, P. W. "Romans 10:4 and the 'End' of the Law." In *The Divine Helmsman: Studies on God's Control of Human Events, Presented to Lou H. Silberman,* ed. J. L. Crenshaw and S. Sandmel, 59-78. New York: Ktav, 1980.

Meyer, P. W. "Romans." In *Harper's Bible Commentary,* ed. J. L. Mays, *et al.,* 1130-67. San Francisco: Harper & Row, 1988.

Mitton, C. L. "Romans 7 Reconsidered." *ExpTim* 65 (1953-54) 78-81; 99-103; 132-35.

Modalsli, O. "Gal. 2-19-21; 5,16-18 ünd Röm. 7,7-25." *TZ* 21 (1965) 22-57.

Modrzjewski, J. "La règle de droit dans l'Egypt Ptolemaique." *Essays in Honor of C. Bradford Welles*, ed. A. E. Samuel. *American Studies in Papyrology* 1 (1966) 125-74.

Monsengwo Pasinya, L. *La Notion de Nomos dans le Pentateuque grec*. Rome: Biblical Institute Press, 1973.

Moo, D. J. "Paul and the Law in the Last Ten Years." *SJT* 40 (1987) 287-307.

Moo, D. J. "'Law,' 'Works of Law,' and Legalism in Paul." *WTJ* 45 (1983) 73-100.

Moore, G. F. *Judaism in the First Centuries of the Christian Era: The Age of the Tannaim*. 3 vols. Cambridge: Harvard University Press, 1927-30.

Morris, T. F. "Law and the Cause of Sin in the Epistle to the Romans." *HeyJ* 28 (1987) 285-91.

Morrison, B., and J. Woodhouse. "The Coherence of Romans 7:1-8:8." *Reformed Theological Review* 47 (1988) 8-16.

Moule, C. F. D. "A Note on Galatians 2:17, 18." *ExpTim* 56 (1944-45) 223.

Moule, C. F. D. "Death 'to Sin', 'to Law', and 'to the World': a Note on Certain Datives." *Mélanges Bibliques en hommage au R. P. Béda Rigaux*, ed. A. Descamps, 367-75. Gembloux: Ducolot, 1970

Moule, C. F. D. "Interpreting Paul by Paul." In *New Testament Christianity for Africa and the World. Essays in honor of H. Sawyerr*, edited by M. E. Glasswell and E. W. Fasholé, 78-90. London: SPCK, 1974.

Moule, C. F. D. *An Idiom Book of New Testament Greek*. 2d ed. Cambridge: Cambridge University Press, 1959.

Moule, H. C. G. "A Study in the Connexion of Doctrines." *The Expositor* 1st ser., 2 (1885) 447-55 [Gal 2:20].

Moulton, J. H. *A Grammar of New Testament Greek*. Vol. I. *Prolegomena*. 3d ed. Edinburgh: Clark, 1908.

Moulton, J. H., and W. F. Howard. *A Grammar of New Testament Greek*. Vol. II. *Accidence and Word-Formation*. Edinburgh: Clark, 1919-29.

Moulton, J. H., and G. Milligan. *The Vocabulary of the Greek Testament Illustrated from the Papyri and Other Non-Literary Sources*. 1914-30. Reprint. Grand Rapids, Mich.: Eerdmans, 1980.

Moulton, J. H. and N. Turner. *A Grammar of New Testament Greek*. Vol. III. *Syntax*. Edinburgh: Clark, 1963.

Muliyil, F. "Torah - Nomos - Law." *BT* 13 (1966) 117-20.

Müller, F. "Zwei Marginalien im Brief des Paulus an die Römer." *ZNW* 40 (1941) 249-54.

Mundle, W. "Zur Auslegung von Gal. 2,17-18." *ZNW* 23 (1924) 152-53.

Murphy-O'Connor, J. "Interpolations in 1 Corinthians." *CBQ* 48 (1986) 81-94.

Murray, J. "Divorce." *WTJ* 11 (1948-49) 105-22 [Rom 7: 1-3].

Murray, J. *The Epistle to the Romans*. 3d ed. Grand Rapids: Eerdmans, 1967.

Mussner, F. "Gesetz - Abraham - Israel." *Kairos* 25 (1983) 200-22.

Mussner, F. *Der Galaterbrief*. HTKNT. Freiburg: Herder, 1974.

Neitzel, H. "Zur Interpretation von Galater 2,11-21." *TQ* 163 (198) 15-39, 131-149.

Nestle-Aland. *Das Neue Testament Griechisch und Deutsch.* Stuttgart: Deutsche Bibelgesellschaft / Katholische Bibelanstalt, 1986.

Neusner, J. "The Use of Later Rabbinic Evidence for the Study of Paul." *Approaches to Ancient Judaism* 2 (1980) 43-63.

Newman, B. M. "Once Again - The Question of 'I' in Romans 7.7-15." *BT* 34 (1983) 124-35.

Nida, E. *Exploring Semantic Structures.* International Library of Linguistics 11. Munich: Fink, 1975.

Nida, E. *The Componential Analysis of Meaning.* The Hague: Mouton, 1975.

Nygren, A. *Commentary on Romans.* Philadelphia: Fortress, 1949.

Ogden, C. K., and I. A. Richards. *The Meaning of Meaning.* 5th ed. New York and London: Harcourt, Brace and Kegan Paul, 1938.

Osten-Sacken, P. von den. "Das paulinische Verständnis des Gesetzes im Spannungsfeld von Eschatologie und Geschichte." *EvT* 37 (1977) 549-87.

Osten-Sacken, P. von den. *Evangelium und Tora. Aufsätze su Paulus.* München: Kaiser, 1987.

Panier, L. "Pour une approche sémiotique de l'épître aux Galates." *Foi et Vie* 84/5 (1985) 19-32.

Pathrapankal, J. "The Polarity of Law and Freedom in Pauline Religion." *Journal of Dharma* 5 (1980) 343-51.

Peirce, C. S. *Collected Papers.* 8 vols. Cambridge: Harvard University Press, 1931-58.

Pelagius. *Expositions of Thirteen Epistles of St. Paul.* Ed. A. Souter. (TextsS 9.1-3; Cambridge: Cambridge University Press, 1922-31) 2.306-43.

Philipose, J. "Romans 5.20: Did God have a bad motive in giving the law?" *BT* 28 (1977) 445.

Préaux, C. *Le Monde Hellénistique.* 2 vols. Paris: Presses Universitaires de France, 1978.

Pringsheim, F. *The Greek Law of Sale.* Weimar: Böhlaus, 1950.

Räisänen, H. "Das 'Gesetz des Glaubens' (Röm 3.27) und das "Gesetz des Geistes' (Röm 8.2)." *NTS* 26 (1979-80) 101-17.

Räisänen, H. "Galatians 2.16 and Paul's Break with Judaism." *NTS* 31 (1985) 543-53.

Räisänen, H. "Legalism and Salvation by the Law. Paul's Portrayal of the Jewish Religion as a Historical and Theological Problem." In *Die Paulinische Literatur und Theologie,* edited by S. Pedersen, 63-83. Aarhus: Forlaget Aros, 1980.

Räisänen, H. "Paul's Conversion and the Development of his View of the Law." *NTS* 33 (1987) 404-19.

Räisänen, H. "Zum Gebrauch von EPITHYMIA und EPITHYMEIN bei Paulus." *ST* 33 (1979) 85-99.

Räisänen, H. *Paul and the Law.* 2d ed. Tübingen: Mohr, 1987.

Räisänen, H. *The Torah and Christ.* Helsinki: Kirjapaino Raamattutalo, 1986.

Ramaroson, L. "La Justification par la foi du Christ Jésus." *ScEs* 39 (1987) 81-92.

Refoulé, F. "Note sur Romains IX, 30-33." *RB* 92 (1985) 161-86.

Reicke, B. "Paulus über das Gesetz." *TZ* 41 (1985) 237-57.

Reicke, B. "The Law and This World According to Paul." *JBL* 70 (1951) 259-76.

Remus, H. E. "Authority, consent, law: *Nomos, physis,* and the striving for a 'giving.'" *SR* 13 (1984) 5-18.

Rétif, A. "A propos de l'interprétation du chapitre VII des *Romains* par saint Augustin." *Recherches de science religieuse* 33 (1946) 368-71.

Rhyne, C. T. "*Nomos Dikaiosynēs* and the Meaning of Romans 10:4." *CBQ* 47 (1985) 486-99.

Rhyne, C. T. *Faith Establishes the Law.* Chico, Cal.: Scholars Press, 1981.

Ridderbos, H. N. *The Epistle of Paul to the Churches of Galatia.* NICNT. Grand Rapids: Eerdmans, 1953.

Riedl, J. "Röm 2,14ff. und das Heil der Heiden bei Augustinus und Thomas." *Scholastik* 40 (1965) 189-213.

Rigaux, B. "Law and Grace in Pauline Eschatology." *Louvain Studies* 2 (1969) 329-33.

Robertson, A. T. *A Grammar of the Greek New Testament in the Light of Historical Research.* 4th ed. Nashville: Broadman, 1934.

Robinson, J. A. T. *Wrestling With Romans.* Philadelphia: Westminster, 1979.

Rüger, H. P. "Hieronymus, die Rabbinen und Paulus. Zur Vorgeschichte des Begriffspaars 'innerer und äusserer Mensch.'" *ZNTW* 68 (1977) 132-37.

Russell, W. B. "An Alternative Suggestion for the Purpose of Romans." *BSac* 145 (1988) 174-84.

Ryle, G. "The Theory of Meaning." In *Philosophy and Ordinary Language,* ed. C. E. Caton, 128-53. Urbana: University of Illinois Press, 1963.

Ryrie, C. C. "The End of the Law." *BSac* 124 (1967) 239-41.

Sampley, J. P. "'Before God, I do not lie' (Gal i. 20). Paul's Self-Defense in the Light of Roman Legal Praxis." *NTS* 23 (1977) 477-82.

Sand, A. "Gesetz und Freiheit. Vom Sinn des Pauluswortes: Christus, des Gesetzes Ende." *TGl* 61 (1971) 1-14.

Sanday, W., and A. C. Headlam. *A Critical and Exegetical Commentary on the Epistle to the Romans.* 13th ed. New York: Scribners, 1911.

Sanders, E. P. "On the Question of Fulfilling the Law in Paul and Rabbinic Judaism." In *Donum Gentilicum. In honor of D. Daube,* edited by E. Bammel, C. K. Barrett and W. D. Davies, 103-26. Oxford: Clarendon Press, 1978.

Sanders, E. P. *Paul and Palestinian Judaism.* Philadelphia: Fortress, 1977.

Sanders, E. P. *Paul, the Law, and the Jewish People.* Philadelphia: Fortress, 1983.

Sanders, E. P. "Romans 7 and the Purpose of the Law." *Proceedings of the Irish Biblical Association* 7 (1983) 44-59.

Sanders, J. A. "Torah and Paul." In *God's Christ and His People. In honor of N. A. Dahl,* edited by J. Jervell and W. A. Meeks, 132-40. Oslo: Universitats Forlaget, 1977.

Saussure, F. de. *Course in General Linguistics.* 1915. La Salle, Ill.: Open Court, 1986.

Schlier, H. *Der Brief an die Galater.* 13th Aufl. Göttingen: Vandenhoeck & Ruprecht, 1965.

Schlier, H. *Der Römerbrief.* HTKNT. Freiburg: Herder, 1977.

Schmidt, R. "Über Gal. 2, 14-21." *Theologische Studien und Kritiken* 50 (1877) 638-705.

Schmithals, W. *Der Römerbrief. Ein Kommentar.* Gütersloh: Mohn, 1988.

Schneider, B. "The Meaning of St. Paul's Antithesis, 'The Letter and the Spirit.'" *CBQ* 15 (1953) 163-207.

Schneider, E. E. "Finis legis Christus." *TZ* 20 (1964) 410-22.

Schoeps, H. J. *Paul.* Philadelphia: Westminster, 1961.

Schoeps, H. J. *Theologie und Geschichte des Judenchristentums.* Tübingen: Mohr, 1949.

Schrage, W. "Die konkreten Einzelgebote in der paul Paränese." Gütersloh: Mohn, 1961.

Schreiner, T. R. "The Abolition and Fulfillment of the Law in Paul." *JSNT* 35 (1989) 47-74.

Schrenk, G. "πατρικός," 5 *TDNT* (1967) 1021-22.

Schroeder, O. "Νόμος ὁ πάντων ὁ βασιλεύς." *Philologus* 74 (1917-18) 195-204.

Schulz, O. "τί οὖν ὁ νόμος; Verhältnis von Gesetz, Sünde und Evangelium nach Gal. 3." *TSK* 75 (1902) 5-56.

Schürmann, H. "'Das Gesetz des Christus' (Gal 6,2). Jesu Verhalten und Wort als letztgültige sittliche Norm nach Paulus." In *Neues Testament und Kirche. Festschrift R. Schnackenburg,* edited by J. Gnilka, 282-300. Freiburg: Herder, 1974.

Schwyzer, E. *Griechische Grammatik.* Vol. 2. *Syntax und Syntaktische Stilistik.* Rev. A. Debrunner. Munchen: Beck'sche, 1950.

Scroggs, R. "New Being: Renewed Mind: New Perception. Paul's View of the Source of Ethical Insight." *Chicago Theological Seminary Register* 72 (1982) 1-12.

Scroggs, R. *Christology in Paul and John.* Philadelphia: Fortress, 1988.

Scroggs, R. *Paul for a New Day.* Philadelphia: Fortress, 1977.

Searight, H. B. "Rom. 7:17: A Short Study in Religious Psychology." *Union Seminary Magazine* 23 (1911-12) 144-49.

Segal, A. F. *Paul the Convert.* New Haven: Yale University Press, 1990.

Segal, A. F. "Romans 7 and Jewish Dietary Law." *SR* 15 (1986) 361-74.

Segal, A. F. "Torah and *nomos* in recent scholarly discussion." *SR* 13 (1984) 19-27.

Selmer, L. "Rom. 7,14-25." *Norsk teologisk tidsskrift* 26 (1925) 88-104.

Sherwin-White, A. N. *Roman Society and Roman Law in the New Testament.* Oxford: Oxford University Press, 1963

Silva, M. *Biblical Words and Their Meaning.* Grand Rapids: Zondervan, 1982.

Slaten, A. W. "The Qualitative Use of νόμος in the Pauline Epistles." *AJT* 23 (1919) 213-19.

Sloyan, G. *Is Christ the End of the Law?* Philadelphia: Westminster, 1978.

Smit, J. "The Letter of Paul to the Galatians: a Deliberative Speech." *NTS* 35 (1989) 1-26.

Smyth, H. W. *Greek Grammar.* Rev. G. M. Messing. Cambridge, Mass.: Harvard University Press, 1956.

Snodgrass, K. "Spheres of Influence: A Possible Solution to the Problem of Paul and the Law." *JSNT* 32 (1988) 93-113.

Snodgrass, K. R. "Justification by Grace—to the Doers: an Analysis of the Place of Romans 2 in the Theology of Paul." *NTS* 32 (1986) 72-93.

Spicq, C. *Notes de Lexicographie Néo Testamentaire.* 2 vols. and suppl. Göttingen: Vandenhoeck & Ruprecht, 1978-82.

Stacey, W. D. *The Pauline View of Man in Relation to its Judaic and Hellenistic Background.* London: St. Martin's, 1956.

Stagg, F. "Freedom and Moral Responsibility Without License or Legalism." *RevExp* 69 (1972) 483-94.

Stanley, D. "Freedom and Slavery in Pauline Usage." *Way* 15 (1975) 83-98.

Stegemann, E. W. "Die umgekehrte Tora. Zum Gesetzesverständnis des Paulus." *Judaica* 43 (1987) 4-20.

Stendahl, K. *Paul Among Jews and Gentiles and other Essays.* Philadelphia: Fortress, 1976.

Stogiannos, B. P. "He peri Nomou didaskalia tes pros Galatas epistoles tou Apostolou Paulou." *Deltion Biblikon Meleton* 1 (1972) 312-28.

Stoike, D. A. "'The Law of Christ': A Study of Paul's Use of the Expression in Galatians 6:2." Ph.D. dissertation, Claremont, 1971.

Strack, H. L. *Introduction to the Talmud and Midrash.* 1931. Reprint. New York: Atheneum, 1969.

Strelan, J. G. "Burden-bearing and the Law of Christ: A Re-examination of Galatians 6:2." *JBL* 94 (1975) 266-76.

Strugnell, J. "Notes en Marge du Volume V des 'Discoveries in the Judean Desert of Jordan." *RQ* 7 (1969-71) 163-276.

Stuhlmacher, P. "'Das End des Gesetzes'. Über Ursprung und Ansatz der paulinischen Theologie." *ZTK* 67 (1970) 14-39.

Stuhlmacher, P. "Der Abfassungzweck des Römerbriefes." *ZNW* 77 (1986) 180-93.

Stuhlmacher, P. "Paul's Understanding of the Law in the Letter to the Romans." *SEÅ* 50 (1985) 87-104.

Stuhlmacher, P. "Paulus, ein Rabbi, der Apostle wurde." In *Paulus—Rabbi und Apostel,* ed. P. Lapide and P. Stuhlmacher, 62-69. Stuttgart: Calwer, 1981.

Synge, E. F. "St Paul's Boyhood and Conversion and his Attitude to Race." *ExpTim* 94 (1983) 260-63.

Taubenschlag, R. *The Law of Graeco-Roman Egypt in the Light of the Papyri.* 2d ed. Warsaw: Panstwowe Wydawnictwo Naukowa: 1955.

Thayer, J. H. *A Greek-English Lexicon of the New Testament.* 4th ed. Edinburgh: Clark, 1901.

Theobald, M. "Warum schrieb Paulus der Römerbrief?" *Bibel und Liturgie* 56 (1983) 150-58.

Thompson, R. W. "How is the Law Fulfilled in Us? An Interpretation of Rom 8:4." *Louvain Studies* 11 (1986) 31-40.

Thompson, R. W. "Paul's Double Critique of Jewish Boasting: A Study of Rom 3,27 in Its Context." *Bib* 67 (1986) 520-31.

Tomlinson, J. "Interpretation of Romans 7:14-25." *LQ* 11 (1918) 558-64.

Tomson, P. J. *Paul and the Jewish Law*. Assen/Maastricht: Van Gorcum, 1990.

Trocmé, E. "From 'I' to 'We': Christian Life According to Romans, Chapters 7 and 8." *AusBR* 35 (1987) 73-76.

Tyson, J. B. "'Works of Law' in Galatians." *JBL* 92 (1973) 423-31.

Ullmann, S. *The Principles of Semantics*. 2d ed. Oxford: Blackwell, 1957.

Ullmann, S. *Semantics: An Introduction to the Science of Meaning*. New York: Barnes & Noble, 1962.

Umbreit, F. W. C. "Des Apostel Paulus Selbstbekenntnis im siebenten Kapitel des Briefes an die Römer." *Theologische Studien und Kritiken* 24 (1851) 633-45.

Urbach, E. *The Sages*. 1979. Reprint. Cambridge, Mass.: Harvard University Press, 1987.

Valgiglio, E. "ΠΟΙΗΤΗΣ (ΠΟΙΕΙΝ) nella Bibbia." *Orpheus* 6 (1985) 396-403.

van de Sandt, H. W. M. "An Explanation of Rom. 8,4a." *Bijdragen* 37 (1976) 361-78.

van de Sandt, H. W. M. "Research into Rom. 8,4a: The Legal Claim of the Law." *Bijdragen* 37 (1976) 252-69.

van den Beld, A. "Romeinen 7:14-25 en het probleem van de akrasía." *Bijdragen* 46 (1985) 19-58.

Vendryes, J. *Language: A Linguistic Introduction to History*. London: Routledge and Kegan Paul, 1925.

Vermes, G. *The Dead Sea Scrolls in English*. 3d ed. Sheffield: JSOT, 1987.

Vollenweider, S. "Zeit und Gesetz. Erwägungen zur Bedeutung apokalyptischer Denkformen bei Paulus." *TZ* 44 (1988) 97-116.

Wagner, G. "Le repas du Seigneur et la justification par la foi. Exégèse de Galates 2-17." *ETR* 36 (1961) 245-54.

Walker, R. "Die Heiden und das Gericht." *EvT* 20 (1960) 302-14.

Walvoord, J. F. "Law in the Epistle to the Romans." *BSac* 94 (1937) 15-30, 281-95.

Warren, G. G. "A Study in Galatians 2:15-21." *Biblical Review* 11 (1926) 356-67.

Watson, F. *Paul, Judaism and Gentiles*. Cambridge: Cambridge University Press, 1976.

Weber, R. "Die Geschichte des Gesetzes und des Ich in Römer 7,7-8,4. Einige Überlegungen zum Zusammenhang von Heilsgeschichte und Anthropologie im Blick auf die theologische Grundstellung des paulinischen Denkens." *Neue Zeitschrift für Systematische Theologie und Religionsphilosophie* 29 (1987) 147-79.

Wedderburn, A. J. M. *The Reasons for Romans*. Edinburgh: Clark, 1988.

Weder, H. "Einsicht in Gesetzlichkeit. Paulus als verständnisvoller Ausleger des menschlichen Lebens." *Judaica* 43 (1987) 21-29.

Weder, H. "Gesetz und Sünde: Gedanken zu einem Qualitativen Sprung im Denken des Paulus." *NTS* 31 (1985) 357-76.

Westerholm, S. "'Letter' and 'Spirit': the Foundation of Pauline Ethics." *NTS* 30 (1984) 229-43.

Westerholm, S. "On Fulfilling the Whole Law." *SEÅ* 51-52 (1986-87) 229-37.

Westerholm, S. "*Torah, nomos* and law: A question of 'meaning'." *SR* 15 (1986) 327-36.

Westerholm, S. *Israel's Law and the Church's Faith*. Grand Rapids: Eerdmans, 1988.

Wetzel, L. "Versuch einer Erklärung der Stelle Gal. 2,14-21." *Theologische Studien und Kritiken* 53 (1880) 432-64.

Whiteley, D. E. H. "Hard Sayings - VIII. Romans 8,3." *Theology* 67 (1964) 114-16.

Wilckens, U. "Statements on the Development of Paul's View of the Law." In *Paul and Paulinism* (Festschrift C. K. Barrett), ed. M. D. Hooker and S. G. Wilson, 17-26. London: SPCK, 1982.

Wilckens, U. "Was heißt bei Paulus: 'Aus Werken des Gesetzes wird kein Mensch gerecht'?" *Rechtfertigung als Freiheit,* 77-109. Neukirchen-Vluyn: Neukirchener, 1974.

Wilckens, U. "Zur Entwicklung des paulinischen Gesetzeverständnisses." *NTS* 28 (1982) 154-90.

Wilckens, U. *Der Brief an die Römer*. 3 vols. Zürich: Benzinger, 1978-82.

Wiles, M. F. "St. Paul's Conception of Law." *ChM* 69 (1955-56) 144-52, 228-34.

Williams, S. K. "Again *Pistis Christou.*" *CBQ* 49 (1987) 431-47.

Williams, S. K. "The Hearing of Faith: ΑΚΟΗ ΠΙΣΤΕΩΣ in Galatians 3." *NTS* 35 (1989) 82-93.

Wilson, J. "Romans 7:24-8:2, a Rearrangement." *ExpTim* 4 (1892-93) 192.

Winger, J. M. "If Anyone Preach; An Examination of Conditional and Related Forms in the Epistles of St. Paul." Master's thesis, Union Theological Seminary, 1983.

Winger, J. M. "Unreal Conditions in the Letters of Paul." *JBL* 105 (1986) 110-112.

Wirtle, B. "Paul's Conception of the Law of Christ and Its Relation to the Law of Moses." *Reformed Theological Review* 38 (1979) 42-50.

Wittgenstein, L. *Philosophical Investigations*. 3d ed. New York: Macmillan, 1958.

Wittgenstein, L. *The Blue and the Brown Books*. New York: Harper & Row, 1958.

Yates, J. C. "The Judgment of the Heathen: The Interpretation of Article XVIII and Romans 2:12-16." *Churchman* 100 (1986) 220-30.

Yates, R. "Paul and the Law in Galatians." *ITQ* 51 (1985) 105-24.

Zahn, A. *Das Gesetz Gottes nach der Lehre und Erfahrung des Apostel Paulus*. Halle: Mühlmann, 1876.

Zahn, T. *Der Brief des Paulus an die Galater*. 3d ed. Leipzig: Deichert, 1922.

Zedda, S. "'Morto alla legge mediante la legge' (Gal 2,19): Testo autobiografico sulla conversione di san Paolo?" *Rivista Biblica*. 37 (1989) 81-95.

Zehnpfund, R. "Das Gesetz in den paulinischen Briefen." *NKZ* 8 (1897) 384-419.

Zeisler, J. A. "The Role of the Tenth Commandment in Romans 7." *JSNT* 33 (1988) 41-56.

Zeller, D. "Der Zusammenhang von Gesetz und Sünde im Römerbrief. Kritischer Nachvollzug der Auslegung von Ulrich Wilckens." *TZ* 38 (1982) 193-212.

Zeller, D. "Zur neueren Diskussion über das Gesetz bei Paulus." *TP* 62 (1987) 481-99.

Zerwick, M. *Biblical Greek*. Rome: Biblical Institute Press, 1963.

Ziesler, J. A. "The Just Requirement of the Law (Romans 8.4)." *AusBR* 35 (1987) 77-82.

Zimmer, F. "Paulus gegen Petrus; Gal 2,14-21 erläutert." *ZWT* 25 (1882) 129-88.

INDEX OF PASSAGES